**Nominated for 3 EISNER AWARDS including
Best New Series and Best Ongoing Series**

"For fans of literature (from classics to contemporary) this series is worth a read. . . .
The Unwritten is **a roller-coaster ride through a library, weaving famous authors
and characters into a tale of mystery** that is, at once, oddly familiar yet highly original."
– USA TODAY

"*The Unwritten* makes a leap from being just a promising new Vertigo title to being on-track to
become the best ongoing Vertigo book since *Sandman*. And given that Vertigo has delivered
the likes of *100 Bullets*, *Y: The Last Man*, and *Fables* since *Sandman* ended,
that's saying something… A-"
–THE A.V. CLUB

"In a time where periodical comics are often being ignored in favor of waiting for the collected
edition, Carey and Gross haven't forgotten how a strong periodical can keep people's interest.
This is a serial that makes me want to read it monthly, because I just have to know
what happens next. Now that's good stuff."
– COMIC BOOK RESOURCES

the
UNWritten
WAR STORIES

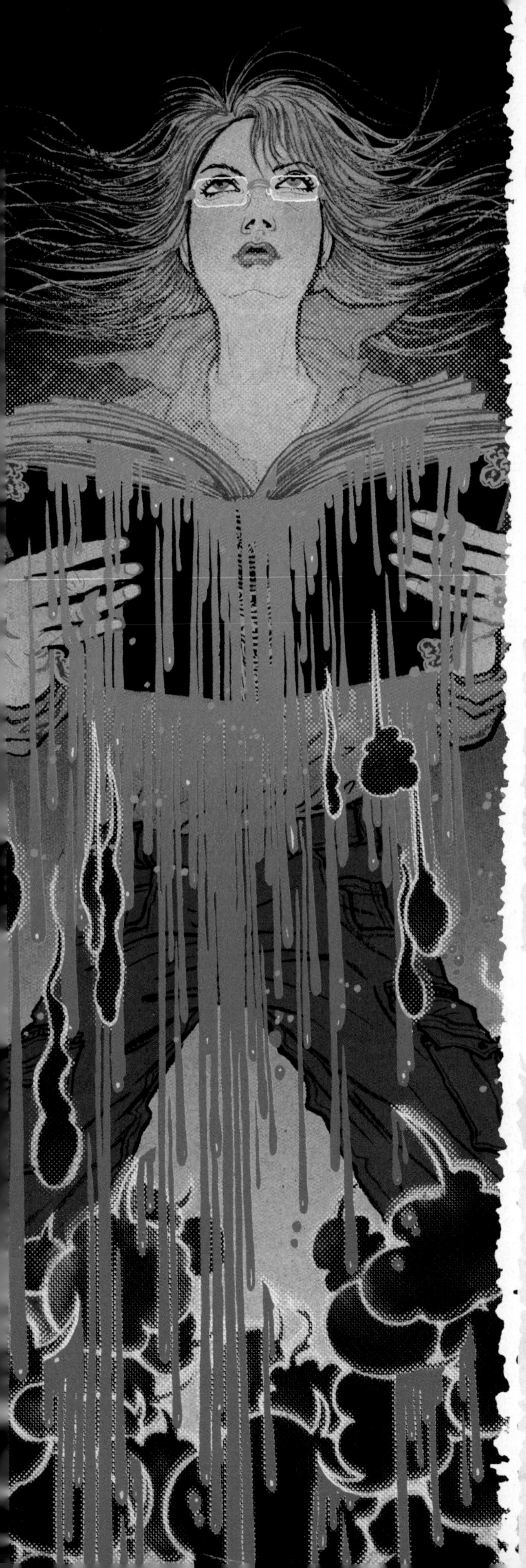

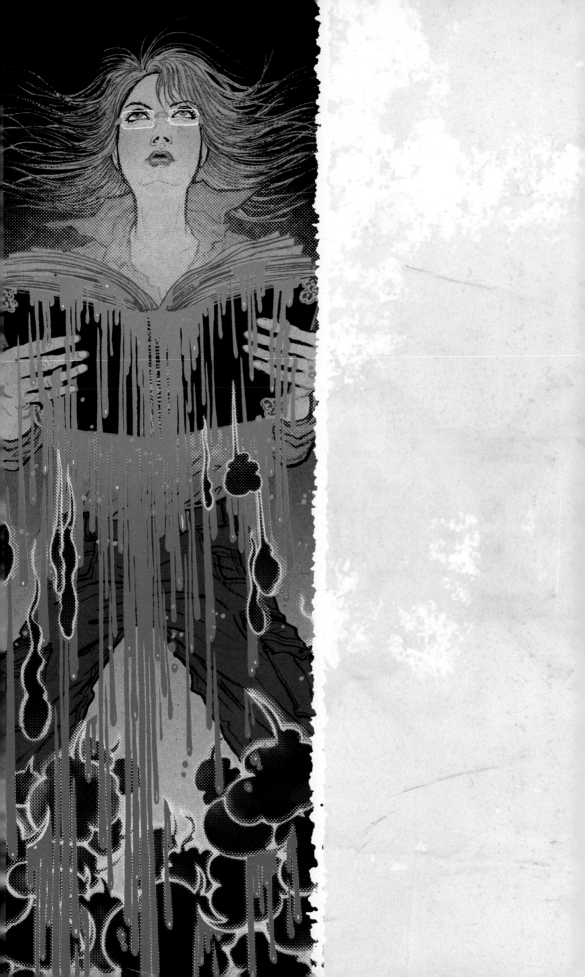

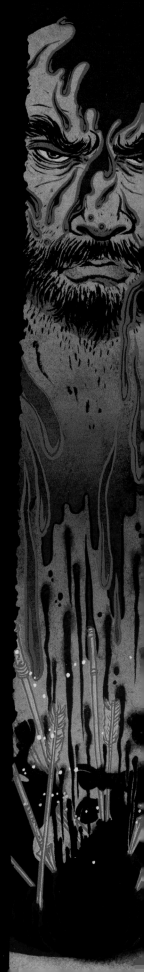

the Unwritten

WAR STORIES

Mike Carey Writer

Peter Gross Al Davison Artists Ryan Kelly Al Davison Finishes

Chris Chuckry Lee Loughridge Colorists

Todd Klein Letterer Yuko Shimizu Cover Artist

THE UNWRITTEN created by Mike Carey and Peter Gross

Greg Lockard Editor – Original Series
Rowena Yow Editor
Robbin Brosterman Design Director – Books
Louis Prandi Publication Design

Shelly Bond Executive Editor – Vertigo
Hank Kanalz Senior VP – Vertigo & Integrated Publishing

Diane Nelson President
Dan DiDio and Jim Lee Co-Publishers
Geoff Johns Chief Creative Officer
Amit Desai Senior VP – Marketing & Franchise Management
Amy Genkins Senior VP – Business & Legal Affairs
Nairi Gardiner Senior VP – Finance
Jeff Boison VP – Publishing Planning
Mark Chiarello VP – Art Direction & Design
John Cunningham VP – Marketing
Terri Cunningham VP – Editorial Administration
Larry Ganem VP – Talent Relations & Services
Alison Gill Senior VP – Manufacturing & Operations
Jay Kogan VP – Business & Legal Affairs, Publishing
Jack Mahan VP – Business Affairs, Talent
Nick Napolitano VP – Manufacturing Administration
Sue Pohja VP – Book Sales
Fred Ruiz VP – Manufacturing Operations
Courtney Simmons Senior VP – Publicity
Bob Wayne Senior VP – Sales

Library of Congress Cataloging-in-Publication Data

Carey, Mike, 1959- author.
  The Unwritten. Volume 10, Apocalypse / Mike Carey, Peter Gross.
    pages cm
  ISBN 978-1-4012-5055-3 (paperback)
  1. Graphic novels. I. Gross, Peter, 1958- illustrator. II. Title. III. Title:
Apocalypse.
  PN6727.C377U589 2014
  741.5'973—dc23

                                                        2014014691

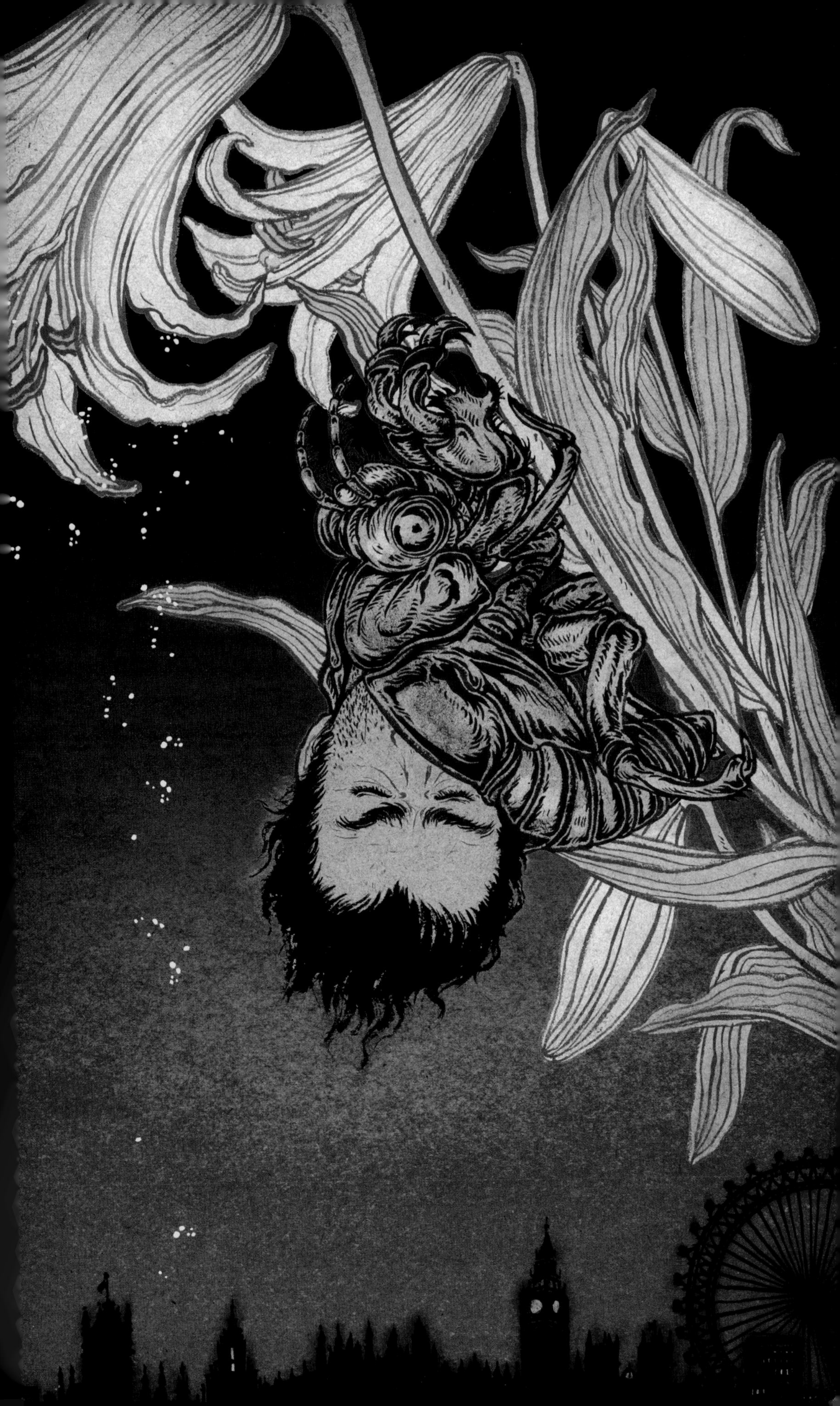

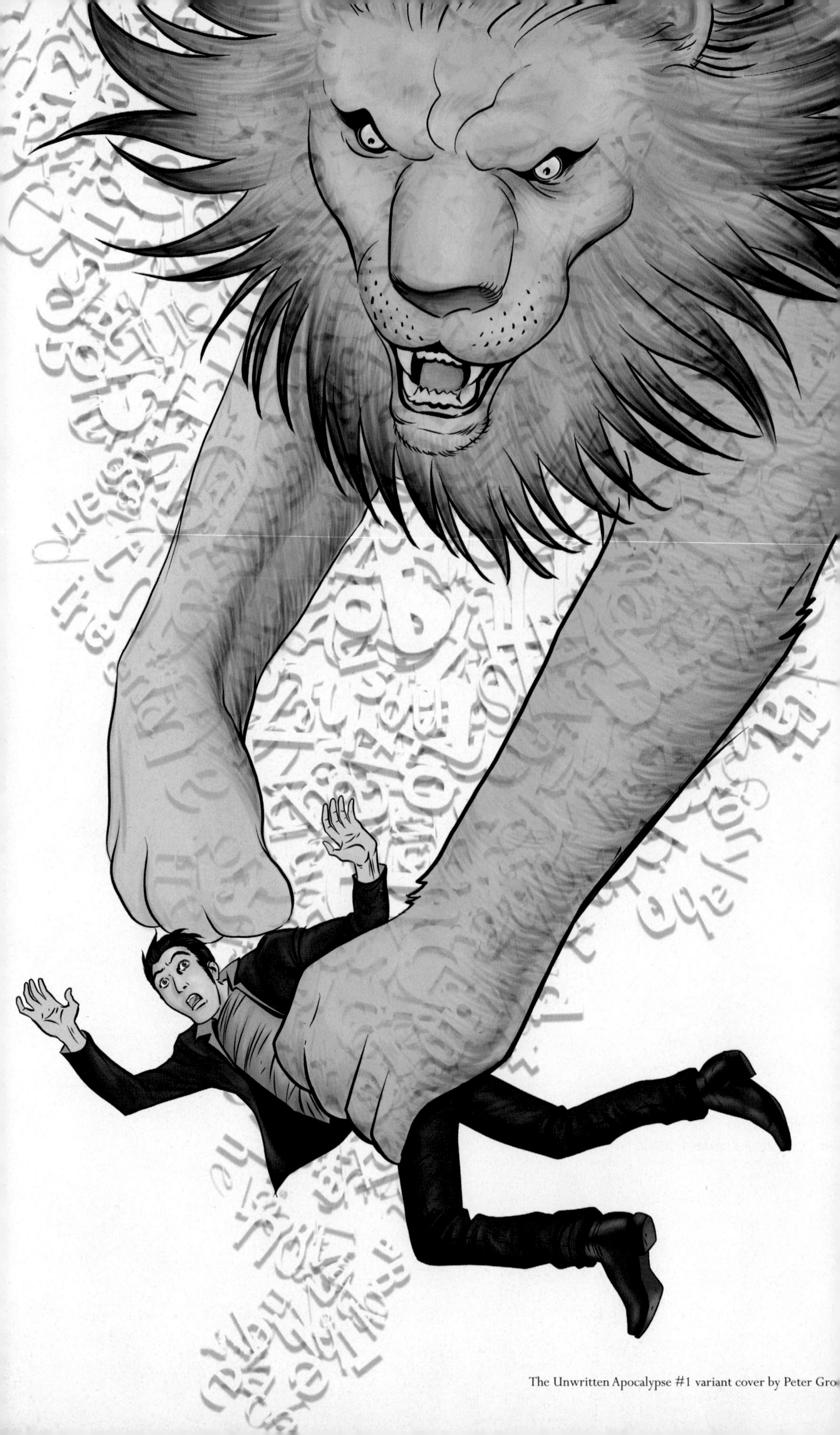

The Unwritten Apocalypse #1 variant cover by Peter Gro

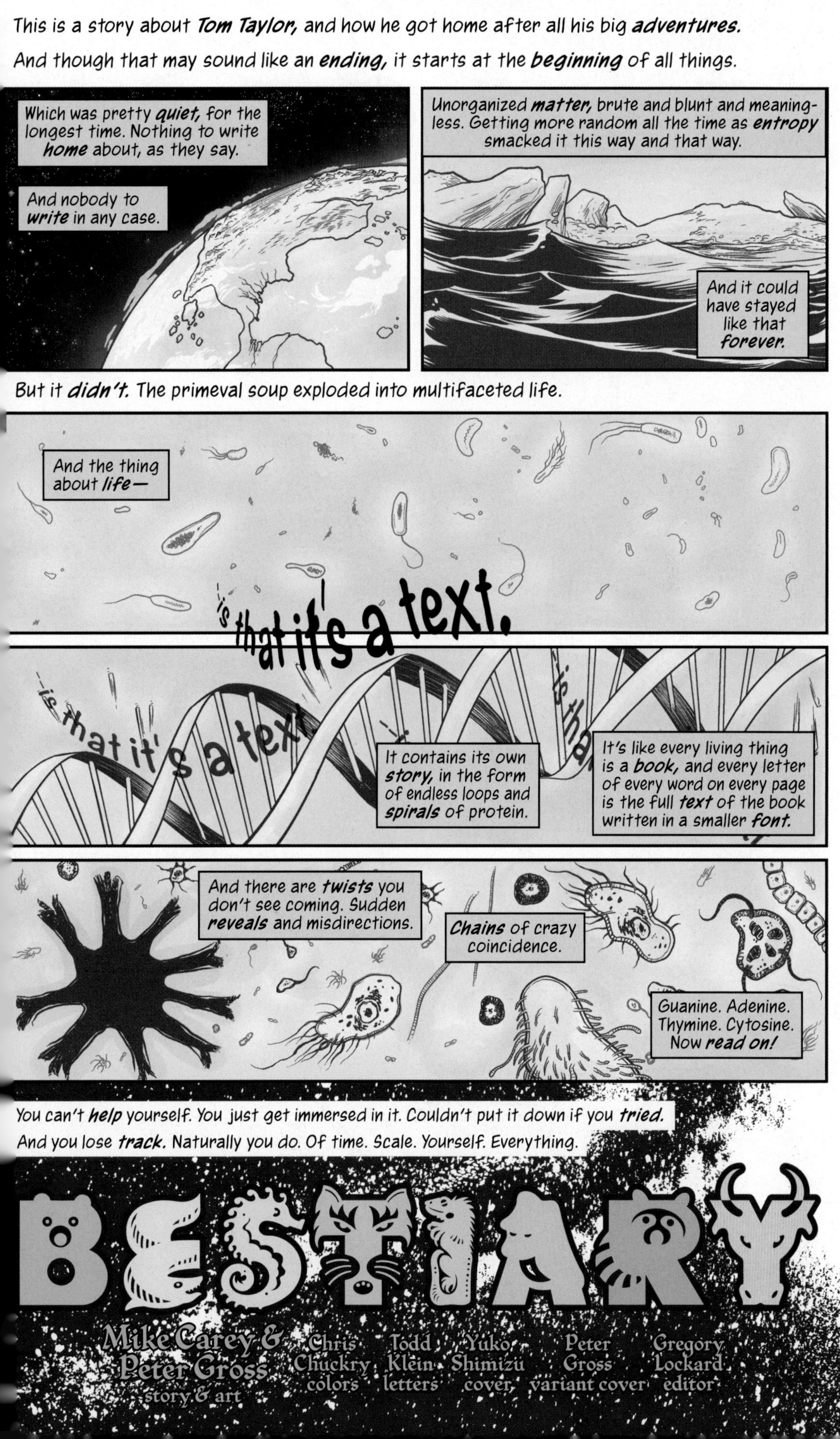
This is a story about Tom Taylor, and how he got home after all his big adventures.
And though that may sound like an ending, it starts at the beginning of all things.
Which was pretty quiet, for the longest time. Nothing to write home about, as they say.
And nobody to write in any case.
Unorganized matter, brute and blunt and meaningless. Getting more random all the time as entropy smacked it this way and that way.
And it could have stayed like that forever.
But it didn't. The primeval soup exploded into multifaceted life.
And the thing about life—
—is that it's a text.
—is that it's a text.
It contains its own story, in the form of endless loops and spirals of protein.
It's like every living thing is a book, and every letter of every word on every page is the full text of the book written in a smaller font.
And there are twists you don't see coming. Sudden reveals and misdirections.
Chains of crazy coincidence.
Guanine. Adenine. Thymine. Cytosine. Now read on!
You can't help yourself. You just get immersed in it. Couldn't put it down if you tried.
And you lose track. Naturally you do. Of time. Scale. Yourself. Everything.
BESTIARY
Mike Carey & Peter Gross story & art
Chris Chuckry colors
Todd Klein letters
Yuko Shimizu cover
Peter Gross variant cover
Gregory Lockard editor

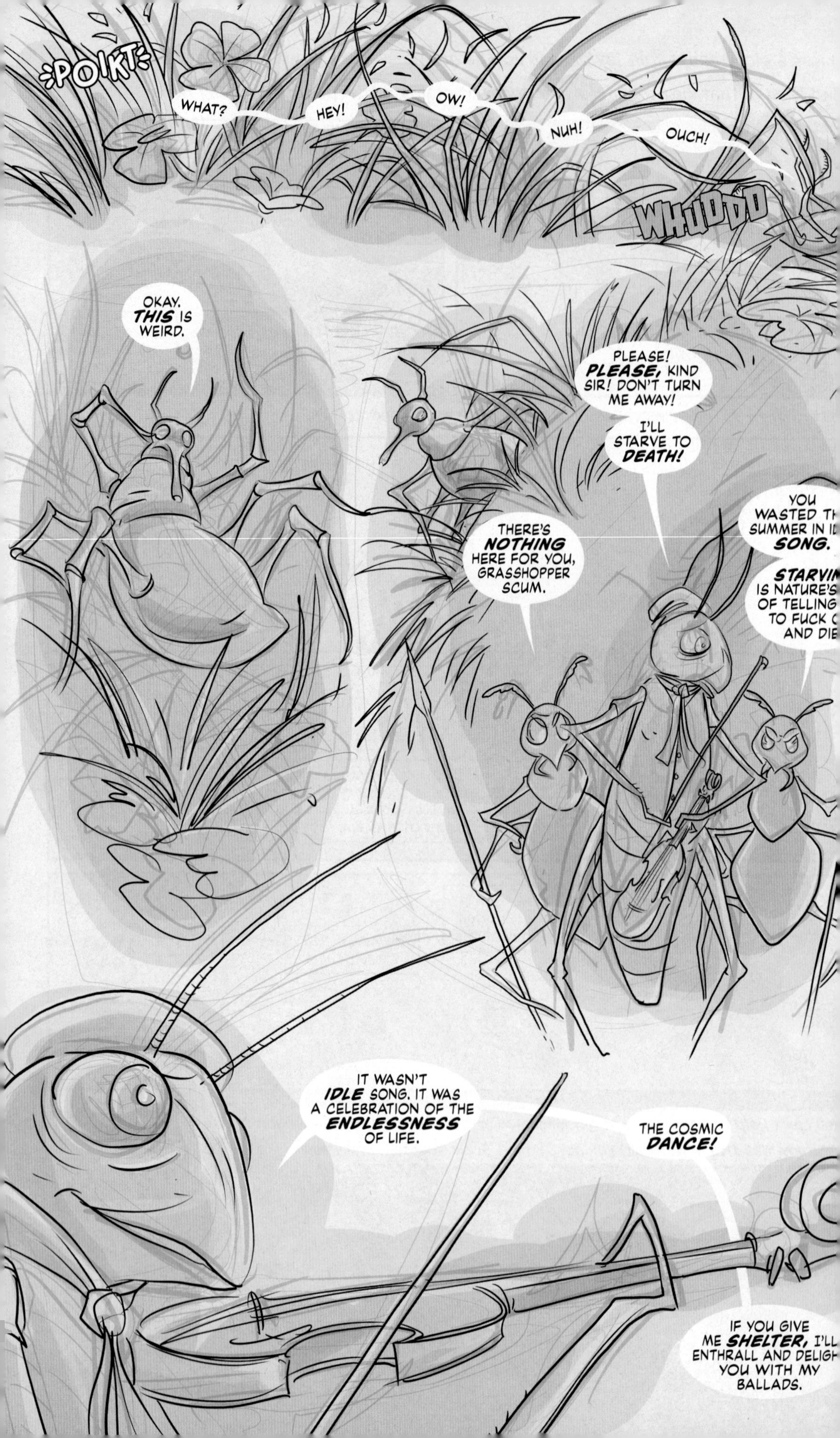
POIKT
WHAT?
HEY!
OW!
NUH!
OUCH!
WHUDDD
OKAY. THIS IS WEIRD.
PLEASE! PLEASE, KIND SIR! DON'T TURN ME AWAY!
I'LL STARVE TO DEATH!
THERE'S NOTHING HERE FOR YOU, GRASSHOPPER SCUM.
YOU WASTED TH SUMMER IN ID SONG.
STARVIN IS NATURE'S OF TELLING TO FUCK O AND DIE
IT WASN'T IDLE SONG. IT WAS A CELEBRATION OF THE ENDLESSNESS OF LIFE.
THE COSMIC DANCE!
IF YOU GIVE ME SHELTER, I'LL ENTHRALL AND DELIGH YOU WITH MY BALLADS.

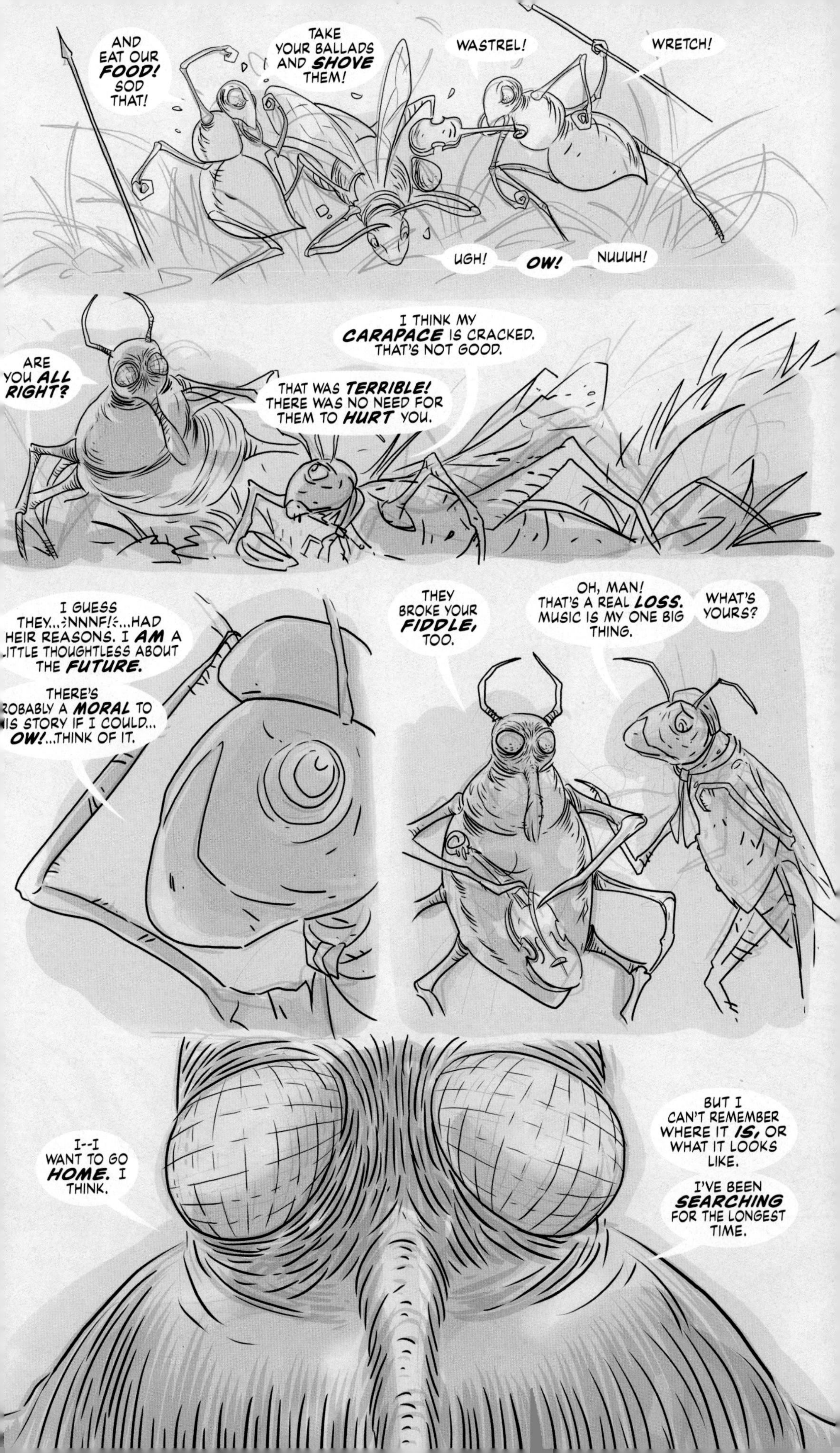
AND EAT OUR FOOD! SOD THAT!
TAKE YOUR BALLADS AND SHOVE THEM!
WASTREL!
WRETCH!
UGH!
OW!
NUUUH!
ARE YOU ALL RIGHT?
THAT WAS TERRIBLE! THERE WAS NO NEED FOR THEM TO HURT YOU.
I THINK MY CARAPACE IS CRACKED. THAT'S NOT GOOD.
I GUESS THEY...NNNF!...HAD HEIR REASONS. I AM A ITTLE THOUGHTLESS ABOUT THE FUTURE.
THERE'S ROBABLY A MORAL TO IS STORY IF I COULD... OW!...THINK OF IT.
THEY BROKE YOUR FIDDLE, TOO.
OH, MAN! THAT'S A REAL LOSS. MUSIC IS MY ONE BIG THING.
WHAT'S YOURS?
I--I WANT TO GO HOME. I THINK.
BUT I CAN'T REMEMBER WHERE IT IS, OR WHAT IT LOOKS LIKE.
I'VE BEEN SEARCHING FOR THE LONGEST TIME.

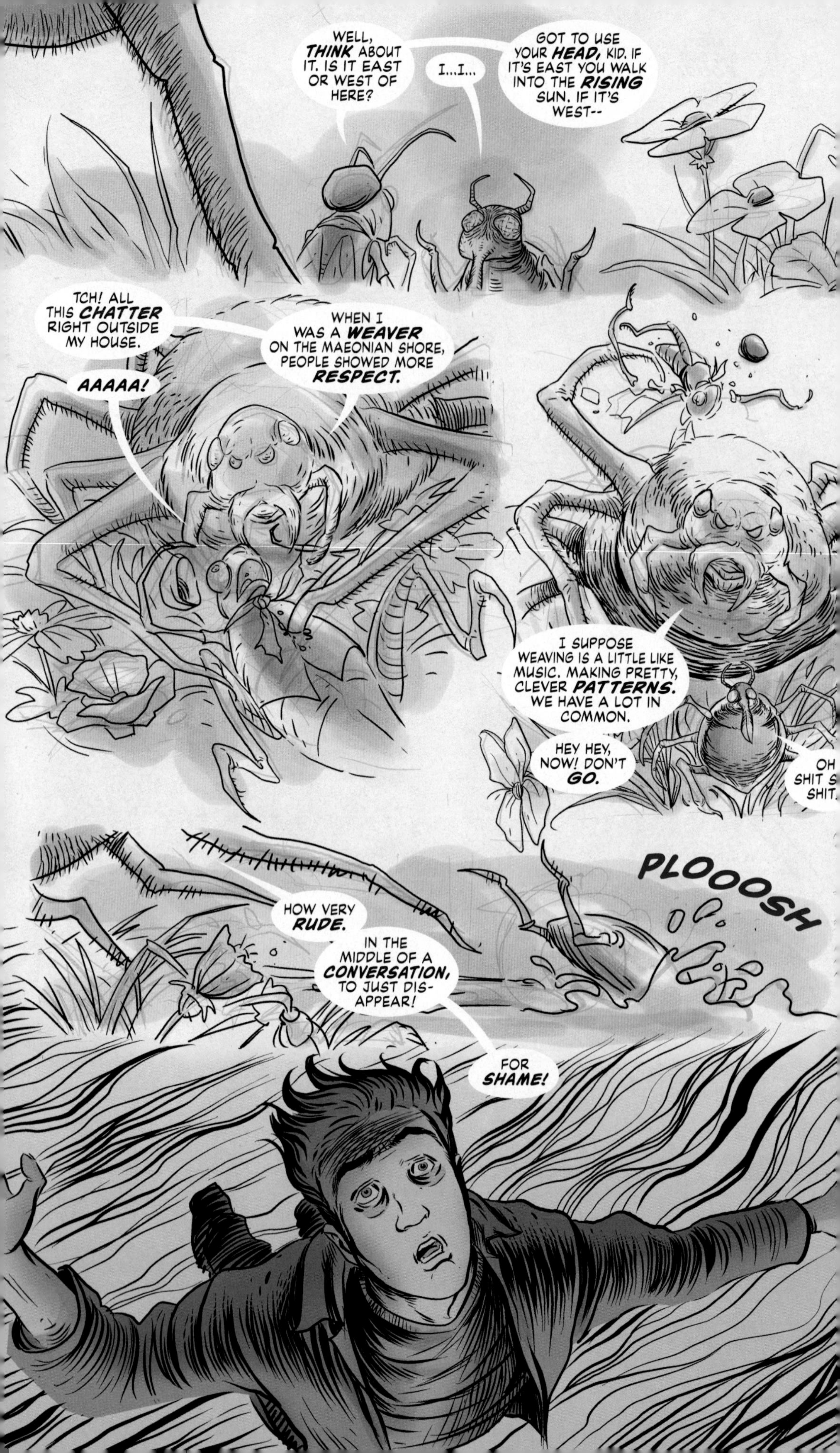
WELL, THINK ABOUT IT. IS IT EAST OR WEST OF HERE?
I...I...
GOT TO USE YOUR HEAD, KID. IF IT'S EAST YOU WALK INTO THE RISING SUN. IF IT'S WEST--
TCH! ALL THIS CHATTER RIGHT OUTSIDE MY HOUSE.
WHEN I WAS A WEAVER ON THE MAEONIAN SHORE, PEOPLE SHOWED MORE RESPECT.
AAAAA!
I SUPPOSE WEAVING IS A LITTLE LIKE MUSIC. MAKING PRETTY, CLEVER PATTERNS. WE HAVE A LOT IN COMMON.
HEY HEY, NOW! DON'T GO.
PLOOOSH
HOW VERY RUDE.
IN THE MIDDLE OF A CONVERSATION, TO JUST DIS-APPEAR!
FOR SHAME!

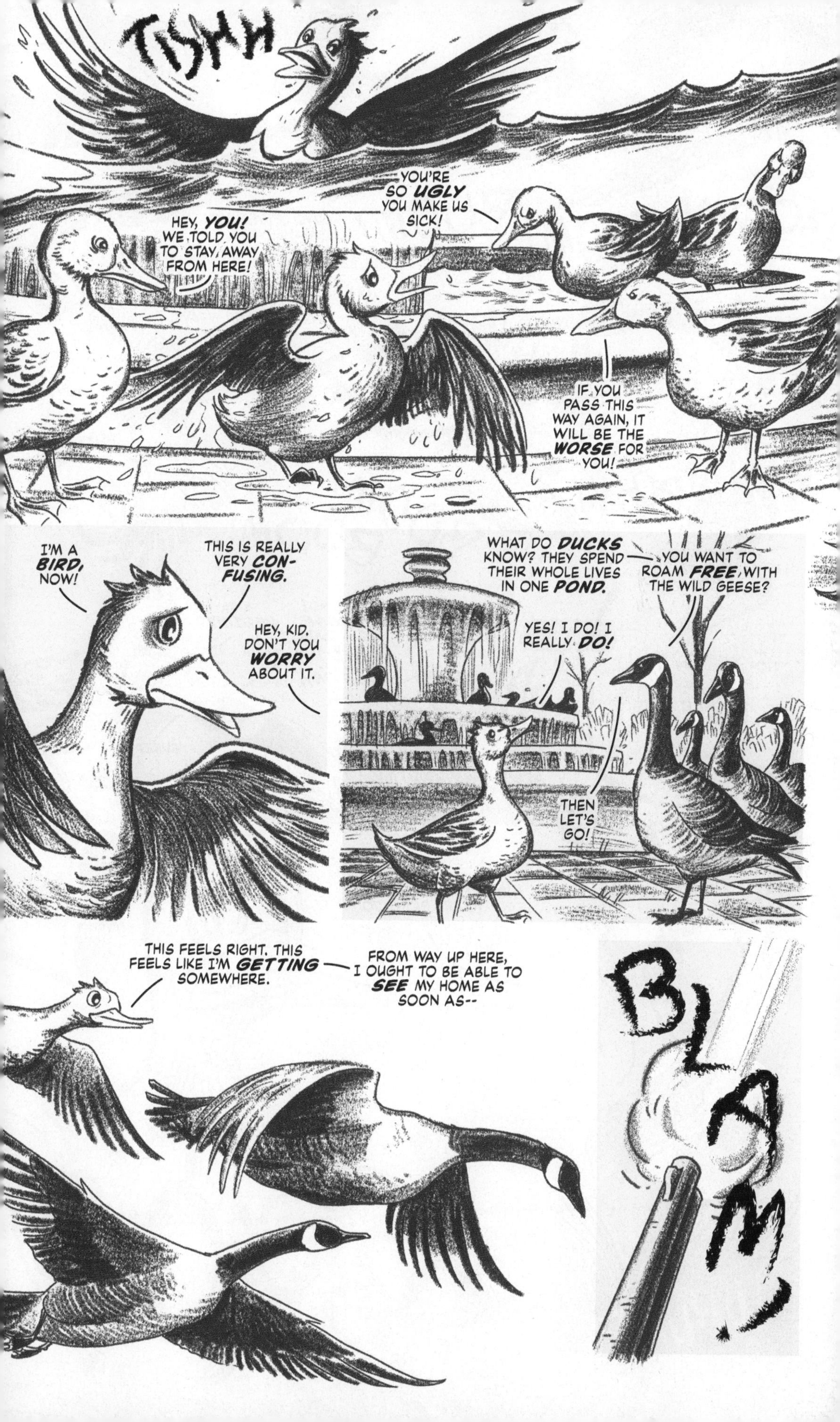
TISHH
HEY, YOU! WE TOLD YOU TO STAY AWAY FROM HERE!
YOU'RE SO UGLY YOU MAKE US SICK!
IF YOU PASS THIS WAY AGAIN, IT WILL BE THE WORSE FOR YOU!
I'M A BIRD, NOW!
THIS IS REALLY VERY CON-FUSING.
HEY, KID. DON'T YOU WORRY ABOUT IT.
WHAT DO DUCKS KNOW? THEY SPEND THEIR WHOLE LIVES IN ONE POND.
YOU WANT TO ROAM FREE WITH THE WILD GEESE?
YES! I DO! I REALLY DO!
THEN LET'S GO!
THIS FEELS RIGHT. THIS FEELS LIKE I'M GETTING SOMEWHERE.
FROM WAY UP HERE, I OUGHT TO BE ABLE TO SEE MY HOME AS SOON AS--
BLAM!

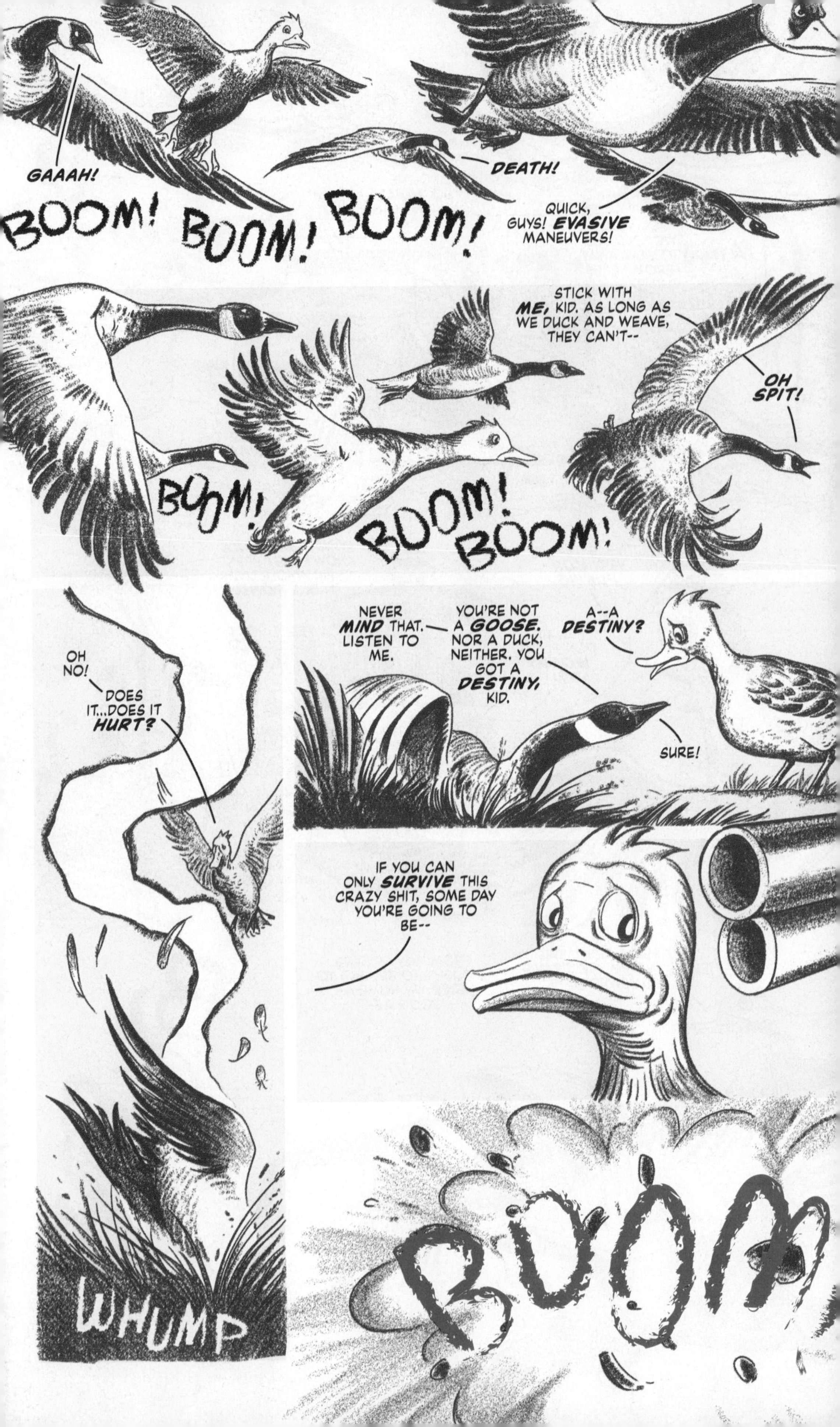
GAAAH!
DEATH!
BOOM! BOOM! BOOM!
QUICK, GUYS! EVASIVE MANEUVERS!
STICK WITH ME, KID. AS LONG AS WE DUCK AND WEAVE, THEY CAN'T--
OH SPIT!
BOOM!
BOOM! BOOM!
OH NO!
DOES IT...DOES IT HURT?
WHUMP
NEVER MIND THAT. LISTEN TO ME.
YOU'RE NOT A GOOSE. NOR A DUCK, NEITHER. YOU GOT A DESTINY, KID.
A--A DESTINY?
SURE!
IF YOU CAN ONLY SURVIVE THIS CRAZY SHIT, SOME DAY YOU'RE GOING TO BE--
BOOM

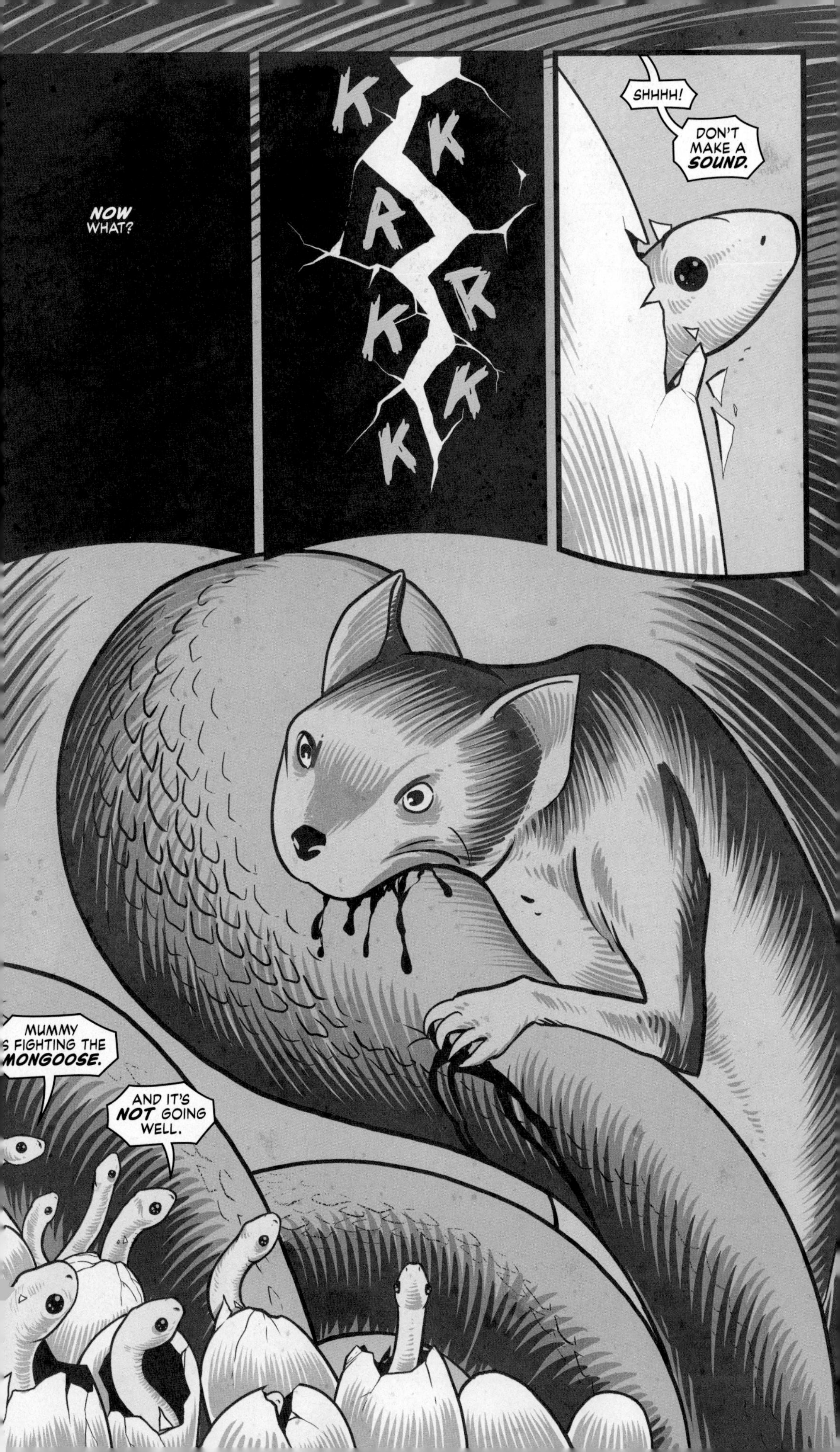
NOW WHAT?
KKRKKRKKK
SHHHH!
DON'T MAKE A SOUND.
MUMMY 'S FIGHTING THE MONGOOSE.
AND IT'S NOT GOING WELL.

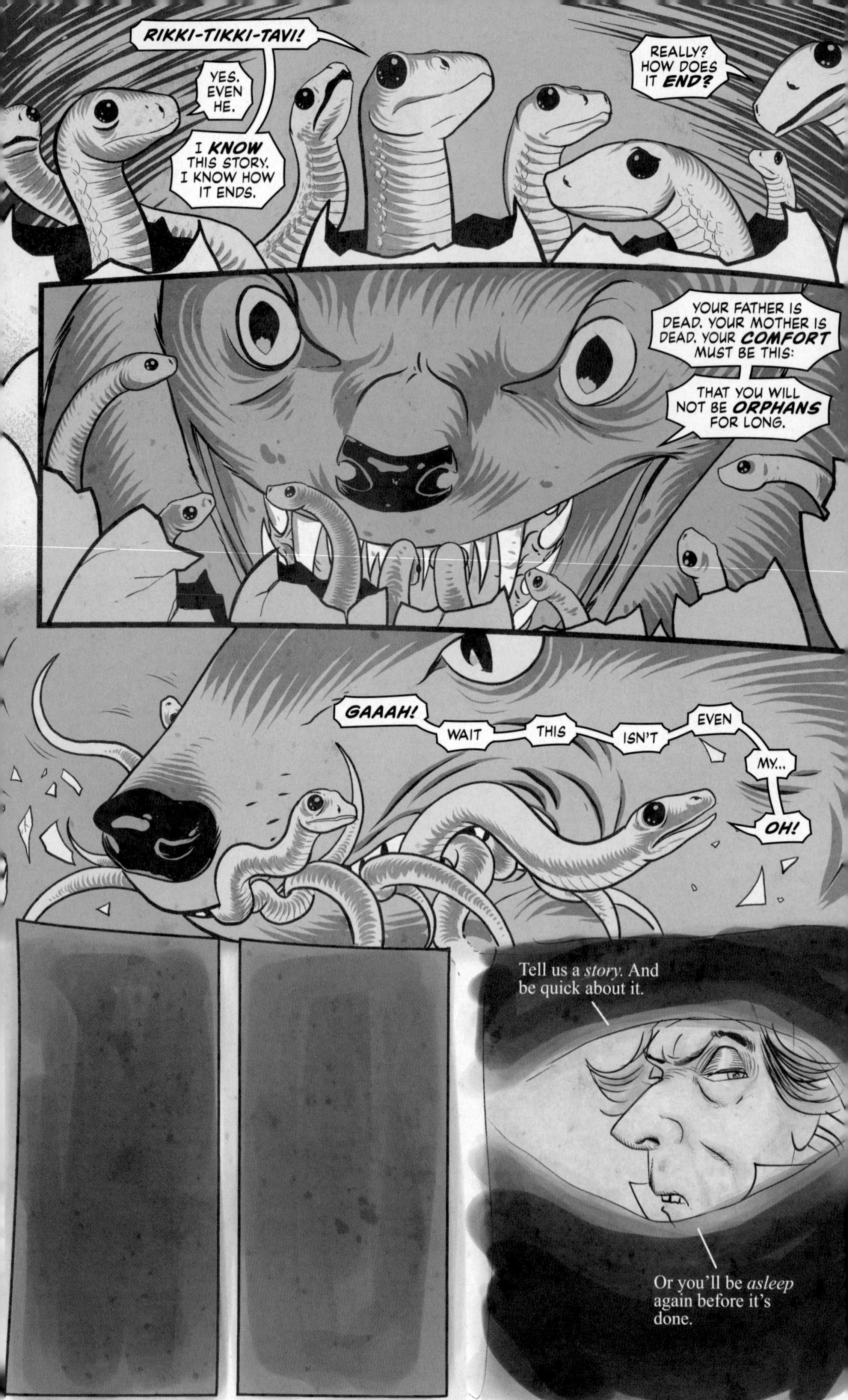
RIKKI-TIKKI-TAVI!
YES. EVEN HE.
I KNOW THIS STORY. I KNOW HOW IT ENDS.
REALLY? HOW DOES IT END?
YOUR FATHER IS DEAD. YOUR MOTHER IS DEAD. YOUR COMFORT MUST BE THIS:
THAT YOU WILL NOT BE ORPHANS FOR LONG.
GAAAH!
WAIT
THIS
ISN'T
EVEN
MY...
OH!
Tell us a story. And be quick about it.
Or you'll be asleep again before it's done.

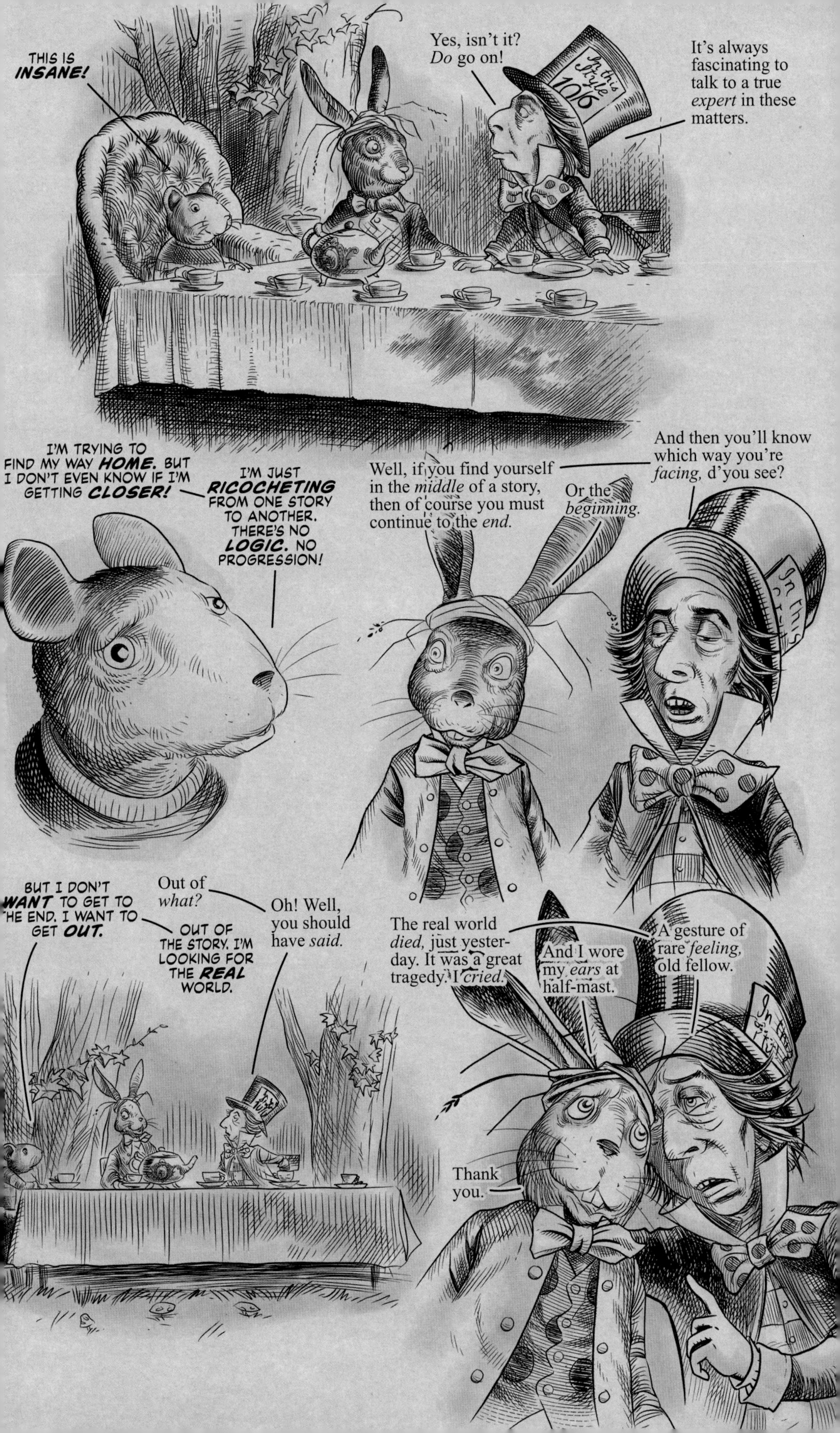
THIS IS INSANE!
Yes, isn't it? Do go on!
It's always fascinating to talk to a true expert in these matters.
I'M TRYING TO FIND MY WAY HOME. BUT I DON'T EVEN KNOW IF I'M GETTING CLOSER!
I'M JUST RICOCHETING FROM ONE STORY TO ANOTHER. THERE'S NO LOGIC. NO PROGRESSION!
Well, if you find yourself in the middle of a story, then of course you must continue to the end.
Or the beginning.
And then you'll know which way you're facing, d'you see?
BUT I DON'T WANT TO GET TO THE END. I WANT TO GET OUT.
Out of what?
OUT OF THE STORY. I'M LOOKING FOR THE REAL WORLD.
Oh! Well, you should have said.
The real world died, just yesterday. It was a great tragedy. I cried.
And I wore my ears at half-mast.
A gesture of rare feeling, old fellow.
Thank you.

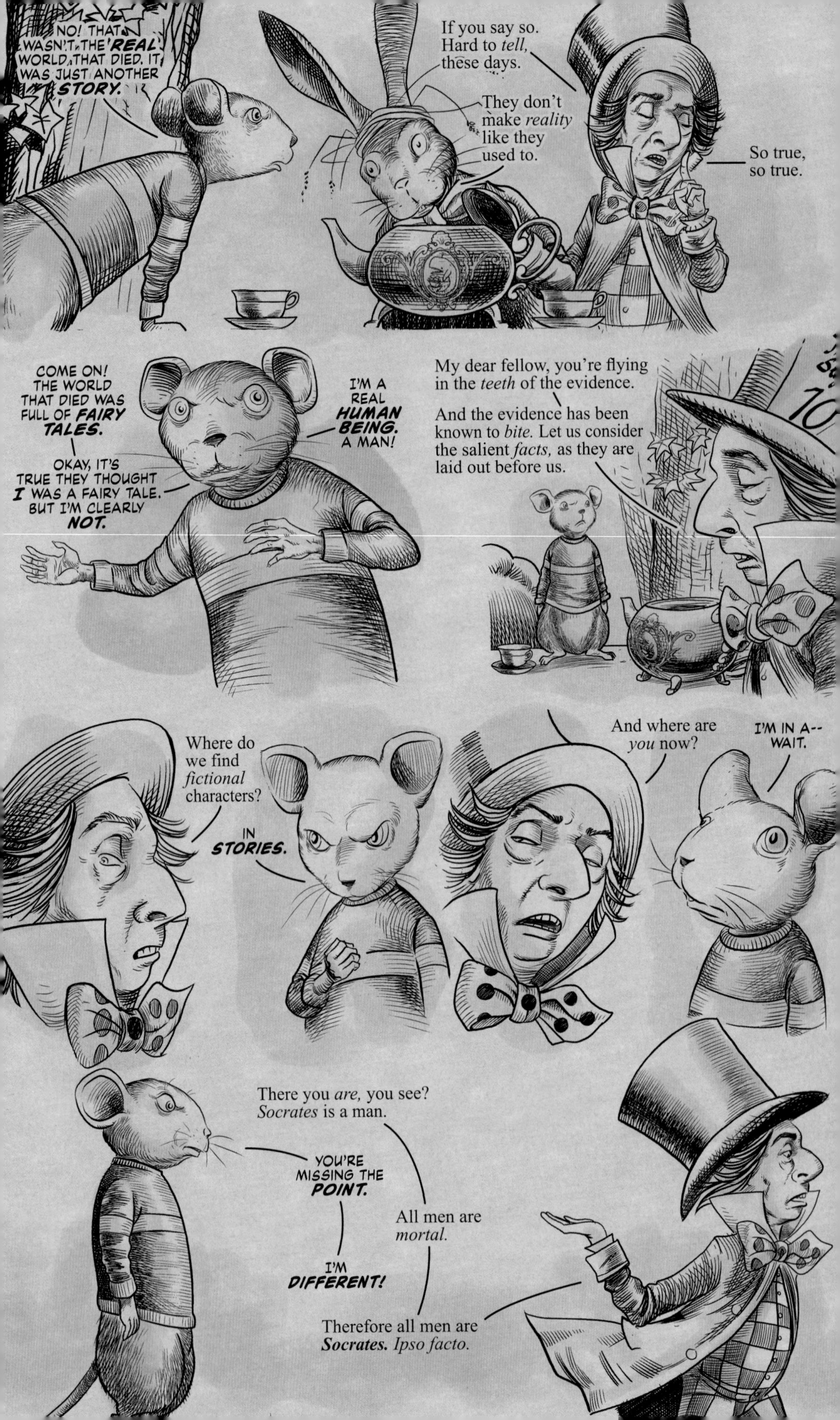
NO! THAT WASN'T THE REAL WORLD THAT DIED. IT WAS JUST ANOTHER STORY.
If you say so. Hard to tell, these days.
They don't make reality like they used to.
So true, so true.
COME ON! THE WORLD THAT DIED WAS FULL OF FAIRY TALES.
OKAY, IT'S TRUE THEY THOUGHT I WAS A FAIRY TALE. BUT I'M CLEARLY NOT.
I'M A REAL HUMAN BEING. A MAN!
My dear fellow, you're flying in the teeth of the evidence.
And the evidence has been known to bite. Let us consider the salient facts, as they are laid out before us.
Where do we find fictional characters?
IN STORIES.
And where are you now?
I'M IN A-- WAIT.
There you are, you see? Socrates is a man.
YOU'RE MISSING THE POINT.
All men are mortal.
I'M DIFFERENT!
Therefore all men are Socrates. Ipso facto.

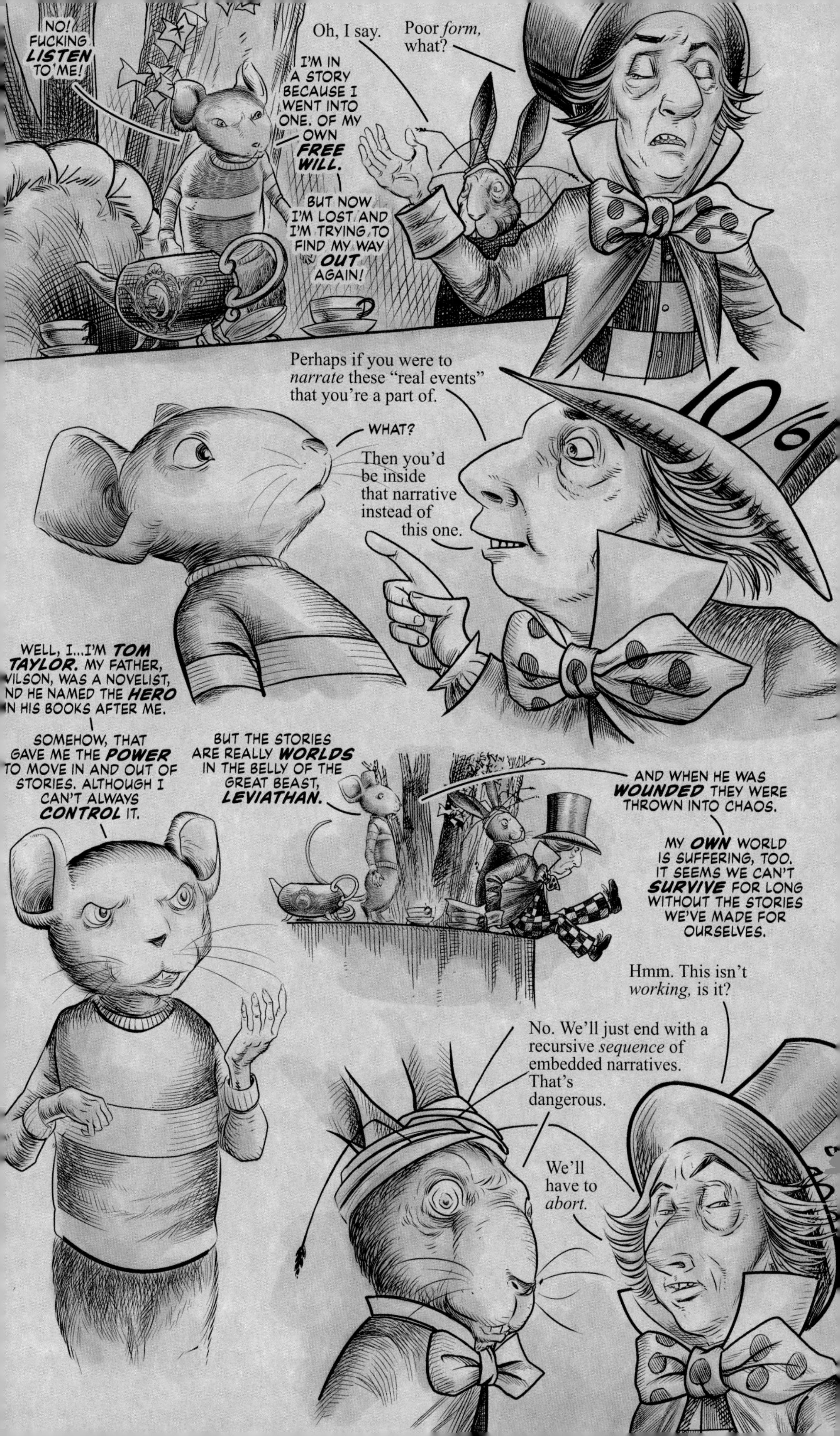
NO! FUCKING LISTEN TO ME!
I'M IN A STORY BECAUSE I WENT INTO ONE. OF MY OWN FREE WILL.
BUT NOW I'M LOST AND I'M TRYING TO FIND MY WAY OUT AGAIN!
Oh, I say.
Poor form, what?
Perhaps if you were to narrate these "real events" that you're a part of.
WHAT?
Then you'd be inside that narrative instead of this one.
10/6
WELL, I...I'M TOM TAYLOR. MY FATHER, VILSON, WAS A NOVELIST, ND HE NAMED THE HERO N HIS BOOKS AFTER ME.
SOMEHOW, THAT GAVE ME THE POWER TO MOVE IN AND OUT OF STORIES. ALTHOUGH I CAN'T ALWAYS CONTROL IT.
BUT THE STORIES ARE REALLY WORLDS IN THE BELLY OF THE GREAT BEAST, LEVIATHAN.
AND WHEN HE WAS WOUNDED THEY WERE THROWN INTO CHAOS.
MY OWN WORLD IS SUFFERING, TOO. IT SEEMS WE CAN'T SURVIVE FOR LONG WITHOUT THE STORIES WE'VE MADE FOR OURSELVES.
Hmm. This isn't working, is it?
No. We'll just end with a recursive sequence of embedded narratives.
That's dangerous.
We'll have to abort.

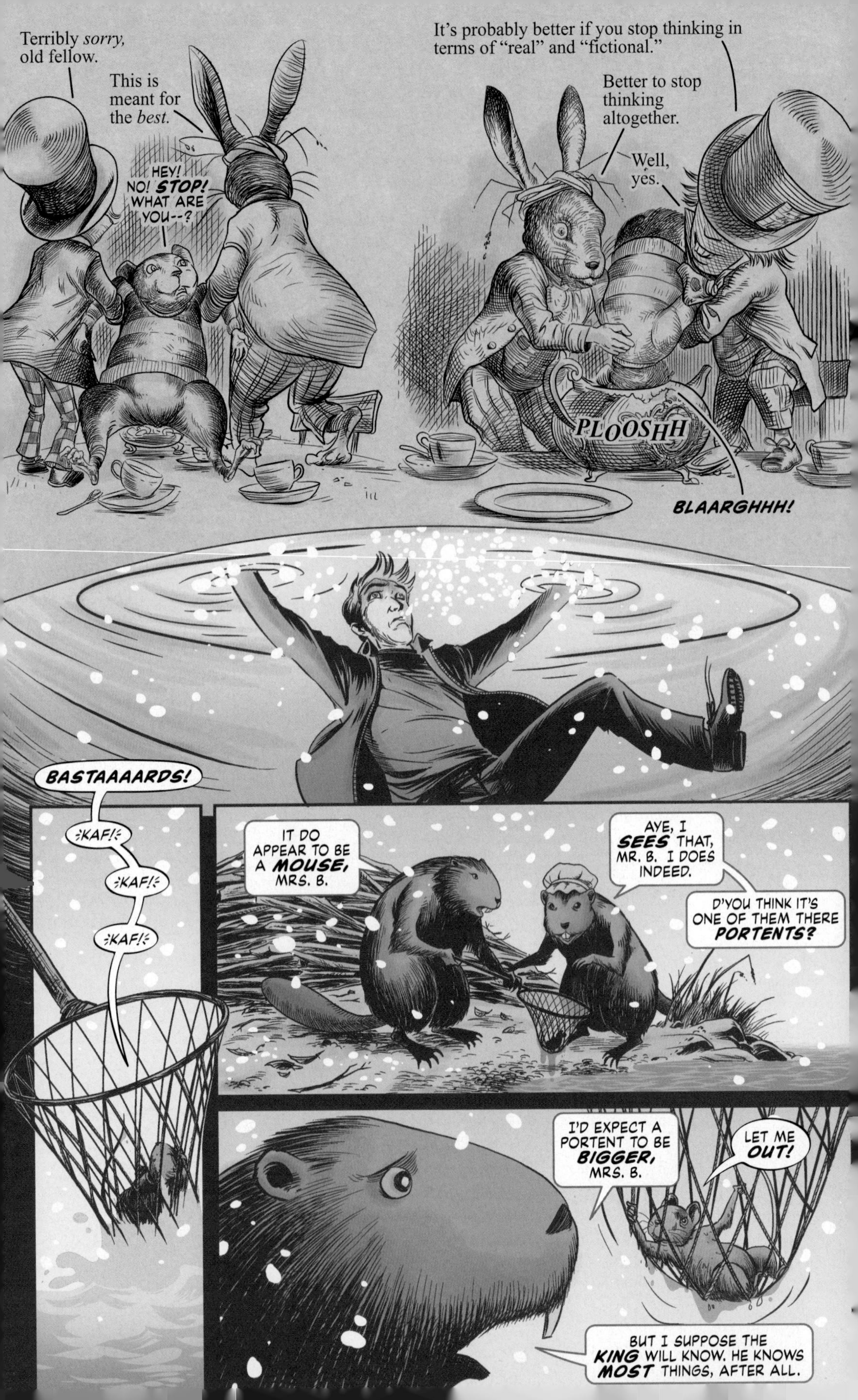
Terribly *sorry,* old fellow.
This is meant for the *best.*
HEY! NO! **STOP!** WHAT ARE YOU--?
It's probably better if you stop thinking in terms of "real" and "fictional."
Better to stop thinking altogether.
Well, yes.
PLOOSHH
BLAARGHHH!
BASTAAAARDS!
KAF!
KAF!
KAF!
IT DO APPEAR TO BE A **MOUSE,** MRS. B.
AYE, I **SEES** THAT, MR. B. I DOES INDEED.
D'YOU THINK IT'S ONE OF THEM THERE **PORTENTS?**
I'D EXPECT A PORTENT TO BE **BIGGER,** MRS. B.
LET ME **OUT!**
BUT I SUPPOSE THE **KING** WILL KNOW. HE KNOWS **MOST** THINGS, AFTER ALL.

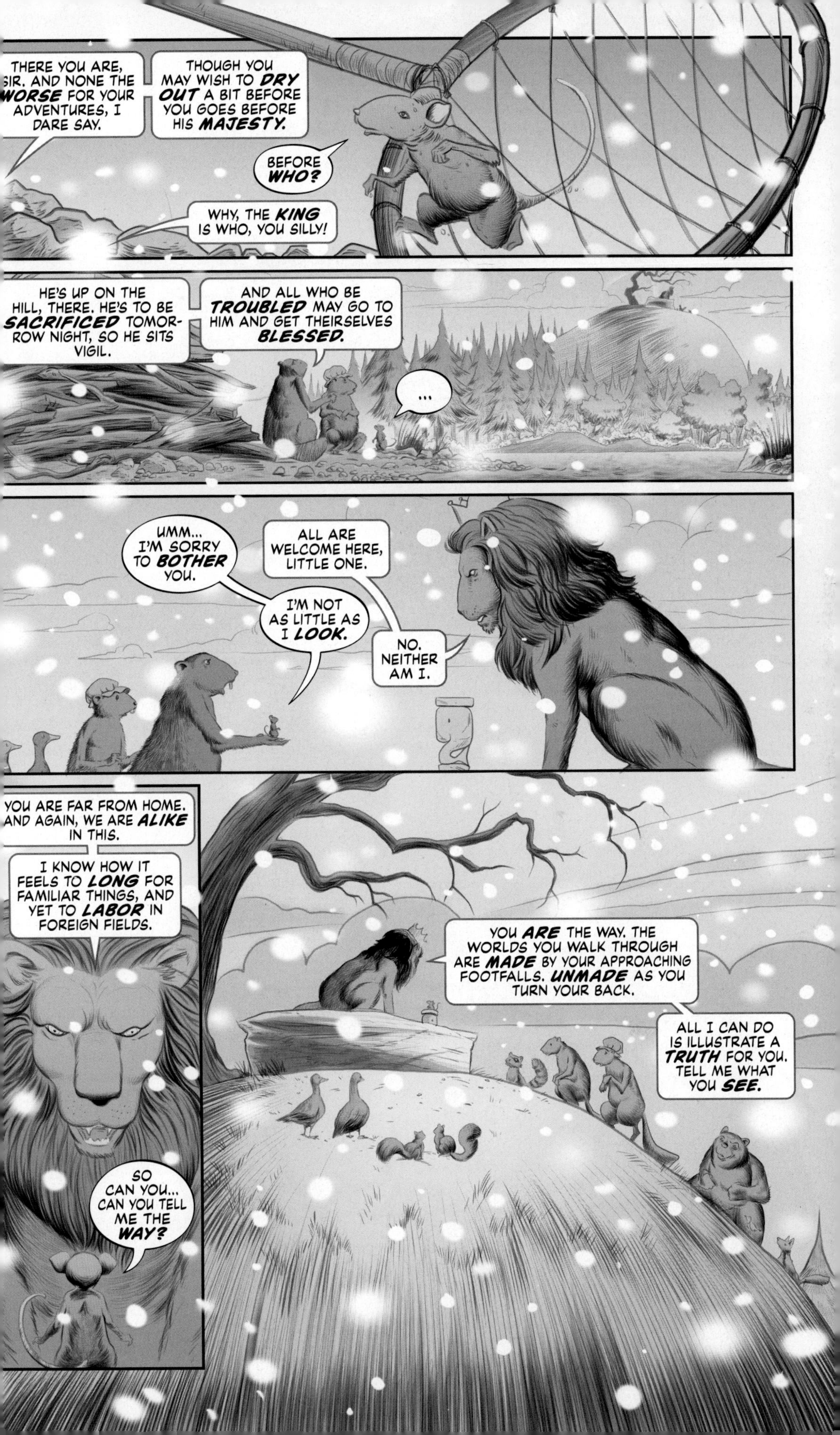

THERE YOU ARE, SIR. AND NONE THE WORSE FOR YOUR ADVENTURES, I DARE SAY.
THOUGH YOU MAY WISH TO DRY OUT A BIT BEFORE YOU GOES BEFORE HIS MAJESTY.
BEFORE WHO?
WHY, THE KING IS WHO, YOU SILLY!
HE'S UP ON THE HILL, THERE. HE'S TO BE SACRIFICED TOMORROW NIGHT, SO HE SITS VIGIL.
AND ALL WHO BE TROUBLED MAY GO TO HIM AND GET THEIRSELVES BLESSED.
...
UMM... I'M SORRY TO BOTHER YOU.
ALL ARE WELCOME HERE, LITTLE ONE.
I'M NOT AS LITTLE AS I LOOK.
NO. NEITHER AM I.
YOU ARE FAR FROM HOME. AND AGAIN, WE ARE ALIKE IN THIS.
I KNOW HOW IT FEELS TO LONG FOR FAMILIAR THINGS, AND YET TO LABOR IN FOREIGN FIELDS.
SO CAN YOU... CAN YOU TELL ME THE WAY?
YOU ARE THE WAY. THE WORLDS YOU WALK THROUGH ARE MADE BY YOUR APPROACHING FOOTFALLS. UNMADE AS YOU TURN YOUR BACK.
ALL I CAN DO IS ILLUSTRATE A TRUTH FOR YOU. TELL ME WHAT YOU SEE.

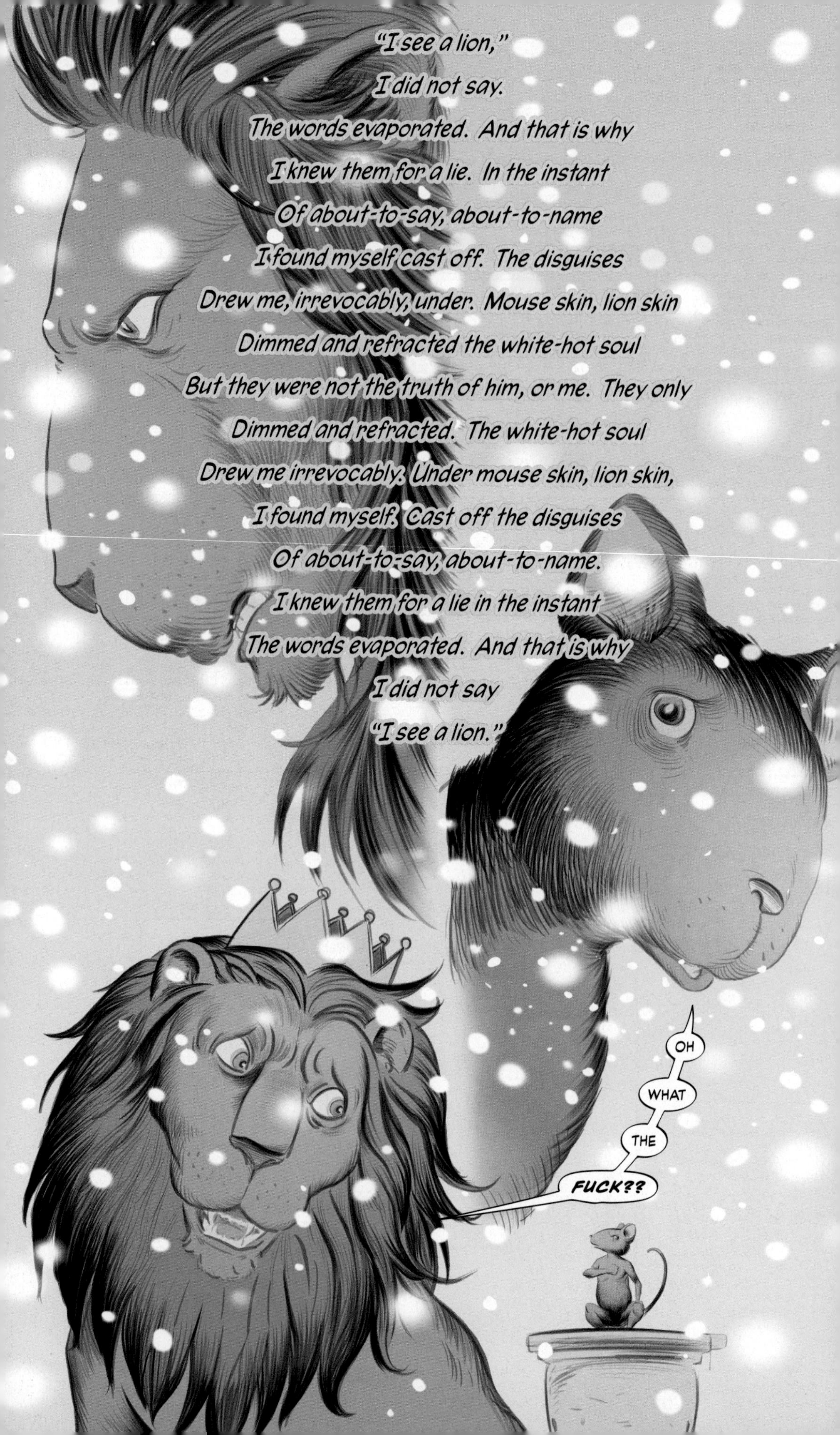
"I see a lion,"
I did not say.
The words evaporated. And that is why
I knew them for a lie. In the instant
Of about-to-say, about-to-name
I found myself cast off. The disguises
Drew me, irrevocably, under. Mouse skin, lion skin
Dimmed and refracted the white-hot soul
But they were not the truth of him, or me. They only
Dimmed and refracted. The white-hot soul
Drew me irrevocably. Under mouse skin, lion skin,
I found myself. Cast off the disguises
Of about-to-say, about-to-name.
I knew them for a lie in the instant
The words evaporated. And that is why
I did not say
"I see a lion."
OH
WHAT
THE
FUCK??

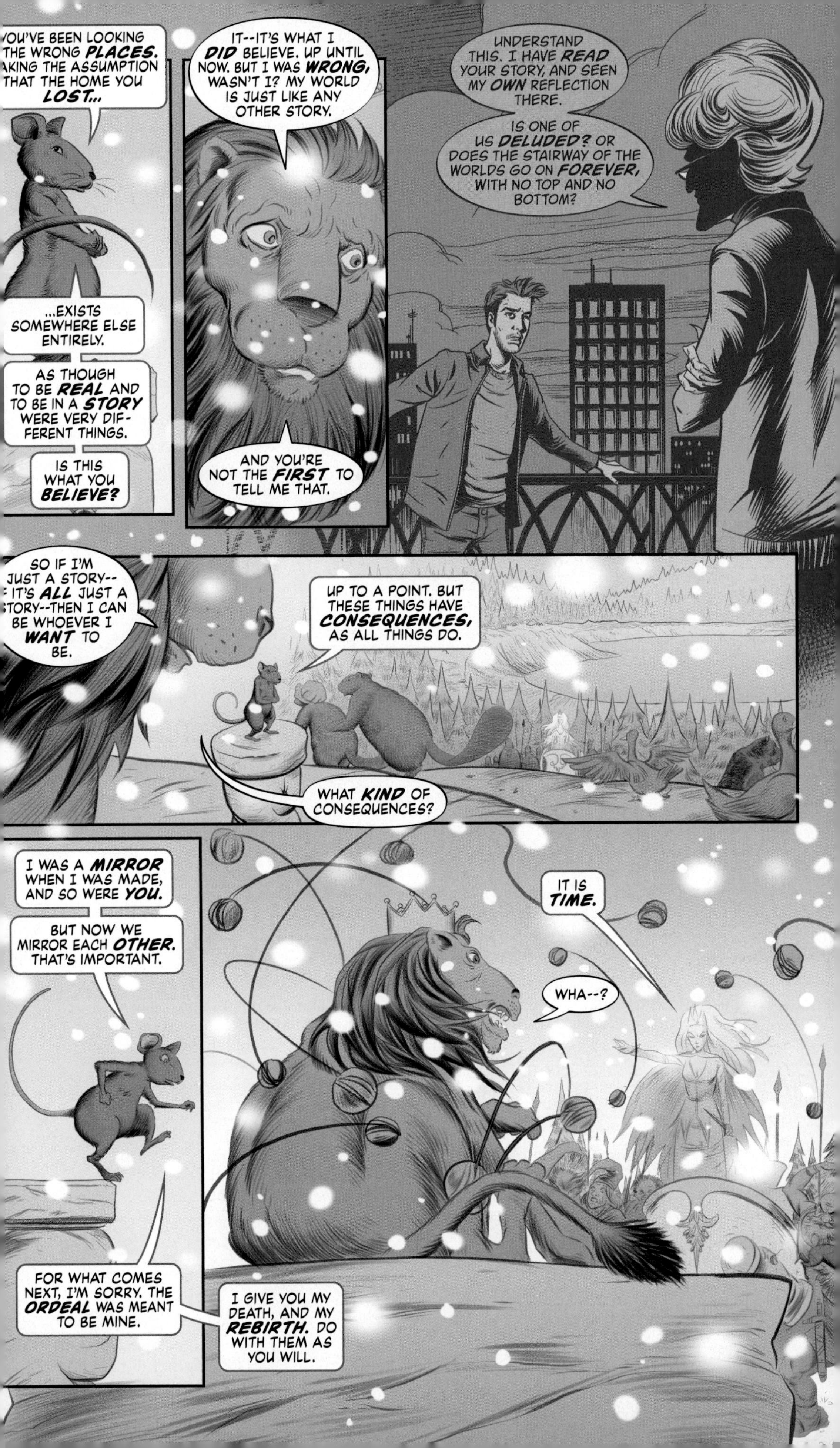

YOU'VE BEEN LOOKING THE WRONG PLACES. AKING THE ASSUMPTION THAT THE HOME YOU LOST...
...EXISTS SOMEWHERE ELSE ENTIRELY.
AS THOUGH TO BE REAL AND TO BE IN A STORY WERE VERY DIF-FERENT THINGS.
IS THIS WHAT YOU BELIEVE?
IT--IT'S WHAT I DID BELIEVE. UP UNTIL NOW. BUT I WAS WRONG, WASN'T I? MY WORLD IS JUST LIKE ANY OTHER STORY.
AND YOU'RE NOT THE FIRST TO TELL ME THAT.
UNDERSTAND THIS. I HAVE READ YOUR STORY, AND SEEN MY OWN REFLECTION THERE.
IS ONE OF US DELUDED? OR DOES THE STAIRWAY OF THE WORLDS GO ON FOREVER, WITH NO TOP AND NO BOTTOM?
SO IF I'M JUST A STORY-- IF IT'S ALL JUST A STORY--THEN I CAN BE WHOEVER I WANT TO BE.
UP TO A POINT. BUT THESE THINGS HAVE CONSEQUENCES, AS ALL THINGS DO.
WHAT KIND OF CONSEQUENCES?
I WAS A MIRROR WHEN I WAS MADE, AND SO WERE YOU.
BUT NOW WE MIRROR EACH OTHER. THAT'S IMPORTANT.
IT IS TIME.
WHA--?
FOR WHAT COMES NEXT, I'M SORRY. THE ORDEAL WAS MEANT TO BE MINE.
I GIVE YOU MY DEATH, AND MY REBIRTH. DO WITH THEM AS YOU WILL.

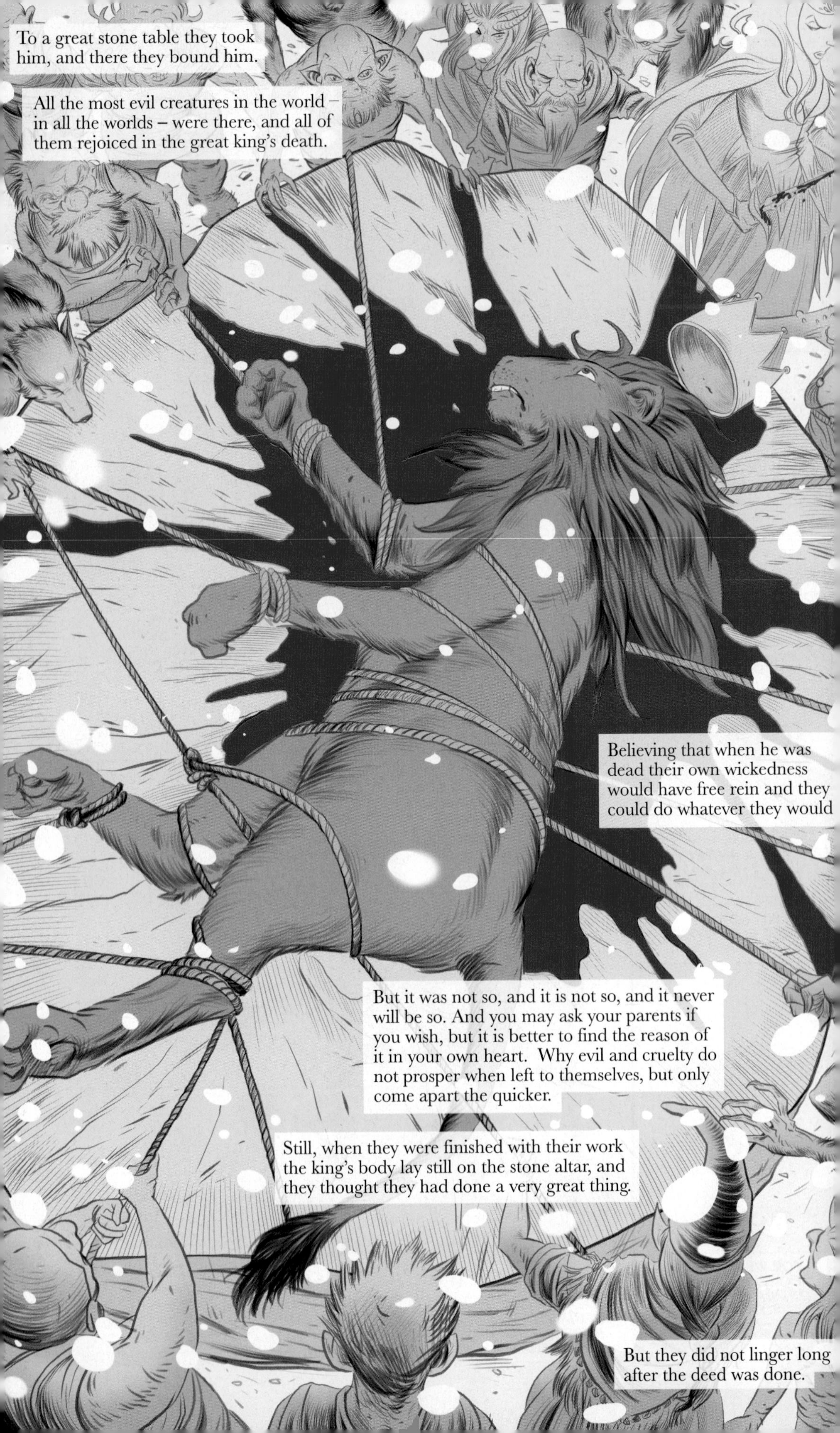
To a great stone table they took him, and there they bound him.
All the most evil creatures in the world – in all the worlds – were there, and all of them rejoiced in the great king's death.
Believing that when he was dead their own wickedness would have free rein and they could do whatever they would
But it was not so, and it is not so, and it never will be so. And you may ask your parents if you wish, but it is better to find the reason of it in your own heart. Why evil and cruelty do not prosper when left to themselves, but only come apart the quicker.
Still, when they were finished with their work the king's body lay still on the stone altar, and they thought they had done a very great thing.
But they did not linger long after the deed was done.

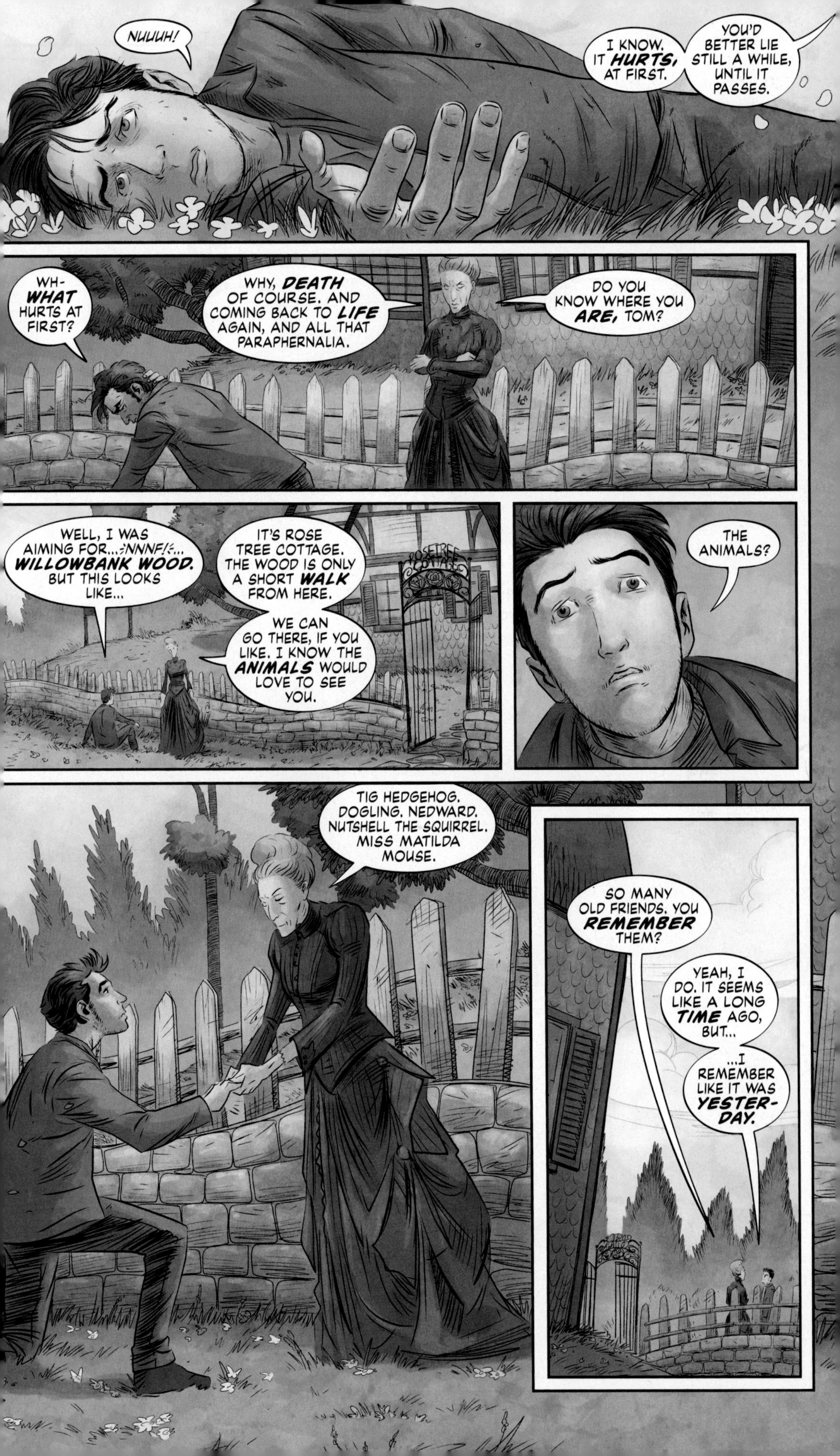
NUUUH!
I KNOW. IT **HURTS,** AT FIRST.
YOU'D BETTER LIE STILL A WHILE, UNTIL IT PASSES.
WH- **WHAT** HURTS AT FIRST?
WHY, **DEATH** OF COURSE. AND COMING BACK TO **LIFE** AGAIN, AND ALL THAT PARAPHERNALIA.
DO YOU KNOW WHERE YOU **ARE,** TOM?
WELL, I WAS AIMING FOR...NNNF!... **WILLOWBANK WOOD.** BUT THIS LOOKS LIKE...
IT'S ROSE TREE COTTAGE. THE WOOD IS ONLY A SHORT **WALK** FROM HERE.
WE CAN GO THERE, IF YOU LIKE. I KNOW THE **ANIMALS** WOULD LOVE TO SEE YOU.
THE ANIMALS?
TIG HEDGEHOG. DOGLING. NEDWARD. NUTSHELL THE SQUIRREL. MISS MATILDA MOUSE.
SO MANY OLD FRIENDS. YOU **REMEMBER** THEM?
YEAH, I DO. IT SEEMS LIKE A LONG **TIME** AGO, BUT...
...I REMEMBER LIKE IT WAS **YESTER-DAY.**

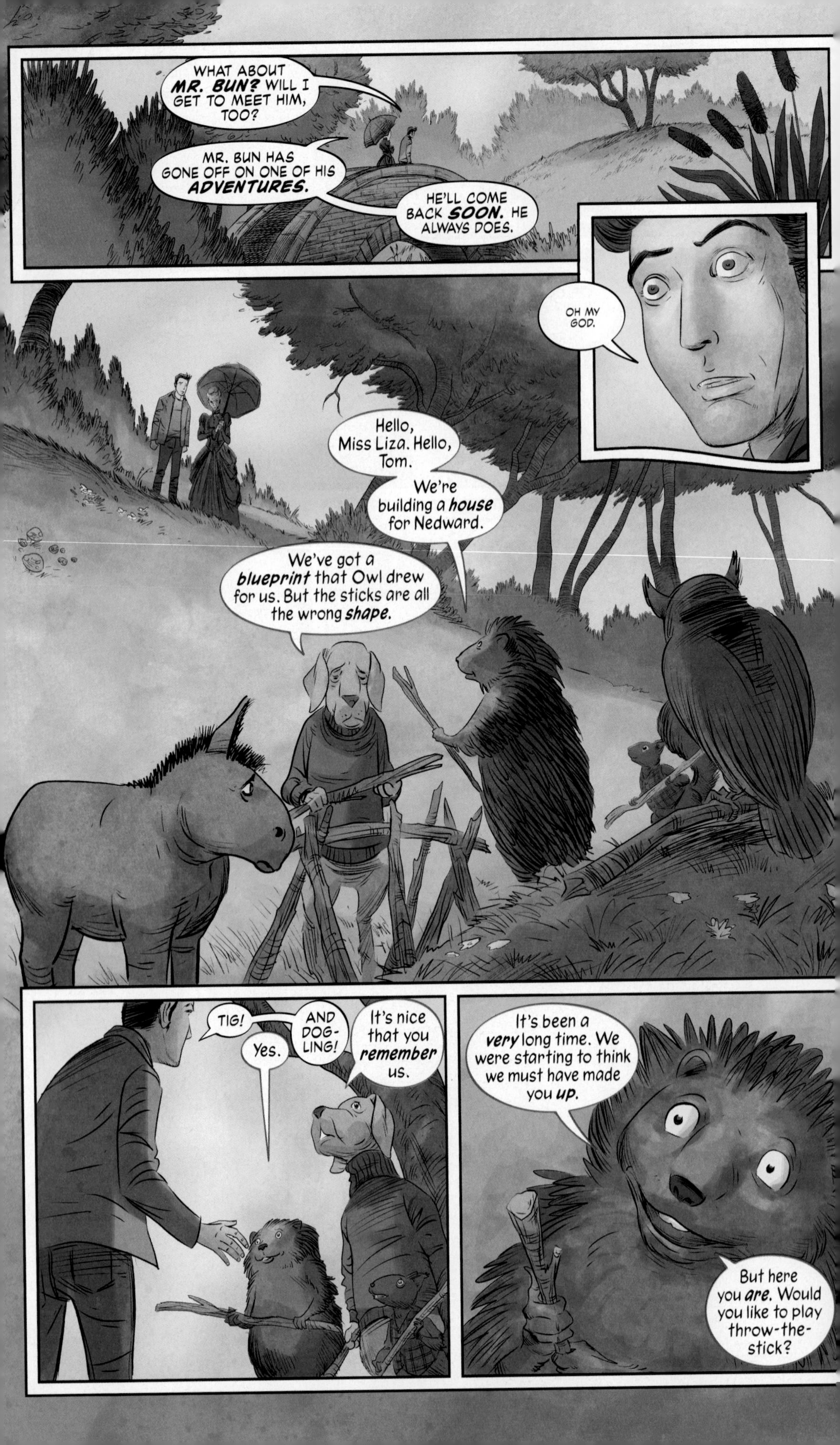
WHAT ABOUT MR. BUN? WILL I GET TO MEET HIM, TOO?
MR. BUN HAS GONE OFF ON ONE OF HIS ADVENTURES.
HE'LL COME BACK SOON. HE ALWAYS DOES.
OH MY GOD.
Hello, Miss Liza. Hello, Tom.
We're building a house for Nedward.
We've got a blueprint that Owl drew for us. But the sticks are all the wrong shape.
TIG!
AND DOG-LING!
Yes.
It's nice that you remember us.
It's been a very long time. We were starting to think we must have made you up.
But here you are. Would you like to play throw-the-stick?

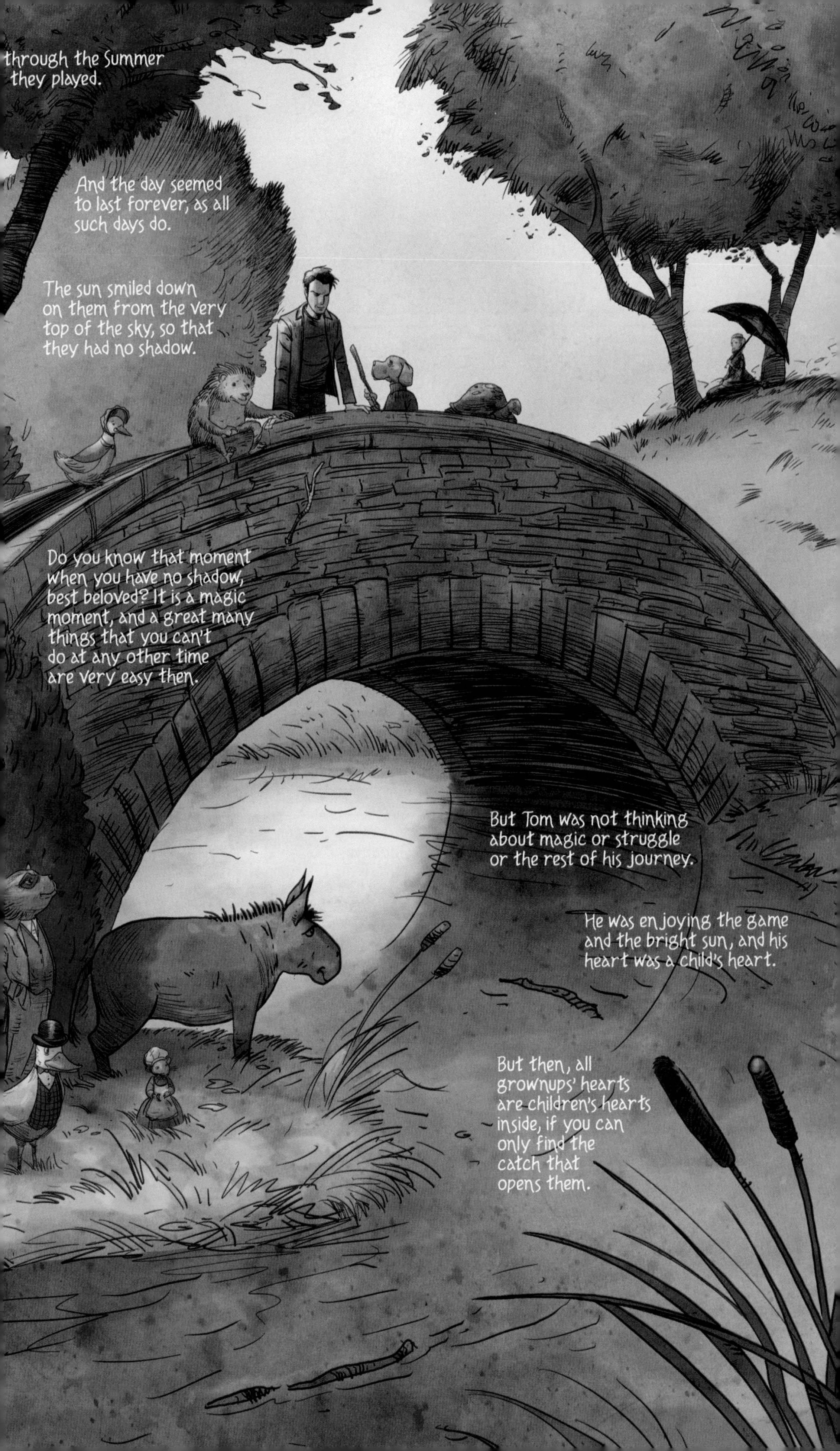
through the Summer they played.
And the day seemed to last forever, as all such days do.
The sun smiled down on them from the very top of the sky, so that they had no shadow.
Do you know that moment when you have no shadow, best beloved? It is a magic moment, and a great many things that you can't do at any other time are very easy then.
But Tom was not thinking about magic or struggle or the rest of his journey.
He was enjoying the game and the bright sun, and his heart was a child's heart.
But then, all grownups' hearts are children's hearts inside, if you can only find the catch that opens them.

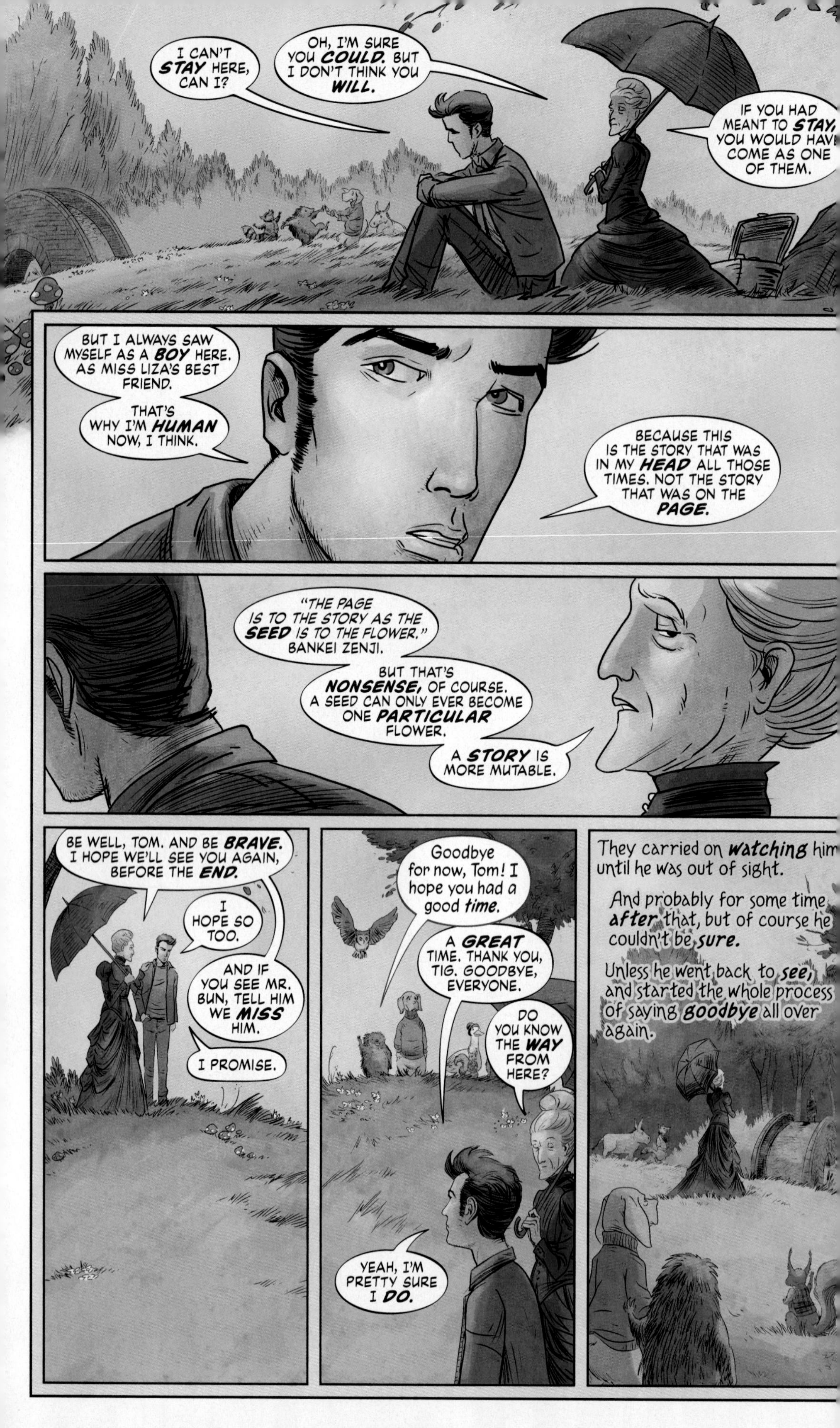
I CAN'T STAY HERE, CAN I?
OH, I'M SURE YOU COULD. BUT I DON'T THINK YOU WILL.
IF YOU HAD MEANT TO STAY, YOU WOULD HAVE COME AS ONE OF THEM.
BUT I ALWAYS SAW MYSELF AS A BOY HERE. AS MISS LIZA'S BEST FRIEND.
THAT'S WHY I'M HUMAN NOW, I THINK.
BECAUSE THIS IS THE STORY THAT WAS IN MY HEAD ALL THOSE TIMES. NOT THE STORY THAT WAS ON THE PAGE.
"THE PAGE IS TO THE STORY AS THE SEED IS TO THE FLOWER." BANKEI ZENJI.
BUT THAT'S NONSENSE, OF COURSE. A SEED CAN ONLY EVER BECOME ONE PARTICULAR FLOWER.
A STORY IS MORE MUTABLE.
BE WELL, TOM. AND BE BRAVE. I HOPE WE'LL SEE YOU AGAIN, BEFORE THE END.
I HOPE SO TOO.
AND IF YOU SEE MR. BUN, TELL HIM WE MISS HIM.
I PROMISE.
Goodbye for now, Tom! I hope you had a good time.
A GREAT TIME. THANK YOU, TIG. GOODBYE, EVERYONE.
DO YOU KNOW THE WAY FROM HERE?
YEAH, I'M PRETTY SURE I DO.
They carried on watching him until he was out of sight.
And probably for some time after that, but of course he couldn't be sure.
Unless he went back to see, and started the whole process of saying goodbye all over again.

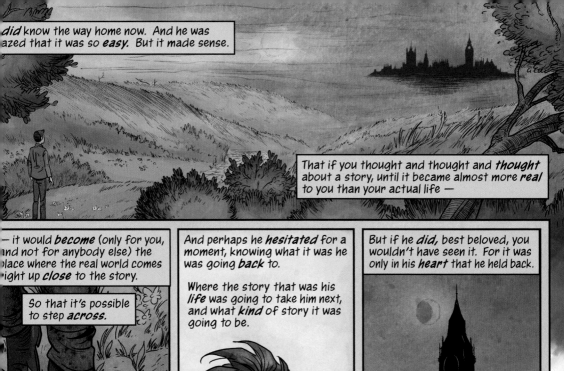

...*did* know the way home now. And he was ...azed that it was so *easy*. But it made sense.

That if you thought and thought and *thought* about a story, until it became almost more *real* to you than your actual life —

— it would *become* (only for you, and not for anybody else) the place where the real world comes right up *close* to the story.

So that it's possible to step *across*.

And perhaps he *hesitated* for a moment, knowing what it was he was going *back* to.

Where the story that was his *life* was going to take him next, and what *kind* of story it was going to be.

But if he *did*, best beloved, you wouldn't have seen it. For it was only in his *heart* that he held back.

His steps did not *slow*, because if they had — even for a moment! — the spell would have been *broken*.

And...

HERE HE IS!

...said a voice he knew, and longed for.

HERE HE IS *AT LAST!*

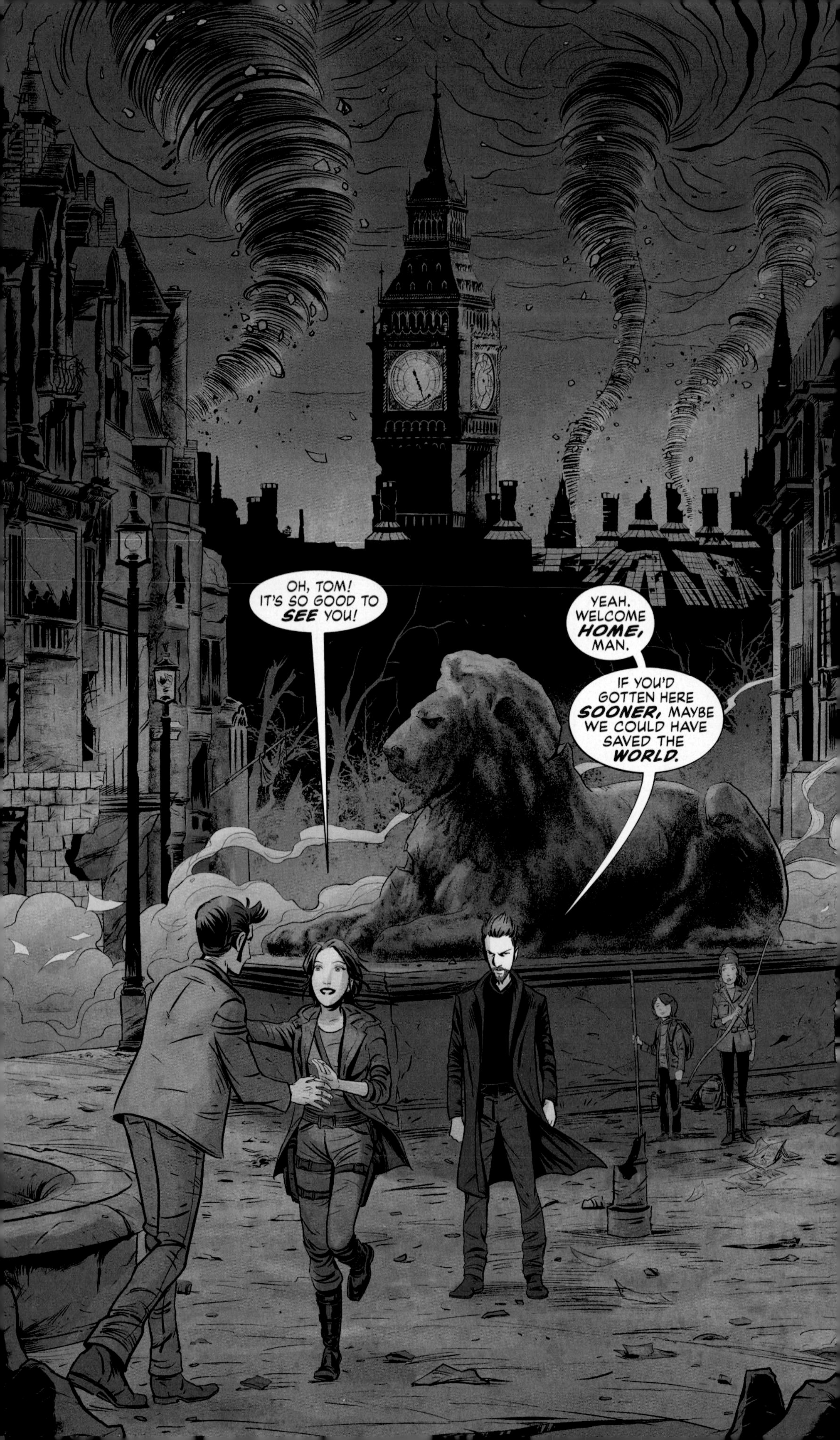
OH, TOM! IT'S SO GOOD TO SEE YOU!
YEAH. WELCOME HOME, MAN.
IF YOU'D GOTTEN HERE SOONER, MAYBE WE COULD HAVE SAVED THE WORLD.

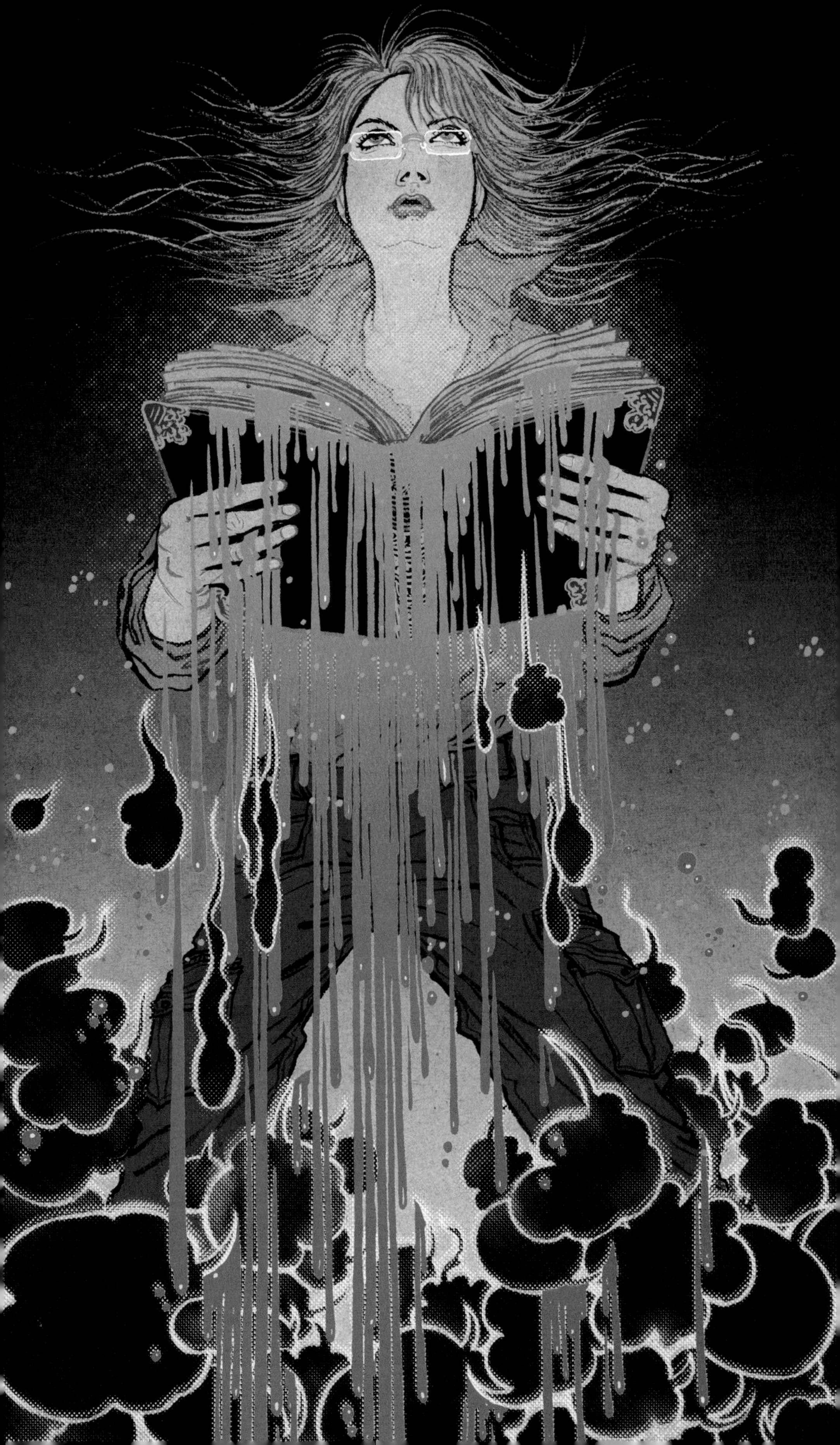

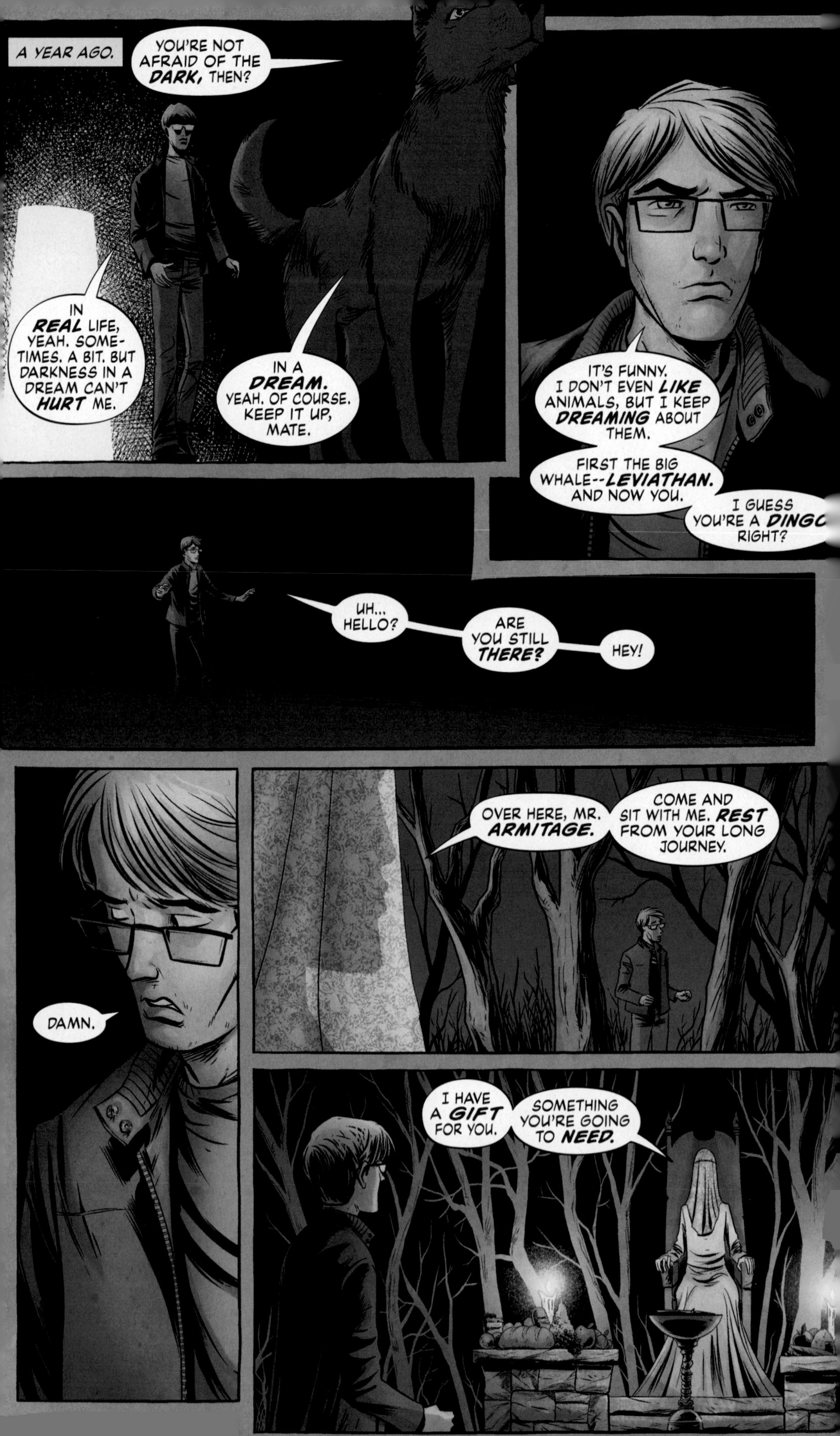
A YEAR AGO.
YOU'RE NOT AFRAID OF THE DARK, THEN?
IN REAL LIFE, YEAH. SOME-TIMES. A BIT. BUT DARKNESS IN A DREAM CAN'T HURT ME.
IN A DREAM. YEAH. OF COURSE. KEEP IT UP, MATE.
IT'S FUNNY. I DON'T EVEN LIKE ANIMALS, BUT I KEEP DREAMING ABOUT THEM.
FIRST THE BIG WHALE--LEVIATHAN. AND NOW YOU.
I GUESS YOU'RE A DINGO RIGHT?
UH... HELLO?
ARE YOU STILL THERE?
HEY!
DAMN.
OVER HERE, MR. ARMITAGE.
COME AND SIT WITH ME. REST FROM YOUR LONG JOURNEY.
I HAVE A GIFT FOR YOU.
SOMETHING YOU'RE GOING TO NEED.

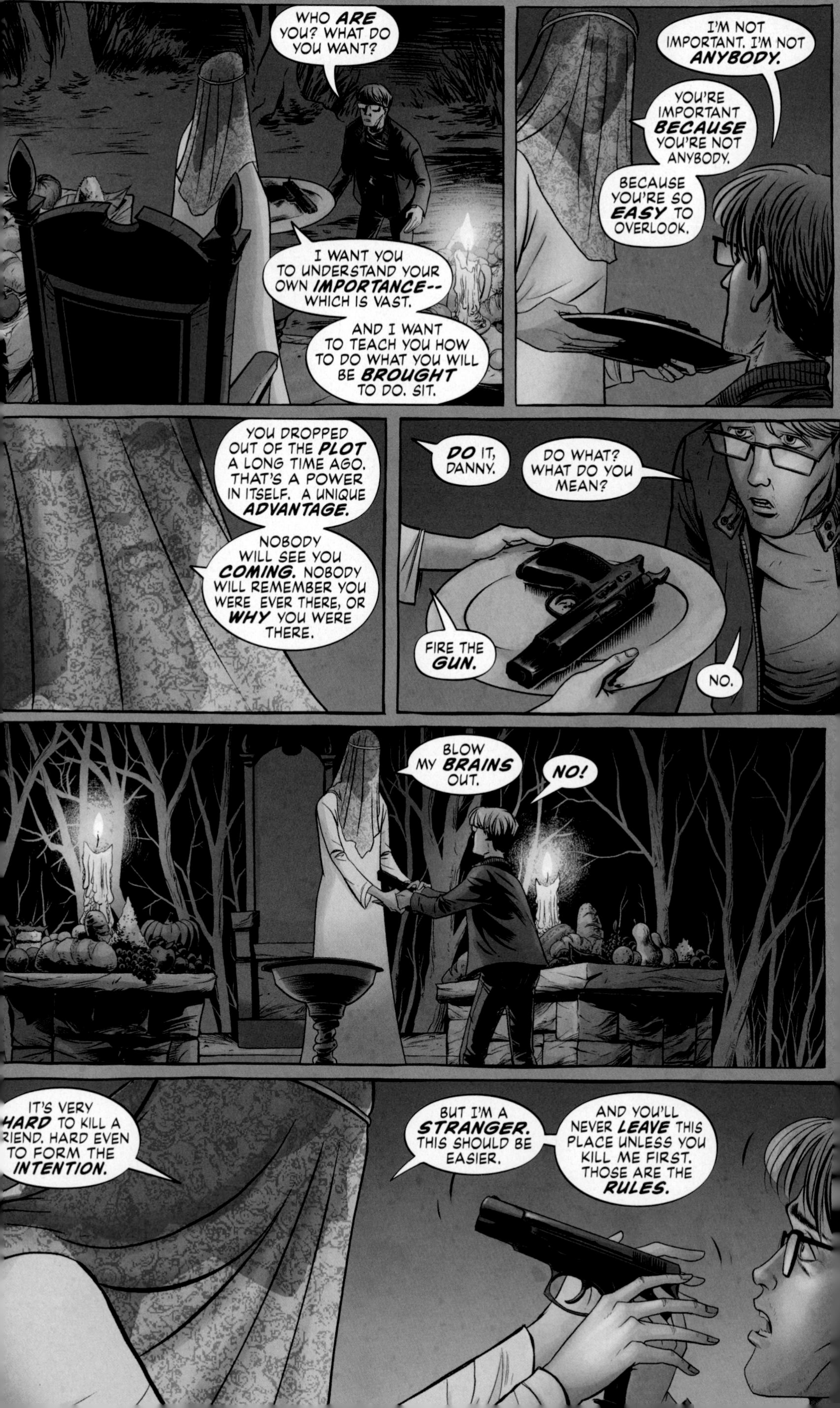
WHO ARE YOU? WHAT DO YOU WANT?
I WANT YOU TO UNDERSTAND YOUR OWN IMPORTANCE-- WHICH IS VAST.
AND I WANT TO TEACH YOU HOW TO DO WHAT YOU WILL BE BROUGHT TO DO. SIT.
I'M NOT IMPORTANT. I'M NOT ANYBODY.
YOU'RE IMPORTANT BECAUSE YOU'RE NOT ANYBODY.
BECAUSE YOU'RE SO EASY TO OVERLOOK.
YOU DROPPED OUT OF THE PLOT A LONG TIME AGO. THAT'S A POWER IN ITSELF. A UNIQUE ADVANTAGE.
NOBODY WILL SEE YOU COMING. NOBODY WILL REMEMBER YOU WERE EVER THERE, OR WHY YOU WERE THERE.
DO IT, DANNY.
DO WHAT? WHAT DO YOU MEAN?
FIRE THE GUN.
NO.
BLOW MY BRAINS OUT.
NO!
IT'S VERY HARD TO KILL A RIEND. HARD EVEN TO FORM THE INTENTION.
BUT I'M A STRANGER. THIS SHOULD BE EASIER.
AND YOU'LL NEVER LEAVE THIS PLACE UNLESS YOU KILL ME FIRST. THOSE ARE THE RULES.

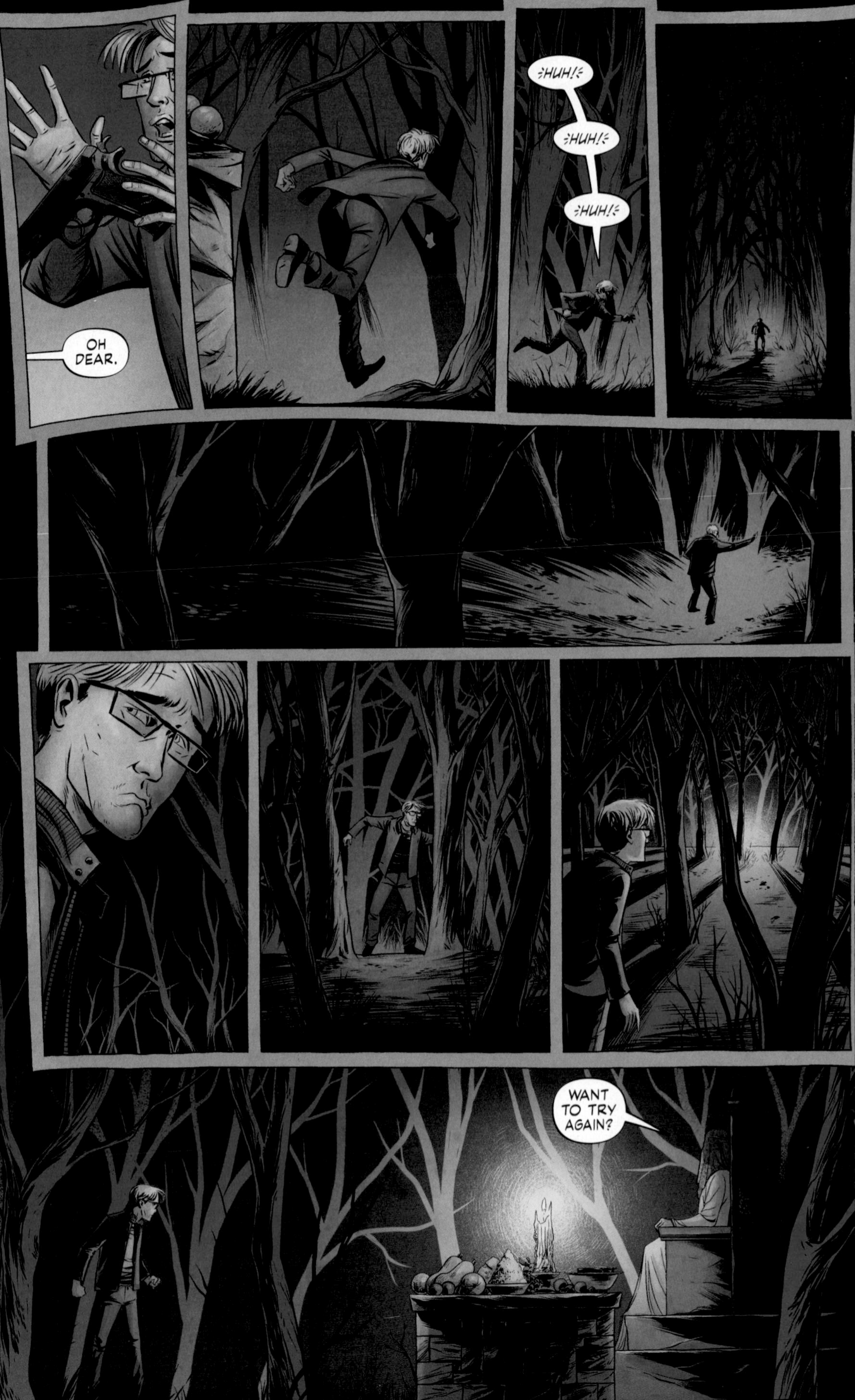
OH DEAR.
HUH!
HUH!
HUH!
WANT TO TRY AGAIN?

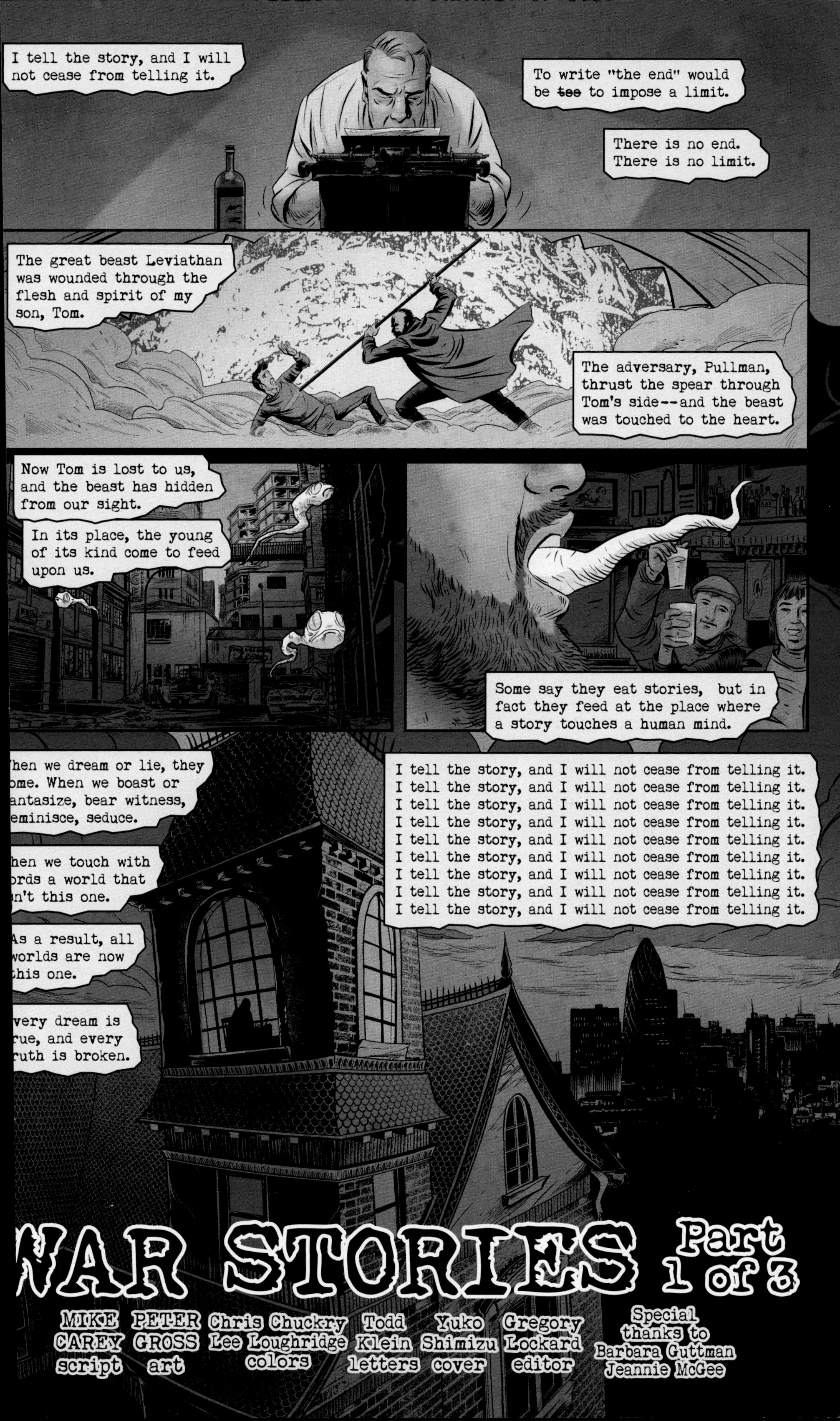
I tell the story, and I will not cease from telling it.
To write "the end" would be ~~too~~ to impose a limit.
There is no end. There is no limit.
The great beast Leviathan was wounded through the flesh and spirit of my son, Tom.
The adversary, Pullman, thrust the spear through Tom's side--and the beast was touched to the heart.
Now Tom is lost to us, and the beast has hidden from our sight.
In its place, the young of its kind come to feed upon us.
Some say they eat stories, but in fact they feed at the place where a story touches a human mind.
hen we dream or lie, they ome. When we boast or antasize, bear witness, eminisce, seduce.
hen we touch with ords a world that n't this one.
As a result, all worlds are now this one.
very dream is rue, and every ruth is broken.
I tell the story, and I will not cease from telling it.
I tell the story, and I will not cease from telling it.
I tell the story, and I will not cease from telling it.
I tell the story, and I will not cease from telling it.
I tell the story, and I will not cease from telling it.
I tell the story, and I will not cease from telling it.
I tell the story, and I will not cease from telling it.
I tell the story, and I will not cease from telling it.
I tell the story, and I will not cease from telling it.
WAR STORIES Part 1 of 3
MIKE CAREY script
PETER GROSS art
Chris Chuckry Lee Loughridge colors
Todd Klein letters
Yuko Shimizu cover
Gregory Lockard editor
Special thanks to Barbara Guttman Jeannie McGee

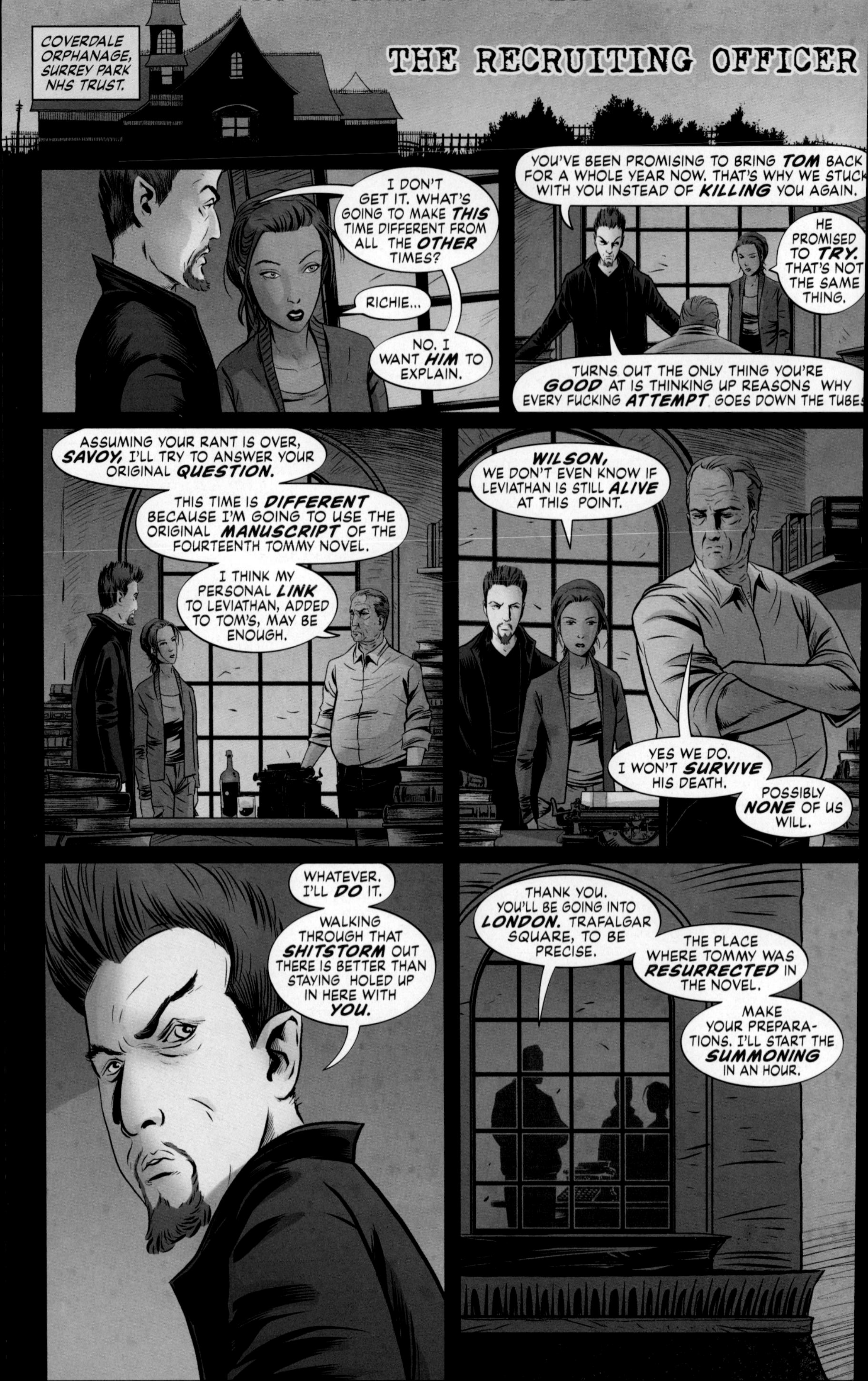
COVERDALE ORPHANAGE, SURREY PARK NHS TRUST.
THE RECRUITING OFFICER
I DON'T GET IT. WHAT'S GOING TO MAKE THIS TIME DIFFERENT FROM ALL THE OTHER TIMES?
RICHIE...
NO. I WANT HIM TO EXPLAIN.
YOU'VE BEEN PROMISING TO BRING TOM BACK FOR A WHOLE YEAR NOW. THAT'S WHY WE STUCK WITH YOU INSTEAD OF KILLING YOU AGAIN.
HE PROMISED TO TRY. THAT'S NOT THE SAME THING.
TURNS OUT THE ONLY THING YOU'RE GOOD AT IS THINKING UP REASONS WHY EVERY FUCKING ATTEMPT GOES DOWN THE TUBES
ASSUMING YOUR RANT IS OVER, SAVOY, I'LL TRY TO ANSWER YOUR ORIGINAL QUESTION.
THIS TIME IS DIFFERENT BECAUSE I'M GOING TO USE THE ORIGINAL MANUSCRIPT OF THE FOURTEENTH TOMMY NOVEL.
I THINK MY PERSONAL LINK TO LEVIATHAN, ADDED TO TOM'S, MAY BE ENOUGH.
WILSON, WE DON'T EVEN KNOW IF LEVIATHAN IS STILL ALIVE AT THIS POINT.
YES WE DO. I WON'T SURVIVE HIS DEATH.
POSSIBLY NONE OF US WILL.
WHATEVER. I'LL DO IT.
WALKING THROUGH THAT SHITSTORM OUT THERE IS BETTER THAN STAYING HOLED UP IN HERE WITH YOU.
THANK YOU. YOU'LL BE GOING INTO LONDON. TRAFALGAR SQUARE, TO BE PRECISE.
THE PLACE WHERE TOMMY WAS RESURRECTED IN THE NOVEL.
MAKE YOUR PREPARATIONS. I'LL START THE SUMMONING IN AN HOUR.

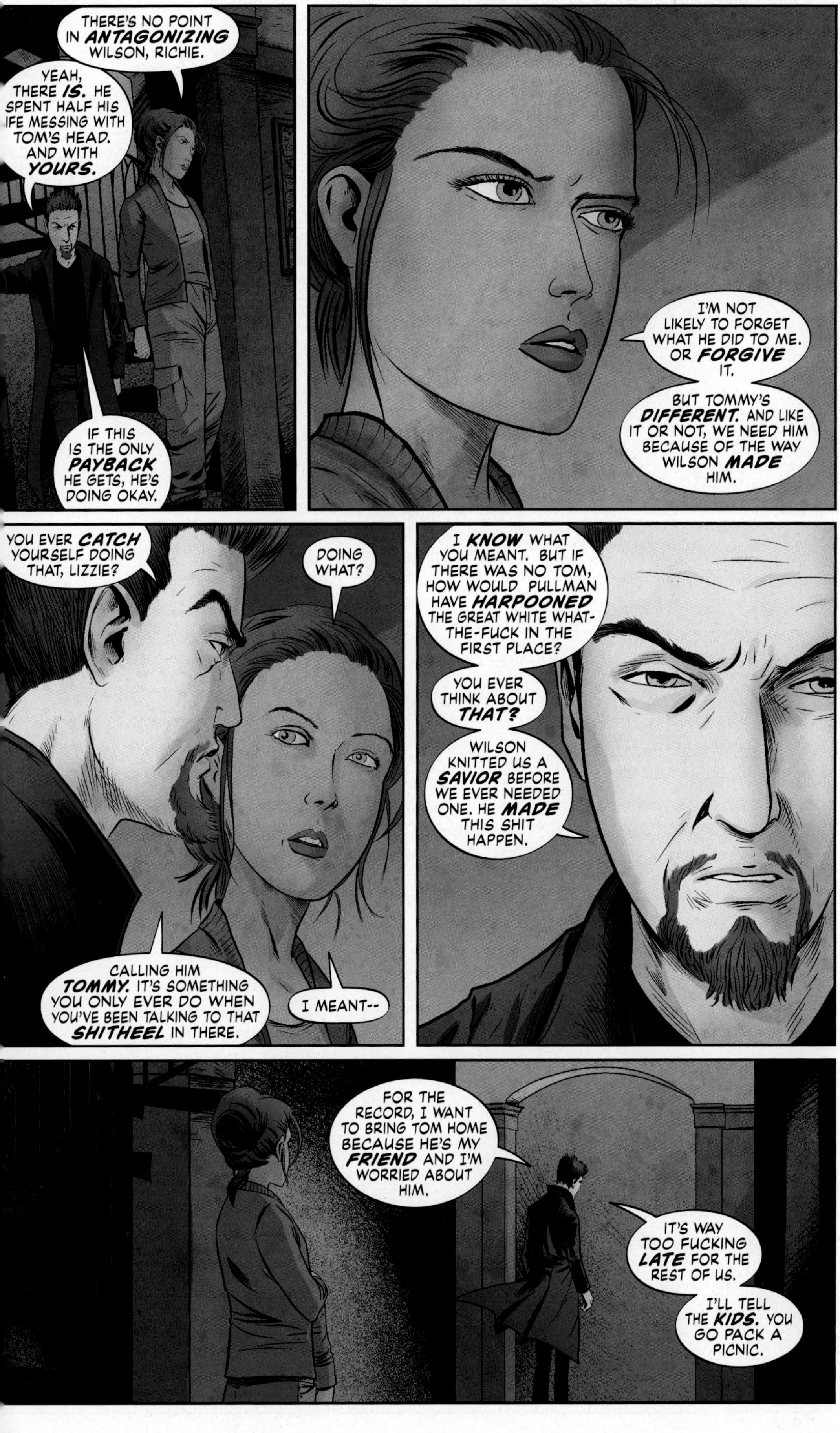

THERE'S NO POINT IN ANTAGONIZING WILSON, RICHIE.
YEAH, THERE IS. HE SPENT HALF HIS LIFE MESSING WITH TOM'S HEAD. AND WITH YOURS.
IF THIS IS THE ONLY PAYBACK HE GETS, HE'S DOING OKAY.
I'M NOT LIKELY TO FORGET WHAT HE DID TO ME. OR FORGIVE IT.
BUT TOMMY'S DIFFERENT. AND LIKE IT OR NOT, WE NEED HIM BECAUSE OF THE WAY WILSON MADE HIM.
YOU EVER CATCH YOURSELF DOING THAT, LIZZIE?
DOING WHAT?
CALLING HIM TOMMY. IT'S SOMETHING YOU ONLY EVER DO WHEN YOU'VE BEEN TALKING TO THAT SHITHEEL IN THERE.
I MEANT--
I KNOW WHAT YOU MEANT. BUT IF THERE WAS NO TOM, HOW WOULD PULLMAN HAVE HARPOONED THE GREAT WHITE WHAT-THE-FUCK IN THE FIRST PLACE?
YOU EVER THINK ABOUT THAT?
WILSON KNITTED US A SAVIOR BEFORE WE EVER NEEDED ONE. HE MADE THIS SHIT HAPPEN.
FOR THE RECORD, I WANT TO BRING TOM HOME BECAUSE HE'S MY FRIEND AND I'M WORRIED ABOUT HIM.
IT'S WAY TOO FUCKING LATE FOR THE REST OF US.
I'LL TELL THE KIDS. YOU GO PACK A PICNIC.

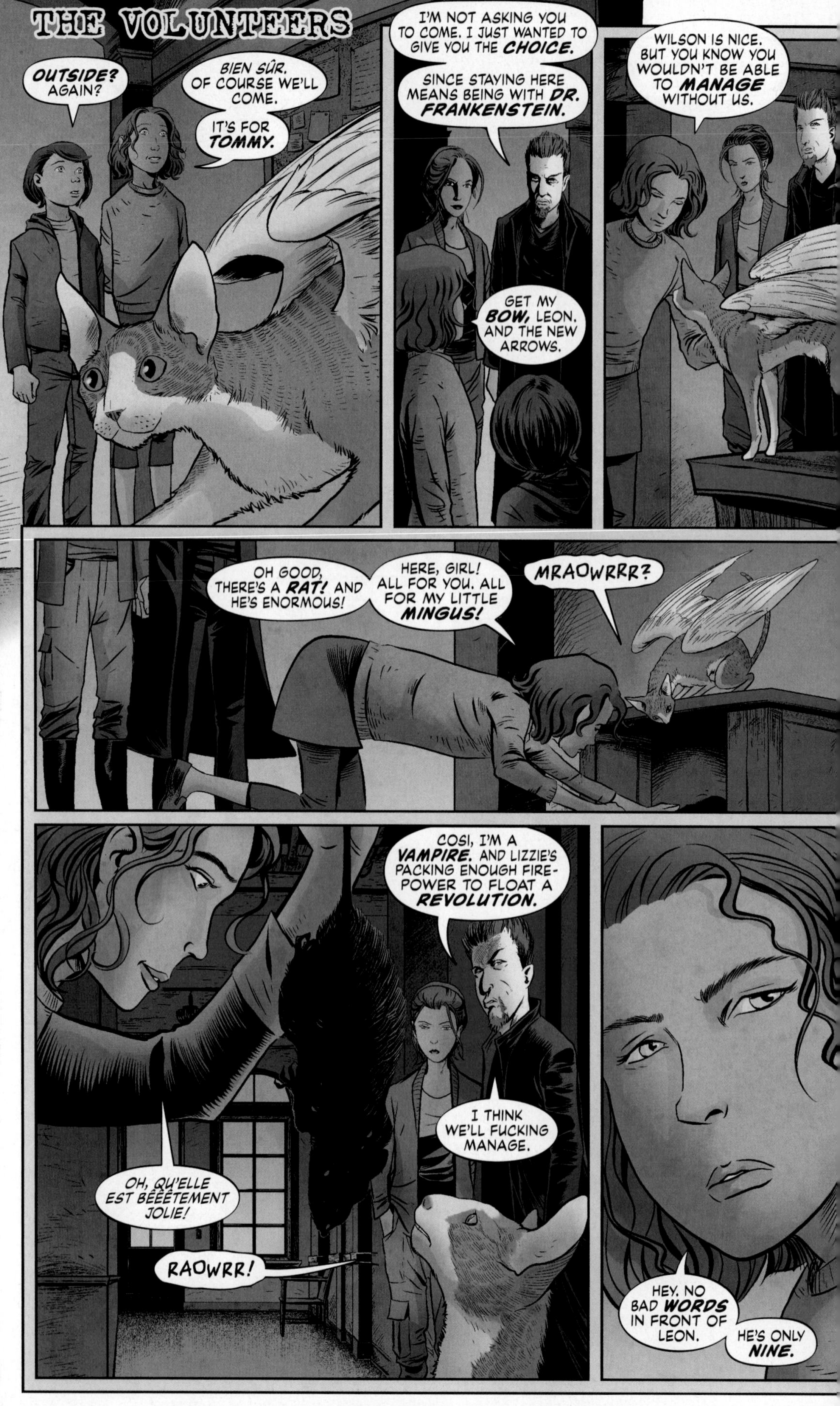
THE VOLUNTEERS
OUTSIDE? AGAIN?
BIEN SÛR. OF COURSE WE'LL COME.
IT'S FOR TOMMY.
I'M NOT ASKING YOU TO COME. I JUST WANTED TO GIVE YOU THE CHOICE.
SINCE STAYING HERE MEANS BEING WITH DR. FRANKENSTEIN.
GET MY BOW, LEON. AND THE NEW ARROWS.
WILSON IS NICE. BUT YOU KNOW YOU WOULDN'T BE ABLE TO MANAGE WITHOUT US.
OH GOOD, THERE'S A RAT! AND HE'S ENORMOUS!
HERE, GIRL! ALL FOR YOU. ALL FOR MY LITTLE MINGUS!
MRAOWRRR?
COSI, I'M A VAMPIRE. AND LIZZIE'S PACKING ENOUGH FIRE-POWER TO FLOAT A REVOLUTION.
I THINK WE'LL FUCKING MANAGE.
OH, QU'ELLE EST BÉÉÉTEMENT JOLIE!
RAOWRR!
HEY. NO BAD WORDS IN FRONT OF LEON.
HE'S ONLY NINE.

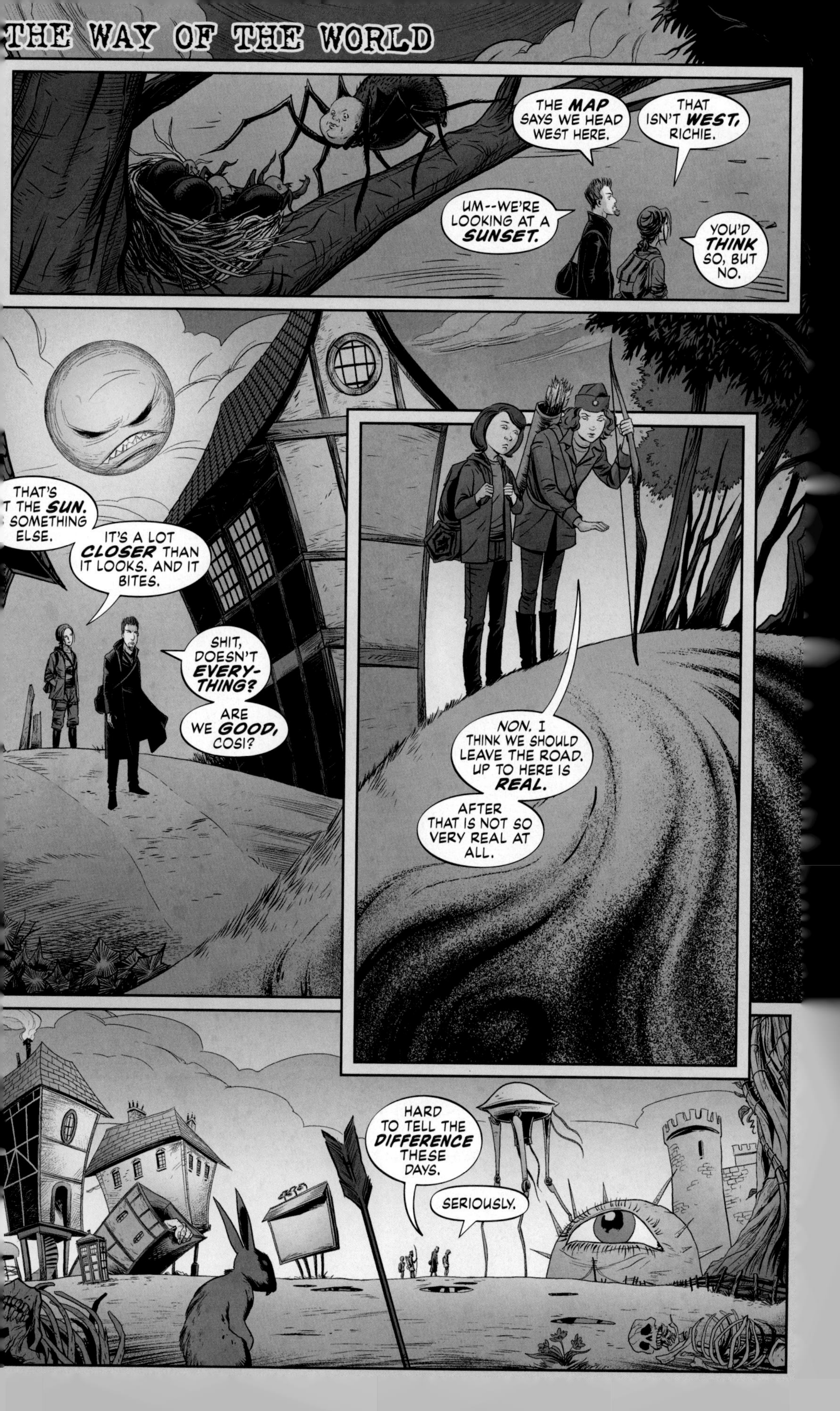
THE WAY OF THE WORLD
THE MAP SAYS WE HEAD WEST HERE.
THAT ISN'T WEST, RICHIE.
UM--WE'RE LOOKING AT A SUNSET.
YOU'D THINK SO, BUT NO.
THAT'S T THE SUN. SOMETHING ELSE.
IT'S A LOT CLOSER THAN IT LOOKS. AND IT BITES.
SHIT, DOESN'T EVERYTHING?
ARE WE GOOD, COSI?
NON. I THINK WE SHOULD LEAVE THE ROAD. UP TO HERE IS REAL.
AFTER THAT IS NOT SO VERY REAL AT ALL.
HARD TO TELL THE DIFFERENCE THESE DAYS.
SERIOUSLY.

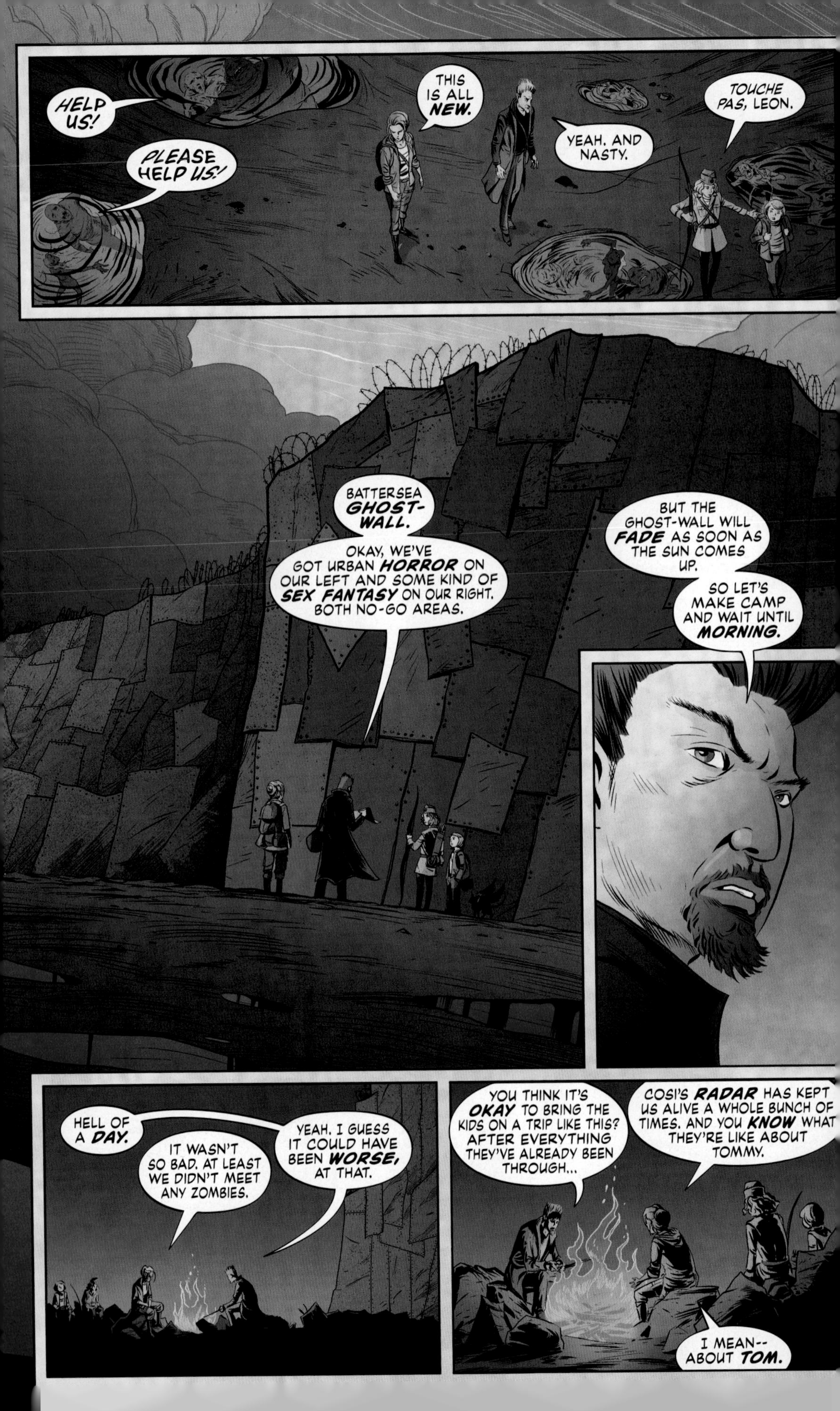
HELP US!
PLEASE HELP US!
THIS IS ALL NEW.
YEAH, AND NASTY.
TOUCHE PAS, LEON.
BATTERSEA GHOST-WALL.
OKAY, WE'VE GOT URBAN HORROR ON OUR LEFT AND SOME KIND OF SEX FANTASY ON OUR RIGHT. BOTH NO-GO AREAS.
BUT THE GHOST-WALL WILL FADE AS SOON AS THE SUN COMES UP.
SO LET'S MAKE CAMP AND WAIT UNTIL MORNING.
HELL OF A DAY.
IT WASN'T SO BAD. AT LEAST WE DIDN'T MEET ANY ZOMBIES.
YEAH. I GUESS IT COULD HAVE BEEN WORSE, AT THAT.
YOU THINK IT'S OKAY TO BRING THE KIDS ON A TRIP LIKE THIS? AFTER EVERYTHING THEY'VE ALREADY BEEN THROUGH...
COSI'S RADAR HAS KEPT US ALIVE A WHOLE BUNCH OF TIMES. AND YOU KNOW WHAT THEY'RE LIKE ABOUT TOMMY.
I MEAN-- ABOUT TOM.

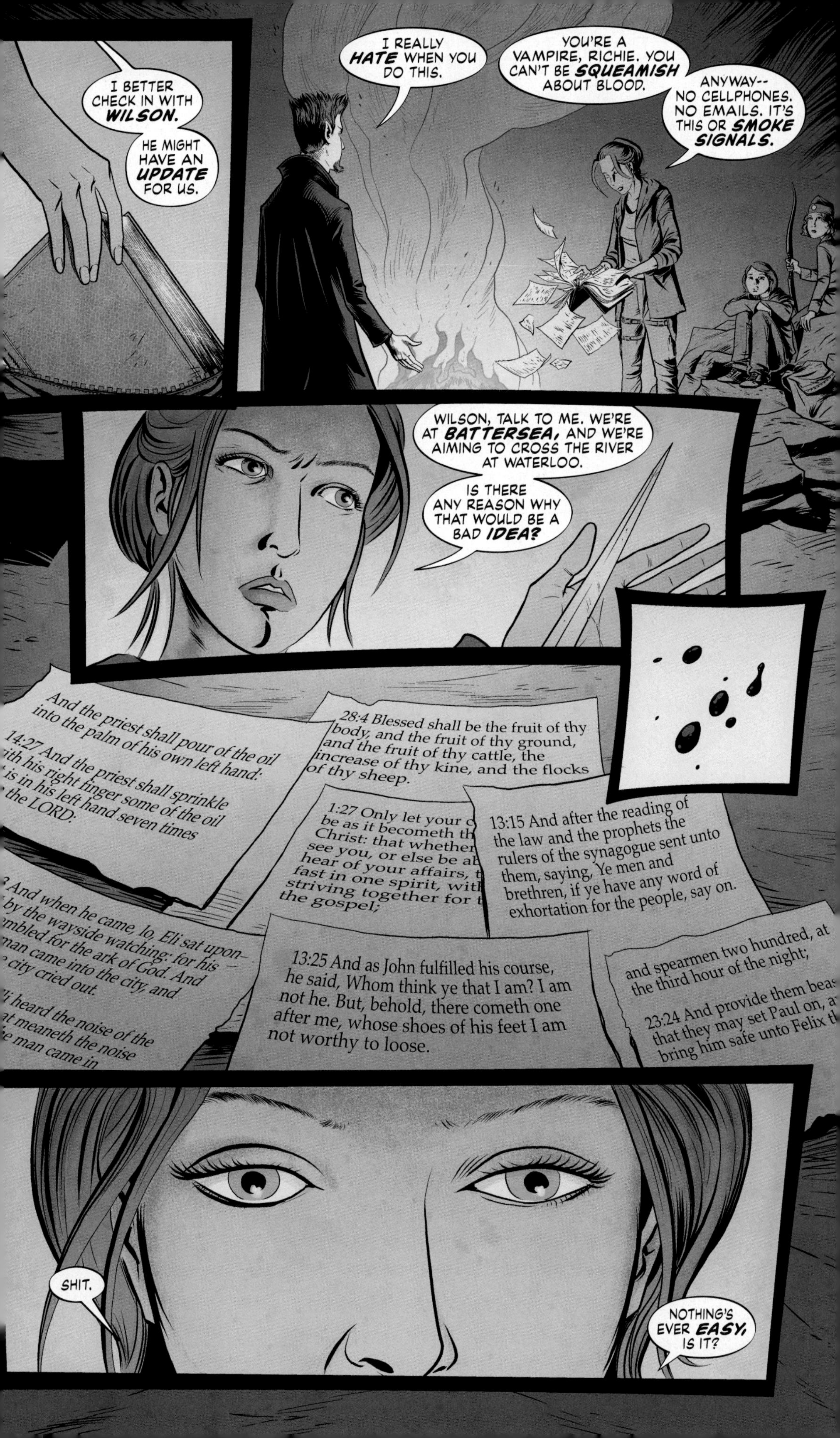
I BETTER CHECK IN WITH WILSON.
HE MIGHT HAVE AN UPDATE FOR US.
I REALLY HATE WHEN YOU DO THIS.
YOU'RE A VAMPIRE, RICHIE. YOU CAN'T BE SQUEAMISH ABOUT BLOOD.
ANYWAY-- NO CELLPHONES. NO EMAILS. IT'S THIS OR SMOKE SIGNALS.
WILSON, TALK TO ME. WE'RE AT BATTERSEA, AND WE'RE AIMING TO CROSS THE RIVER AT WATERLOO.
IS THERE ANY REASON WHY THAT WOULD BE A BAD IDEA?
And the priest shall pour of the oil into the palm of his own left hand:
14:27 And the priest shall sprinkle
28:4 Blessed shall be the fruit of thy body, and the fruit of thy ground, and the fruit of thy cattle, the increase of thy kine, and the flocks of thy sheep.
13:15 And after the reading of the law and the prophets the rulers of the synagogue sent unto them, saying, Ye men and brethren, if ye have any word of exhortation for the people, say on.
13:25 And as John fulfilled his course, he said, Whom think ye that I am? I am not he. But, behold, there cometh one after me, whose shoes of his feet I am not worthy to loose.
and spearmen two hundred, at the third hour of the night;
SHIT.
NOTHING'S EVER EASY, IS IT?

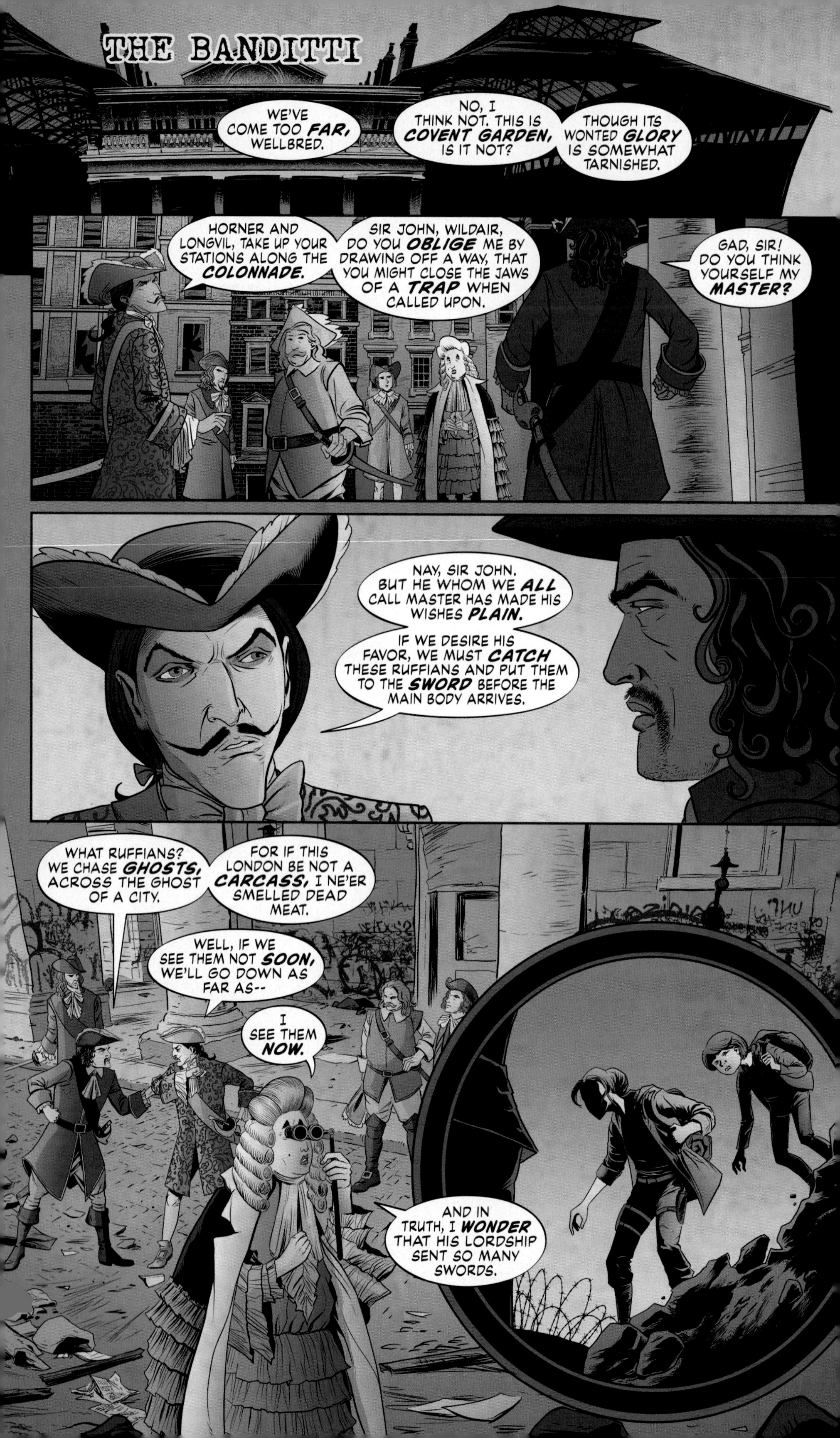
THE BANDITTI
WE'VE COME TOO FAR, WELLBRED.
NO, I THINK NOT. THIS IS COVENT GARDEN, IS IT NOT?
THOUGH ITS WONTED GLORY IS SOMEWHAT TARNISHED.
HORNER AND LONGVIL, TAKE UP YOUR STATIONS ALONG THE COLONNADE.
SIR JOHN, WILDAIR, DO YOU OBLIGE ME BY DRAWING OFF A WAY, THAT YOU MIGHT CLOSE THE JAWS OF A TRAP WHEN CALLED UPON.
GAD, SIR! DO YOU THINK YOURSELF MY MASTER?
NAY, SIR JOHN. BUT HE WHOM WE ALL CALL MASTER HAS MADE HIS WISHES PLAIN.
IF WE DESIRE HIS FAVOR, WE MUST CATCH THESE RUFFIANS AND PUT THEM TO THE SWORD BEFORE THE MAIN BODY ARRIVES.
WHAT RUFFIANS? WE CHASE GHOSTS, ACROSS THE GHOST OF A CITY.
FOR IF THIS LONDON BE NOT A CARCASS, I NE'ER SMELLED DEAD MEAT.
WELL, IF WE SEE THEM NOT SOON, WE'LL GO DOWN AS FAR AS--
I SEE THEM NOW.
AND IN TRUTH, I WONDER THAT HIS LORDSHIP SENT SO MANY SWORDS.

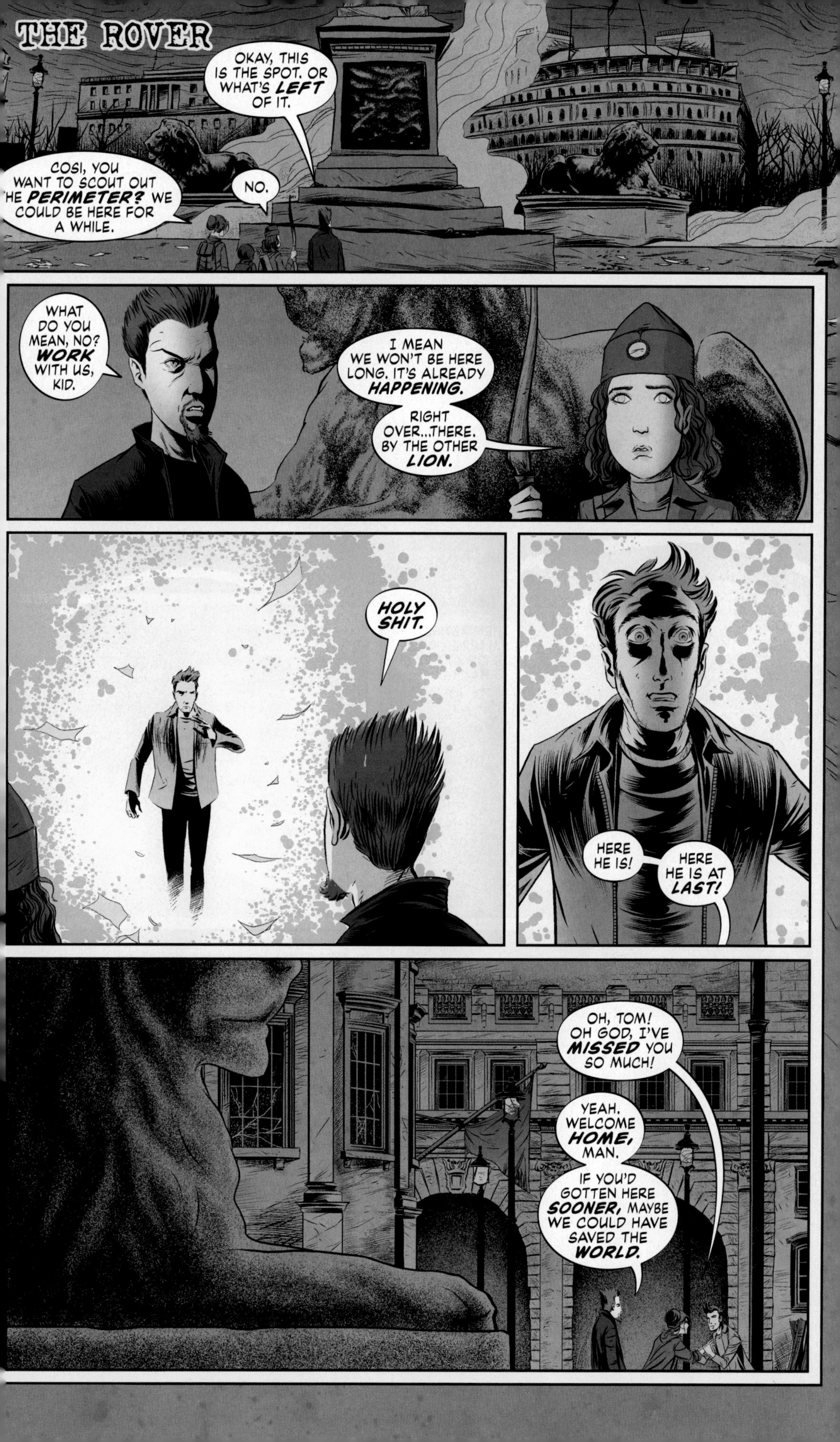
OKAY, THIS IS THE SPOT. OR WHAT'S LEFT OF IT.
COSI, YOU WANT TO SCOUT OUT HE PERIMETER? WE COULD BE HERE FOR A WHILE.
NO.
WHAT DO YOU MEAN, NO? WORK WITH US, KID.
I MEAN WE WON'T BE HERE LONG. IT'S ALREADY HAPPENING.
RIGHT OVER...THERE. BY THE OTHER LION.
HOLY SHIT.
HERE HE IS!
HERE HE IS AT LAST!
OH, TOM! OH GOD, I'VE MISSED YOU SO MUCH!
YEAH. WELCOME HOME, MAN.
IF YOU'D GOTTEN HERE SOONER, MAYBE WE COULD HAVE SAVED THE WORLD.

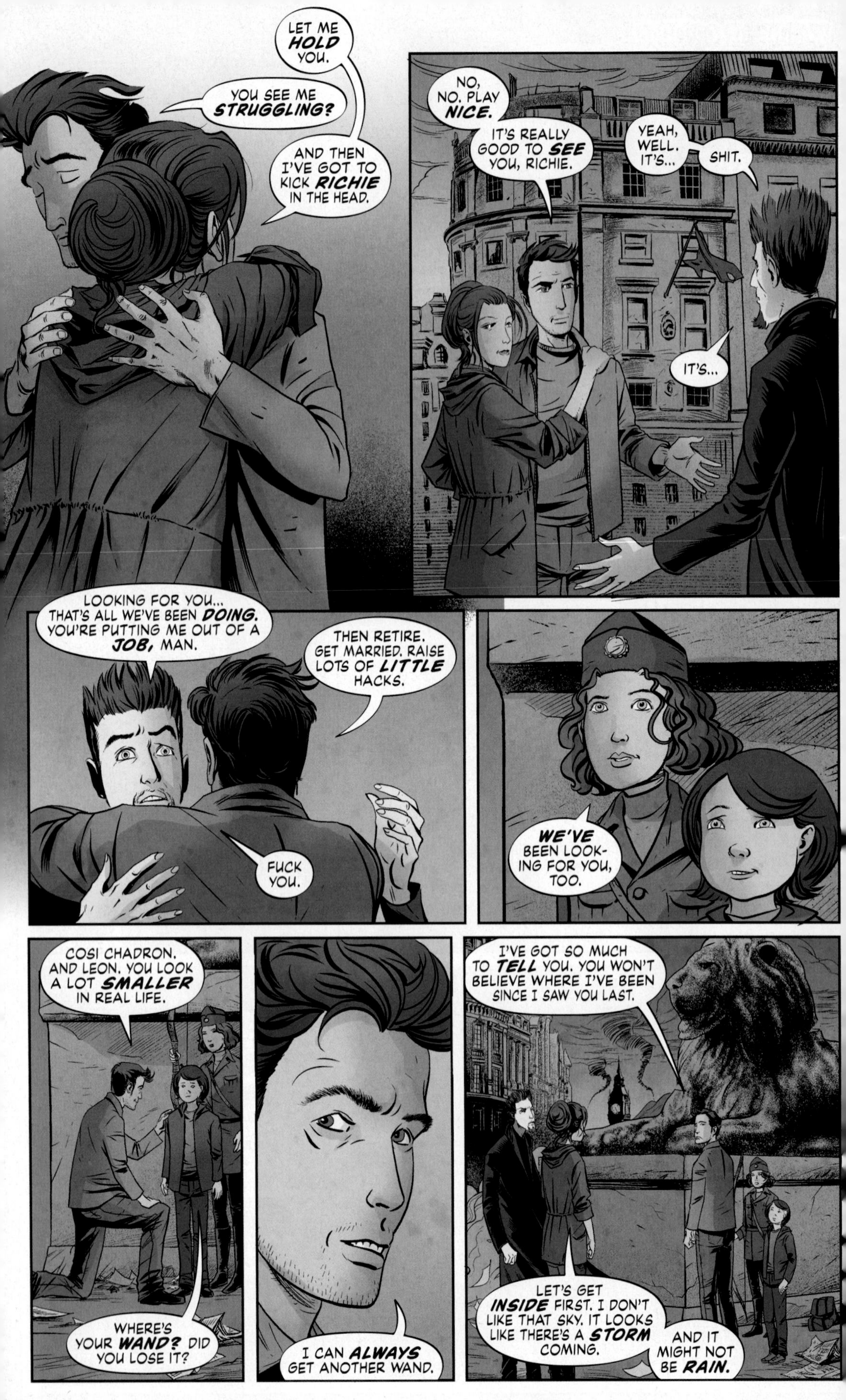
LET ME HOLD YOU.
YOU SEE ME STRUGGLING?
AND THEN I'VE GOT TO KICK RICHIE IN THE HEAD.
NO, NO. PLAY NICE.
IT'S REALLY GOOD TO SEE YOU, RICHIE.
YEAH, WELL. IT'S...
SHIT.
IT'S...
LOOKING FOR YOU... THAT'S ALL WE'VE BEEN DOING. YOU'RE PUTTING ME OUT OF A JOB, MAN.
THEN RETIRE. GET MARRIED. RAISE LOTS OF LITTLE HACKS.
FUCK YOU.
WE'VE BEEN LOOKING FOR YOU, TOO.
COSI CHADRON. AND LEON. YOU LOOK A LOT SMALLER IN REAL LIFE.
WHERE'S YOUR WAND? DID YOU LOSE IT?
I CAN ALWAYS GET ANOTHER WAND.
I'VE GOT SO MUCH TO TELL YOU. YOU WON'T BELIEVE WHERE I'VE BEEN SINCE I SAW YOU LAST.
LET'S GET INSIDE FIRST. I DON'T LIKE THAT SKY. IT LOOKS LIKE THERE'S A STORM COMING.
AND IT MIGHT NOT BE RAIN.

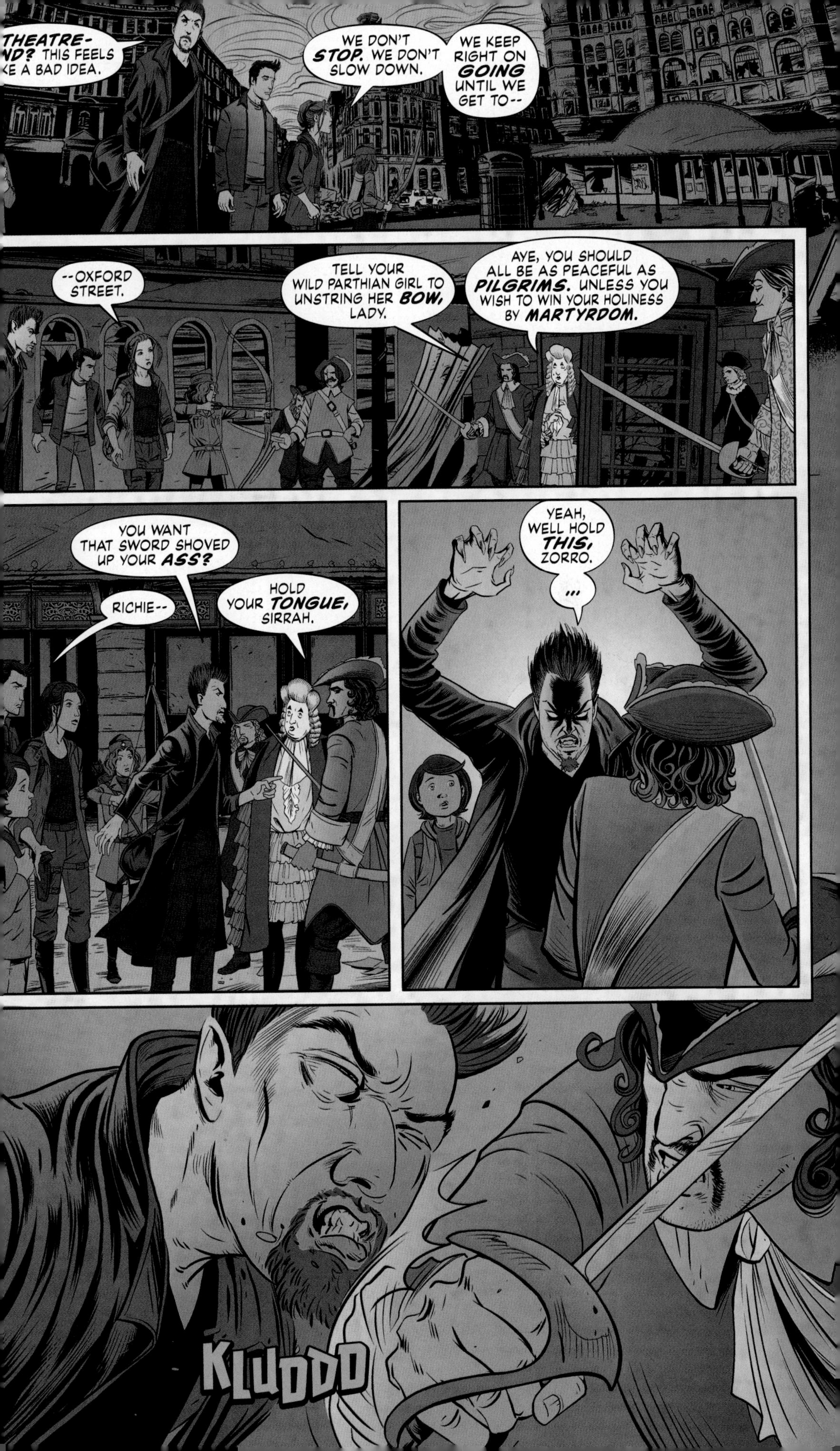
THEATRE-
ND? THIS FEELS
KE A BAD IDEA.
WE DON'T STOP. WE DON'T SLOW DOWN.
WE KEEP RIGHT ON GOING UNTIL WE GET TO--
--OXFORD STREET.
TELL YOUR WILD PARTHIAN GIRL TO UNSTRING HER BOW, LADY.
AYE, YOU SHOULD ALL BE AS PEACEFUL AS PILGRIMS. UNLESS YOU WISH TO WIN YOUR HOLINESS BY MARTYRDOM.
YOU WANT THAT SWORD SHOVED UP YOUR ASS?
RICHIE--
HOLD YOUR TONGUE, SIRRAH.
YEAH, WELL HOLD THIS, ZORRO.
...
KLUDDD

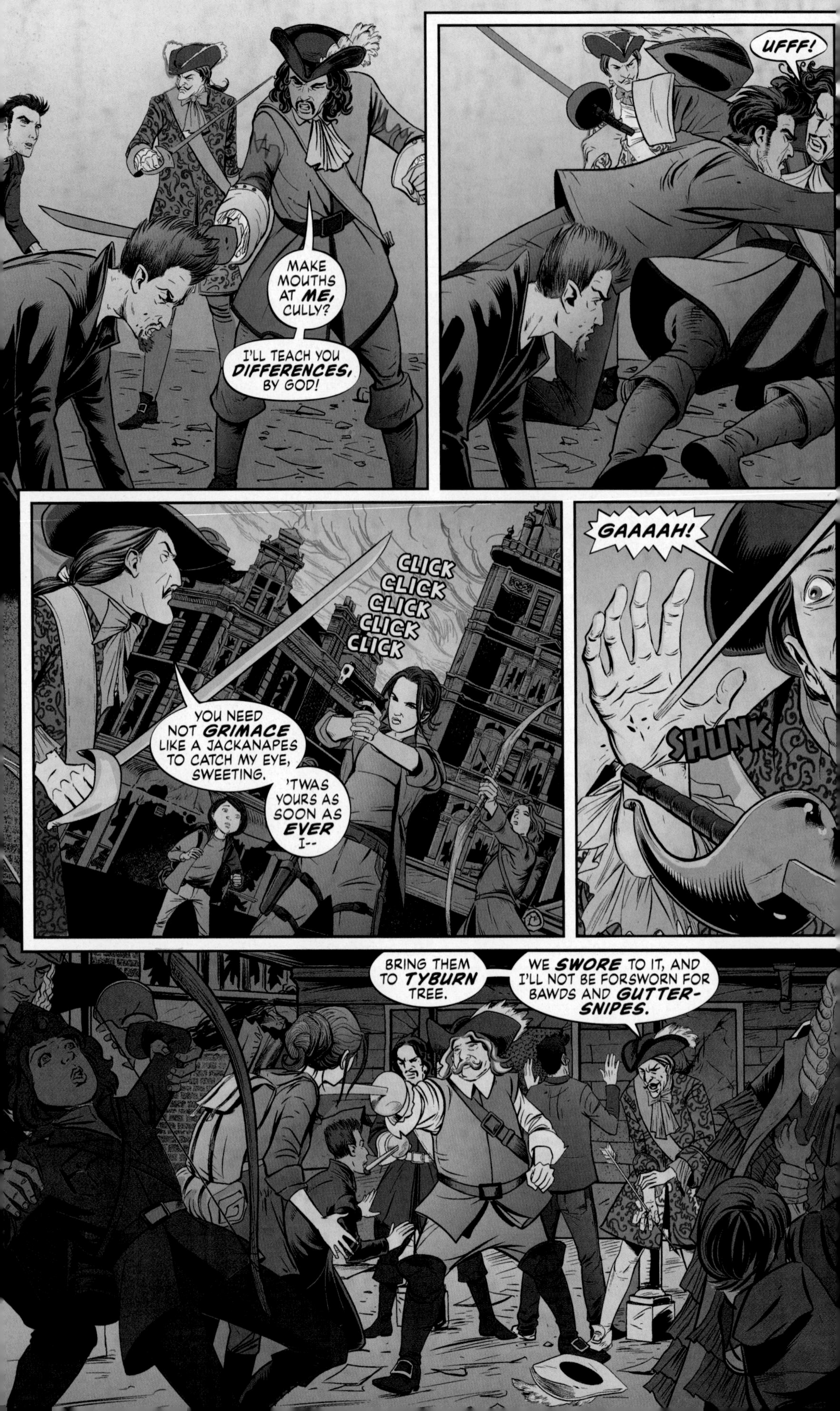
MAKE MOUTHS AT ME, CULLY?
I'LL TEACH YOU DIFFERENCES, BY GOD!
UFFF!
CLICK CLICK CLICK CLICK CLICK
YOU NEED NOT GRIMACE LIKE A JACKANAPES TO CATCH MY EYE, SWEETING.
'TWAS YOURS AS SOON AS EVER I--
GAAAAH!
SHUNK
BRING THEM TO TYBURN TREE.
WE SWORE TO IT, AND I'LL NOT BE FORSWORN FOR BAWDS AND GUTTER-SNIPES.

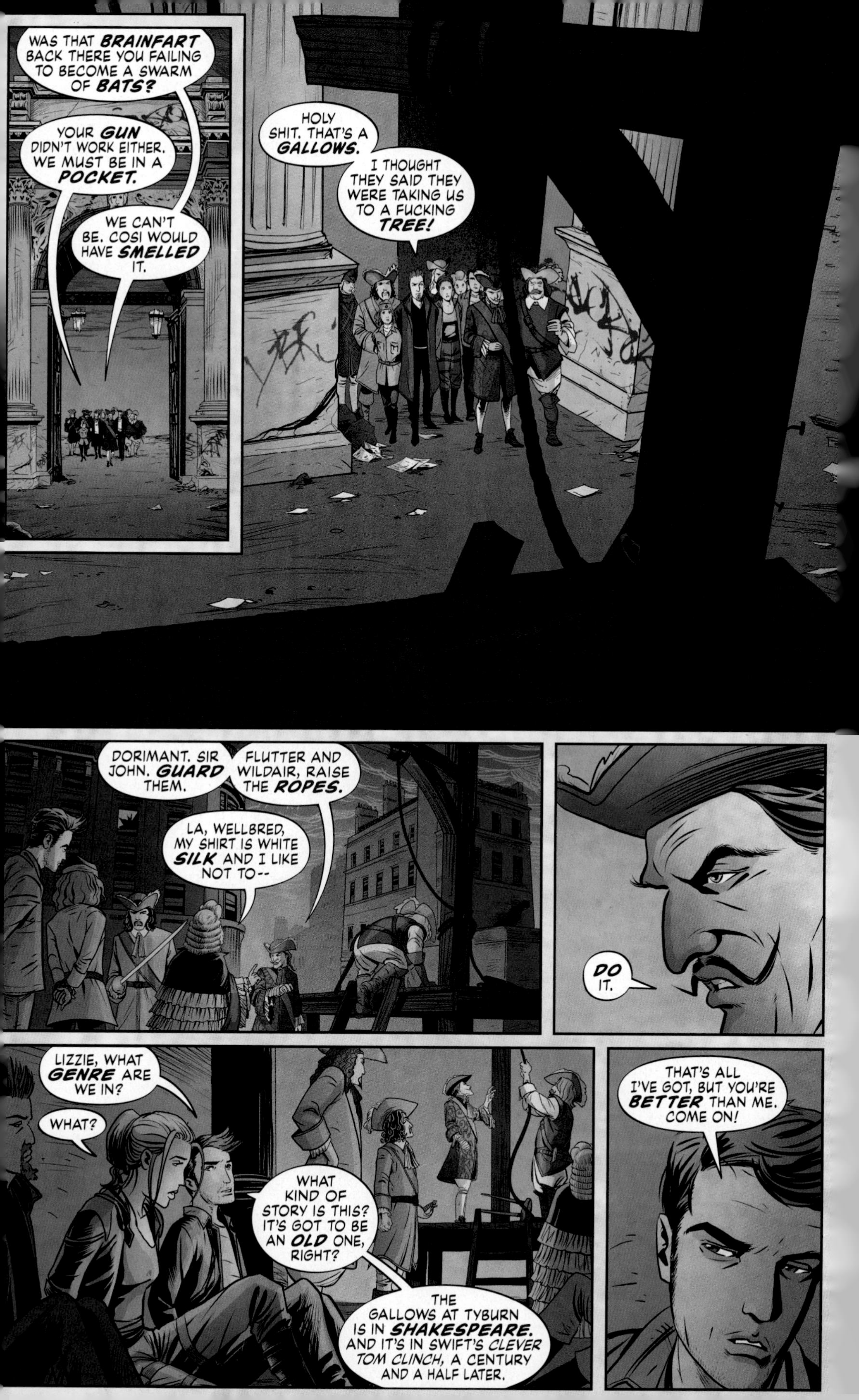

WAS THAT BRAINFART BACK THERE YOU FAILING TO BECOME A SWARM OF BATS?
YOUR GUN DIDN'T WORK EITHER. WE MUST BE IN A POCKET.
WE CAN'T BE. COSI WOULD HAVE SMELLED IT.
HOLY SHIT. THAT'S A GALLOWS.
I THOUGHT THEY SAID THEY WERE TAKING US TO A FUCKING TREE!
DORIMANT. SIR JOHN. GUARD THEM.
FLUTTER AND WILDAIR, RAISE THE ROPES.
LA, WELLBRED, MY SHIRT IS WHITE SILK AND I LIKE NOT TO--
DO IT.
LIZZIE, WHAT GENRE ARE WE IN?
WHAT?
WHAT KIND OF STORY IS THIS? IT'S GOT TO BE AN OLD ONE, RIGHT?
THE GALLOWS AT TYBURN IS IN SHAKESPEARE. AND IT'S IN SWIFT'S CLEVER TOM CLINCH, A CENTURY AND A HALF LATER.
THAT'S ALL I'VE GOT, BUT YOU'RE BETTER THAN ME. COME ON!

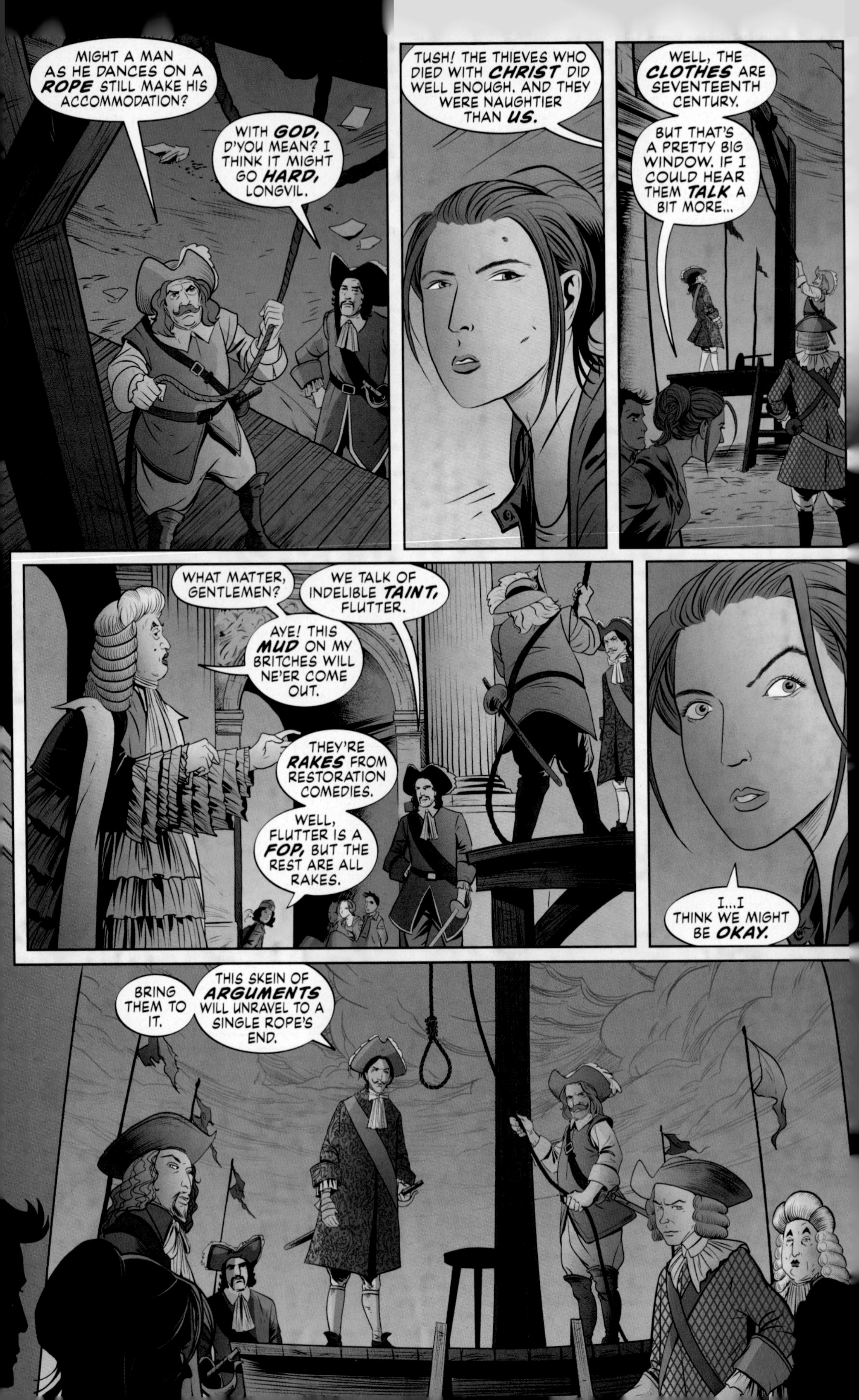
MIGHT A MAN AS HE DANCES ON A ROPE STILL MAKE HIS ACCOMMODATION?
WITH GOD, D'YOU MEAN? I THINK IT MIGHT GO HARD, LONGVIL.
TUSH! THE THIEVES WHO DIED WITH CHRIST DID WELL ENOUGH. AND THEY WERE NAUGHTIER THAN US.
WELL, THE CLOTHES ARE SEVENTEENTH CENTURY.
BUT THAT'S A PRETTY BIG WINDOW. IF I COULD HEAR THEM TALK A BIT MORE...
WHAT MATTER, GENTLEMEN?
WE TALK OF INDELIBLE TAINT, FLUTTER.
AYE! THIS MUD ON MY BRITCHES WILL NE'ER COME OUT.
THEY'RE RAKES FROM RESTORATION COMEDIES.
WELL, FLUTTER IS A FOP, BUT THE REST ARE ALL RAKES.
I...I THINK WE MIGHT BE OKAY.
BRING THEM TO IT.
THIS SKEIN OF ARGUMENTS WILL UNRAVEL TO A SINGLE ROPE'S END.

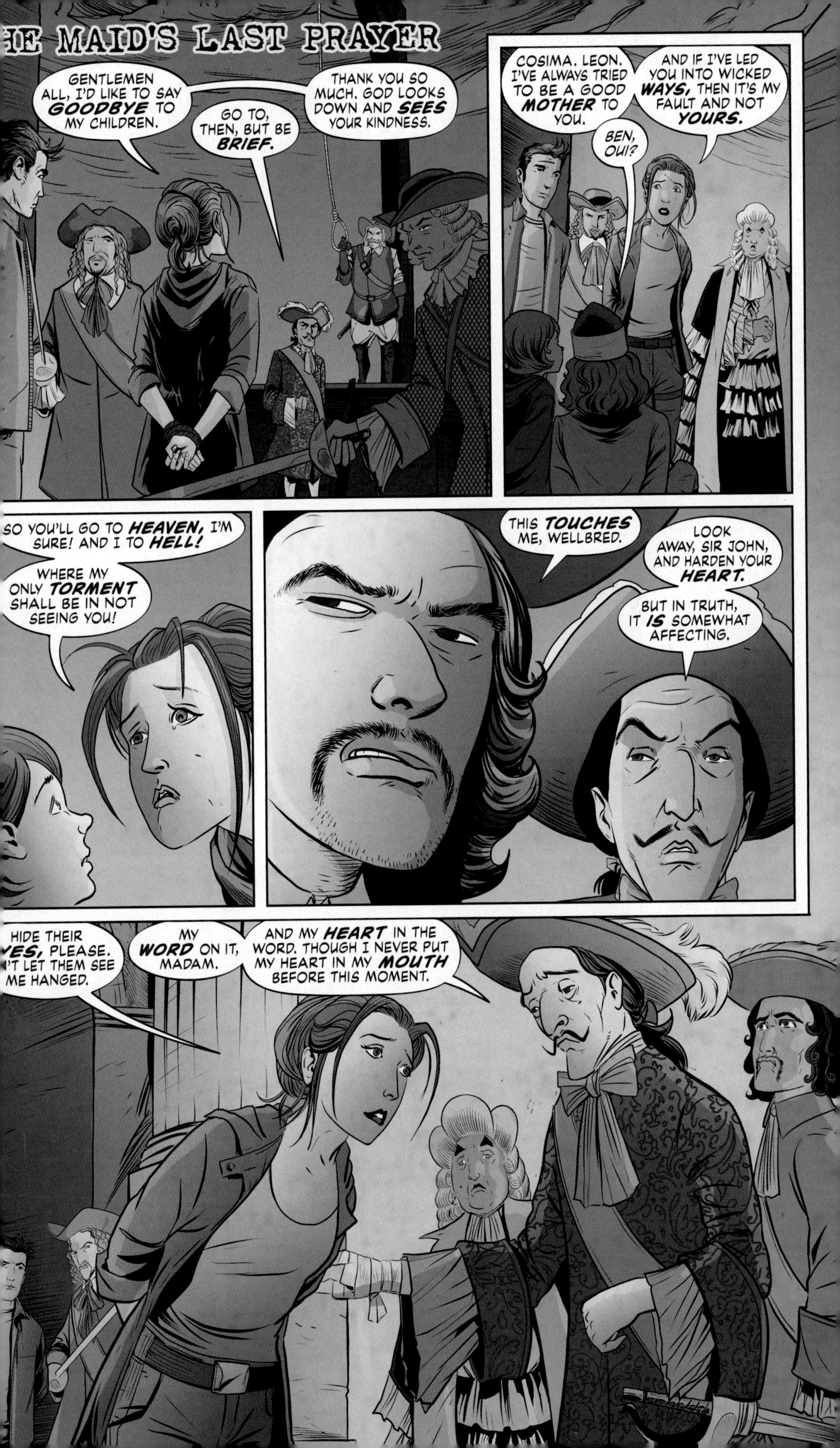

HE MAID'S LAST PRAYER
GENTLEMEN ALL, I'D LIKE TO SAY GOODBYE TO MY CHILDREN.
GO TO, THEN, BUT BE BRIEF.
THANK YOU SO MUCH. GOD LOOKS DOWN AND SEES YOUR KINDNESS.
COSIMA. LEON. I'VE ALWAYS TRIED TO BE A GOOD MOTHER TO YOU.
AND IF I'VE LED YOU INTO WICKED WAYS, THEN IT'S MY FAULT AND NOT YOURS.
BEN, OUI?
SO YOU'LL GO TO HEAVEN, I'M SURE! AND I TO HELL!
WHERE MY ONLY TORMENT SHALL BE IN NOT SEEING YOU!
THIS TOUCHES ME, WELLBRED.
LOOK AWAY, SIR JOHN, AND HARDEN YOUR HEART.
BUT IN TRUTH, IT IS SOMEWHAT AFFECTING.
HIDE THEIR
YES, PLEASE.
'T LET THEM SEE
ME HANGED.
MY WORD ON IT, MADAM.
AND MY HEART IN THE WORD. THOUGH I NEVER PUT MY HEART IN MY MOUTH BEFORE THIS MOMENT.

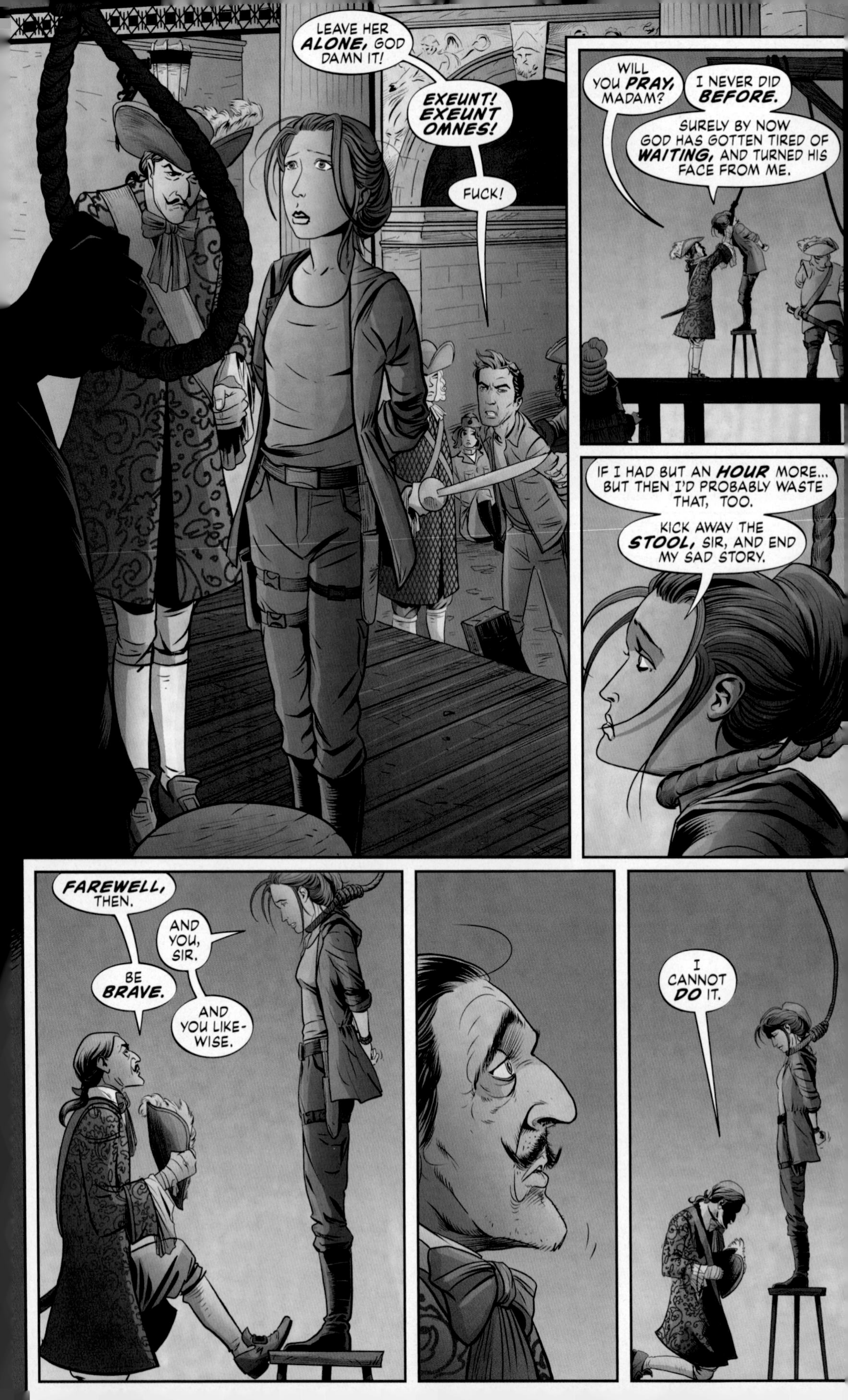
LEAVE HER ALONE, GOD DAMN IT!
EXEUNT! EXEUNT OMNES!
FUCK!
WILL YOU PRAY, MADAM?
I NEVER DID BEFORE.
SURELY BY NOW GOD HAS GOTTEN TIRED OF WAITING, AND TURNED HIS FACE FROM ME.
IF I HAD BUT AN HOUR MORE... BUT THEN I'D PROBABLY WASTE THAT, TOO.
KICK AWAY THE STOOL, SIR, AND END MY SAD STORY.
FAREWELL, THEN.
BE BRAVE.
AND YOU, SIR.
AND YOU LIKEWISE.
I CANNOT DO IT.

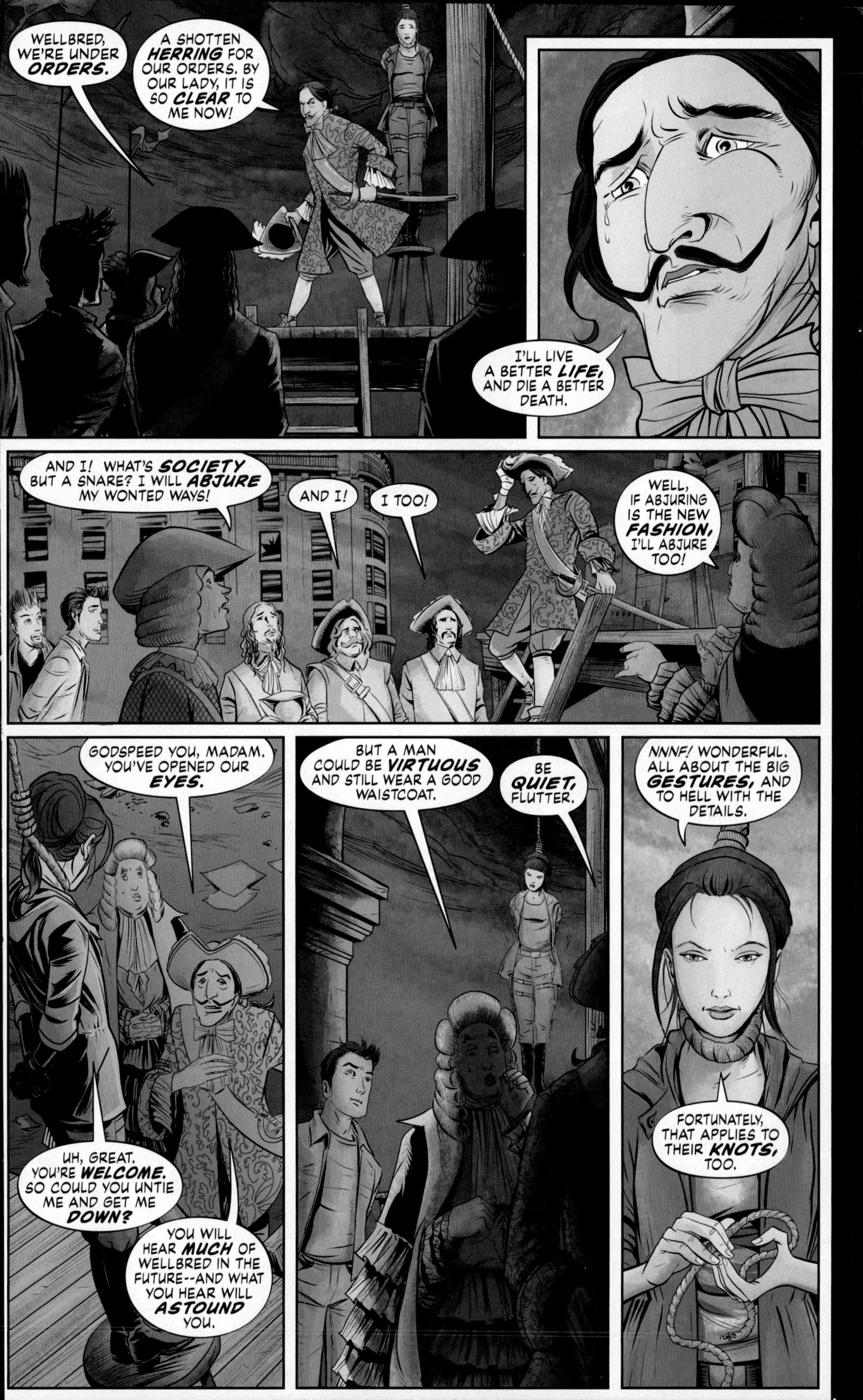
WELLBRED, WE'RE UNDER ORDERS.
A SHOTTEN HERRING FOR OUR ORDERS. BY OUR LADY, IT IS SO CLEAR TO ME NOW!
I'LL LIVE A BETTER LIFE, AND DIE A BETTER DEATH.
AND I! WHAT'S SOCIETY BUT A SNARE? I WILL ABJURE MY WONTED WAYS!
AND I!
I TOO!
WELL, IF ABJURING IS THE NEW FASHION, I'LL ABJURE TOO!
GODSPEED YOU, MADAM. YOU'VE OPENED OUR EYES.
UH, GREAT. YOU'RE WELCOME. SO COULD YOU UNTIE ME AND GET ME DOWN?
YOU WILL HEAR MUCH OF WELLBRED IN THE FUTURE--AND WHAT YOU HEAR WILL ASTOUND YOU.
BUT A MAN COULD BE VIRTUOUS AND STILL WEAR A GOOD WAISTCOAT.
BE QUIET, FLUTTER.
NNNF! WONDERFUL. ALL ABOUT THE BIG GESTURES, AND TO HELL WITH THE DETAILS.
FORTUNATELY, THAT APPLIES TO THEIR KNOTS, TOO.

HOW THE FUCK DID YOU **DO** THAT, HEXAM?

I **KNOW** HOW SHE DID IT.

SHE TOLD ME ONCE SHE LEARNED ABOUT **STORIES** THE WAY A SOLDIER LEARNS HOW TO STRIP A **RIFLE**.

EXACTLY.

THE RAKE ALMOST ALWAYS **REPENTS** AT THE END.

THAT'S HOW RESTORATION PLAYWRIGHTS GOT AWAY WITH HAVING **LIBERTINES** AS HEROES.

THAT WAS FUCKING WEIRD, THOUGH. THE **OLD** CHARACTERS BELONG TO LEVIATHAN.

WE BARELY **EVER** SEE THEM.

THAT CLOUD IS REAL **CLOSE** NOW. I THINK WE SHOULD GET MOVING.

IT'S **NOT** A CLOUD. IT'S...I THINK... POUSSIÈRE.

DUST.

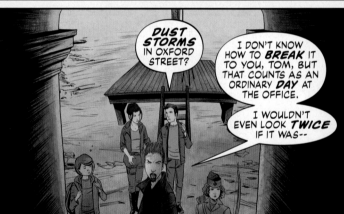

DUST STORMS IN OXFORD STREET?

I DON'T KNOW HOW TO **BREAK** IT TO YOU, TOM, BUT THAT COUNTS AS AN ORDINARY **DAY** AT THE OFFICE.

I WOULDN'T EVEN LOOK **TWICE** IF IT WAS--

OH FUCK MY RELIABLE **LUCK.**

WHAT IS IT?

WELL, IT'S STILL A FAIR WAY OFF, AND I'D **HATE** TO RUSH TO JUDGMENT--

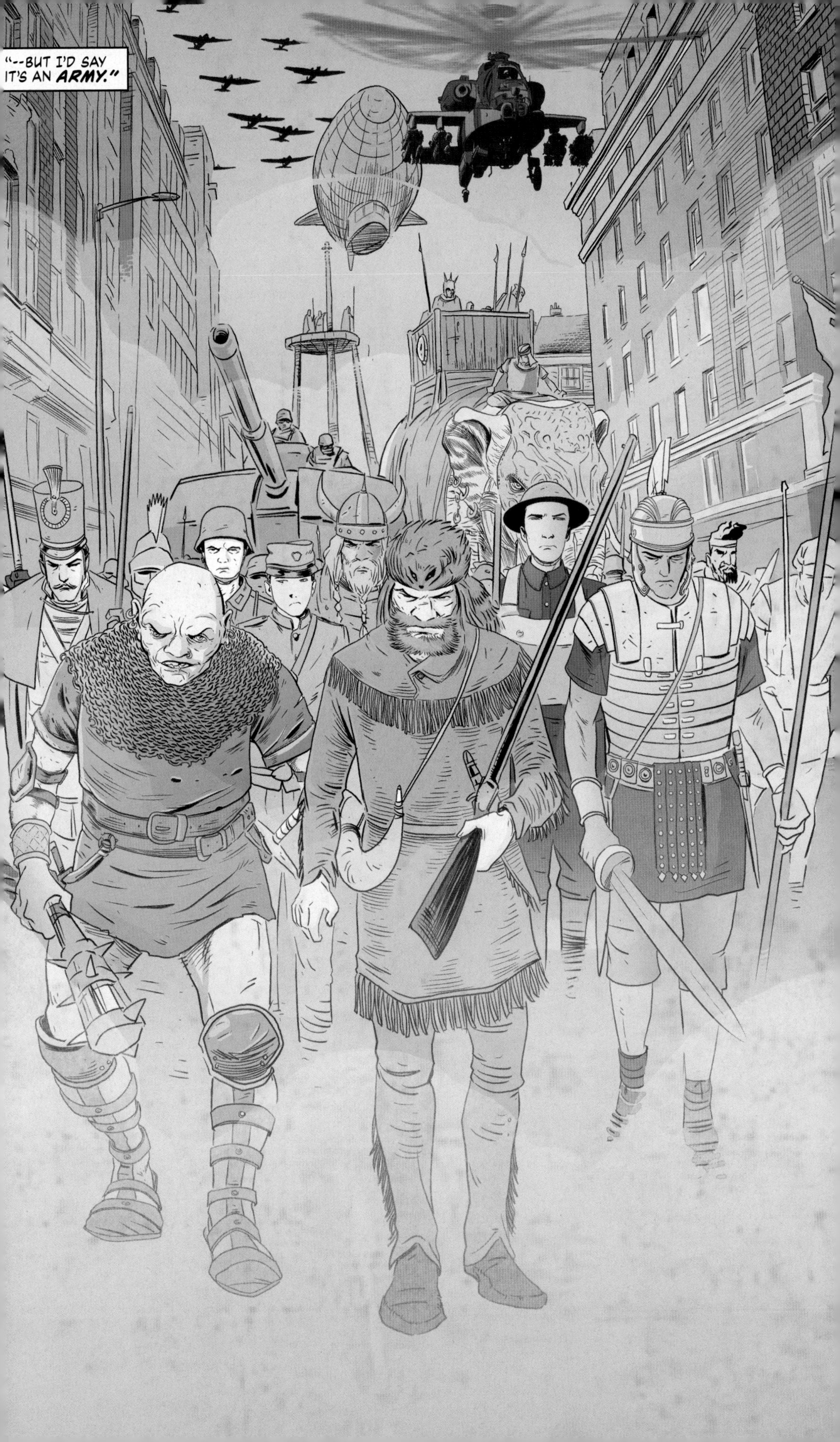
"--BUT I'D SAY IT'S AN ARMY."

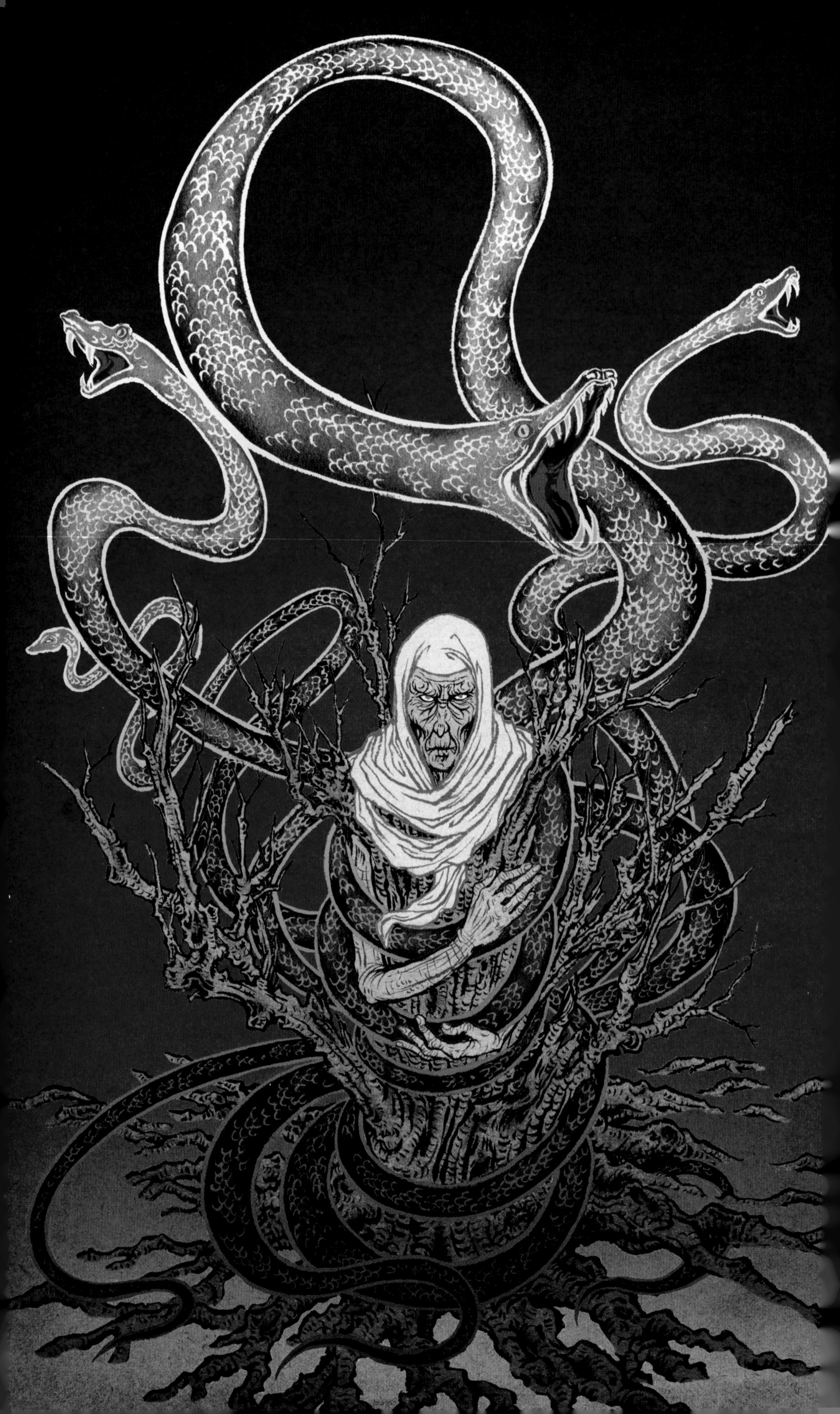

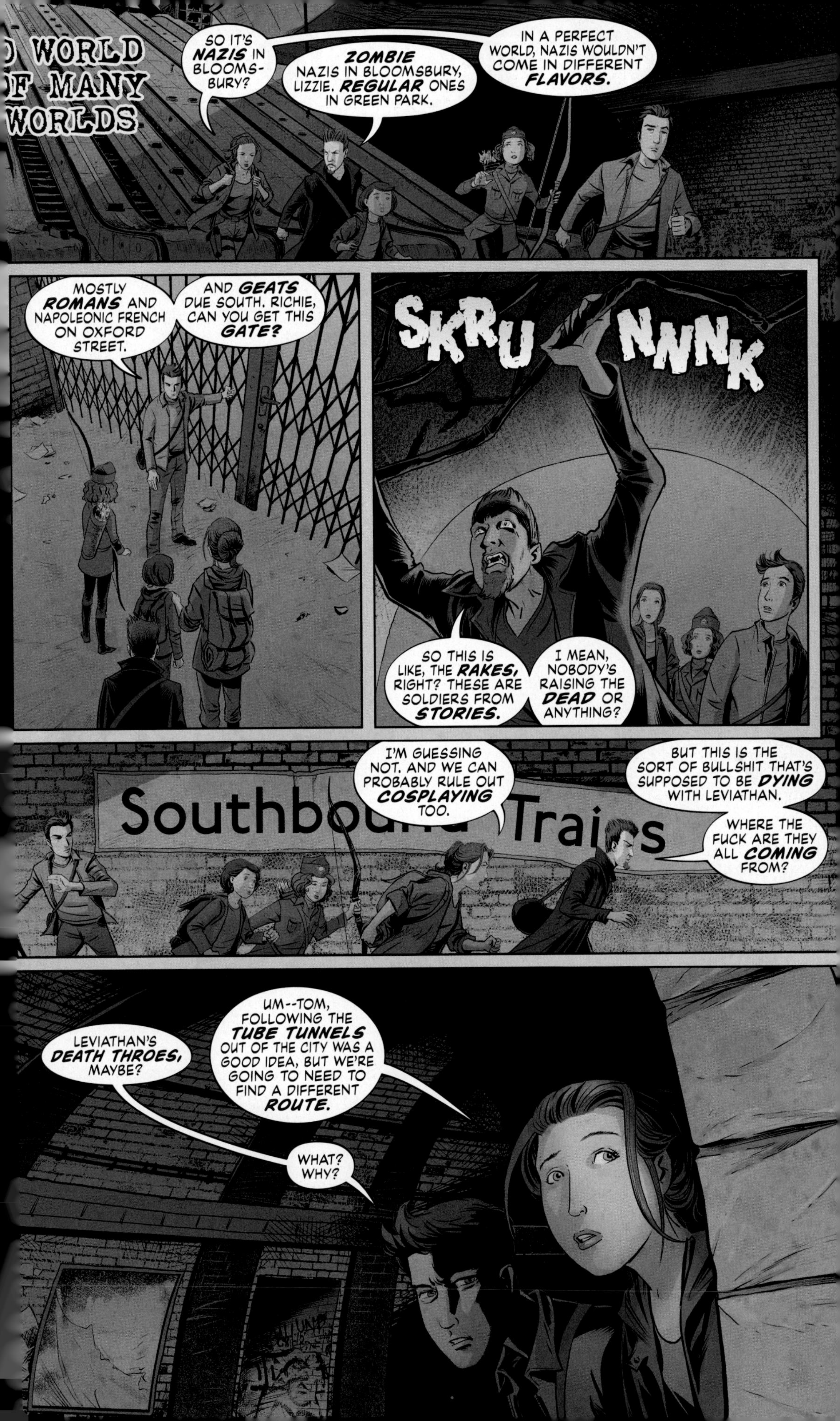

O WORLD OF MANY WORLDS
SO IT'S NAZIS IN BLOOMS-BURY?
ZOMBIE NAZIS IN BLOOMSBURY, LIZZIE. REGULAR ONES IN GREEN PARK.
IN A PERFECT WORLD, NAZIS WOULDN'T COME IN DIFFERENT FLAVORS.
MOSTLY ROMANS AND NAPOLEONIC FRENCH ON OXFORD STREET.
AND GEATS DUE SOUTH. RICHIE, CAN YOU GET THIS GATE?
SKRUNNNK
SO THIS IS LIKE, THE RAKES, RIGHT? THESE ARE SOLDIERS FROM STORIES.
I MEAN, NOBODY'S RAISING THE DEAD OR ANYTHING?
Southbound Trains
I'M GUESSING NOT. AND WE CAN PROBABLY RULE OUT COSPLAYING TOO.
BUT THIS IS THE SORT OF BULLSHIT THAT'S SUPPOSED TO BE DYING WITH LEVIATHAN.
WHERE THE FUCK ARE THEY ALL COMING FROM?
LEVIATHAN'S DEATH THROES, MAYBE?
UM--TOM, FOLLOWING THE TUBE TUNNELS OUT OF THE CITY WAS A GOOD IDEA, BUT WE'RE GOING TO NEED TO FIND A DIFFERENT ROUTE.
WHAT? WHY?

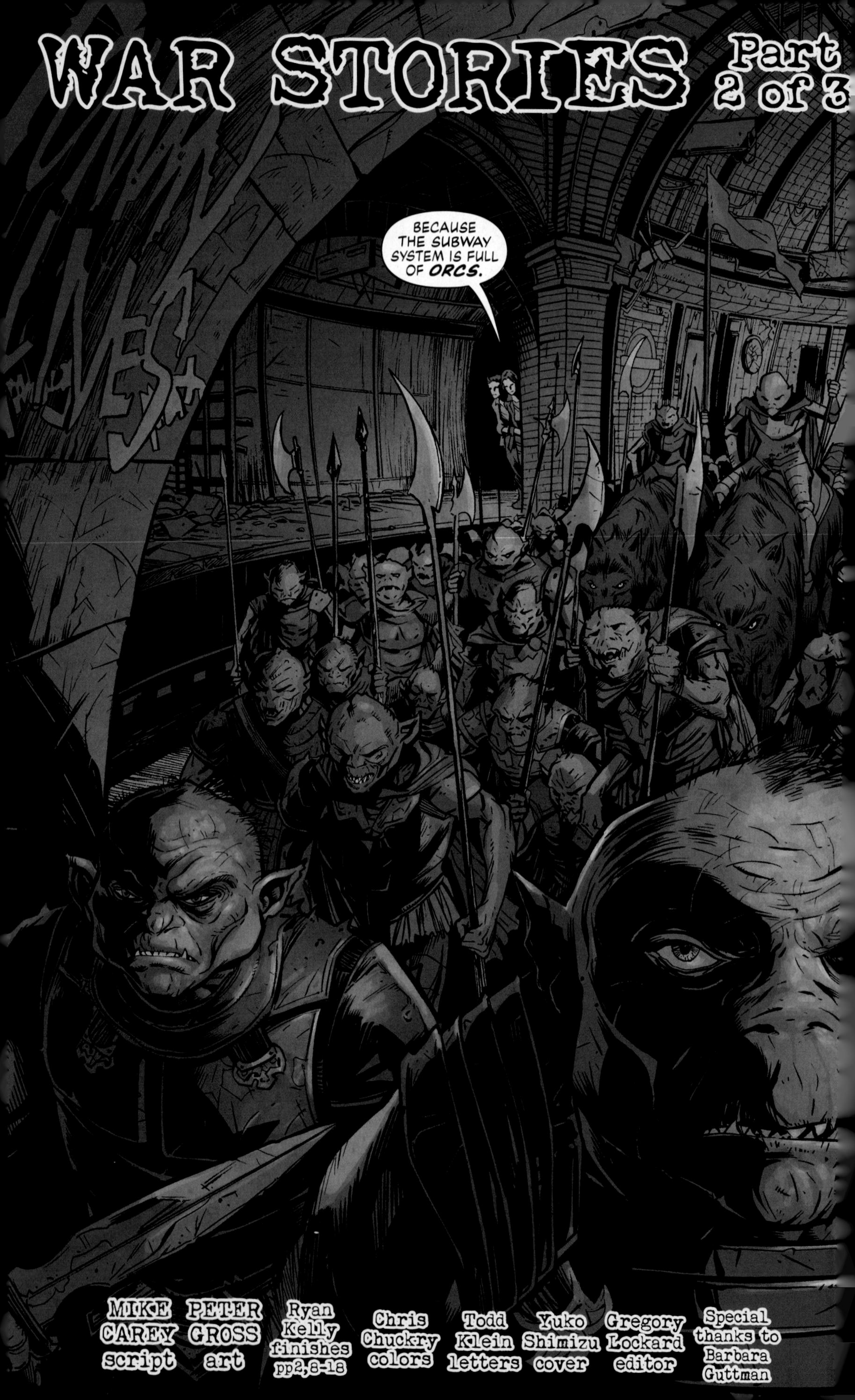
WAR STORIES Part 2 of 3
BECAUSE THE SUBWAY SYSTEM IS FULL OF ORCS.
MIKE CAREY script
PETER GROSS art
Ryan Kelly finishes pp2,8-18
Chris Chuckry colors
Todd Klein letters
Yuko Shimizu cover
Gregory Lockard editor
Special thanks to Barbara Guttman

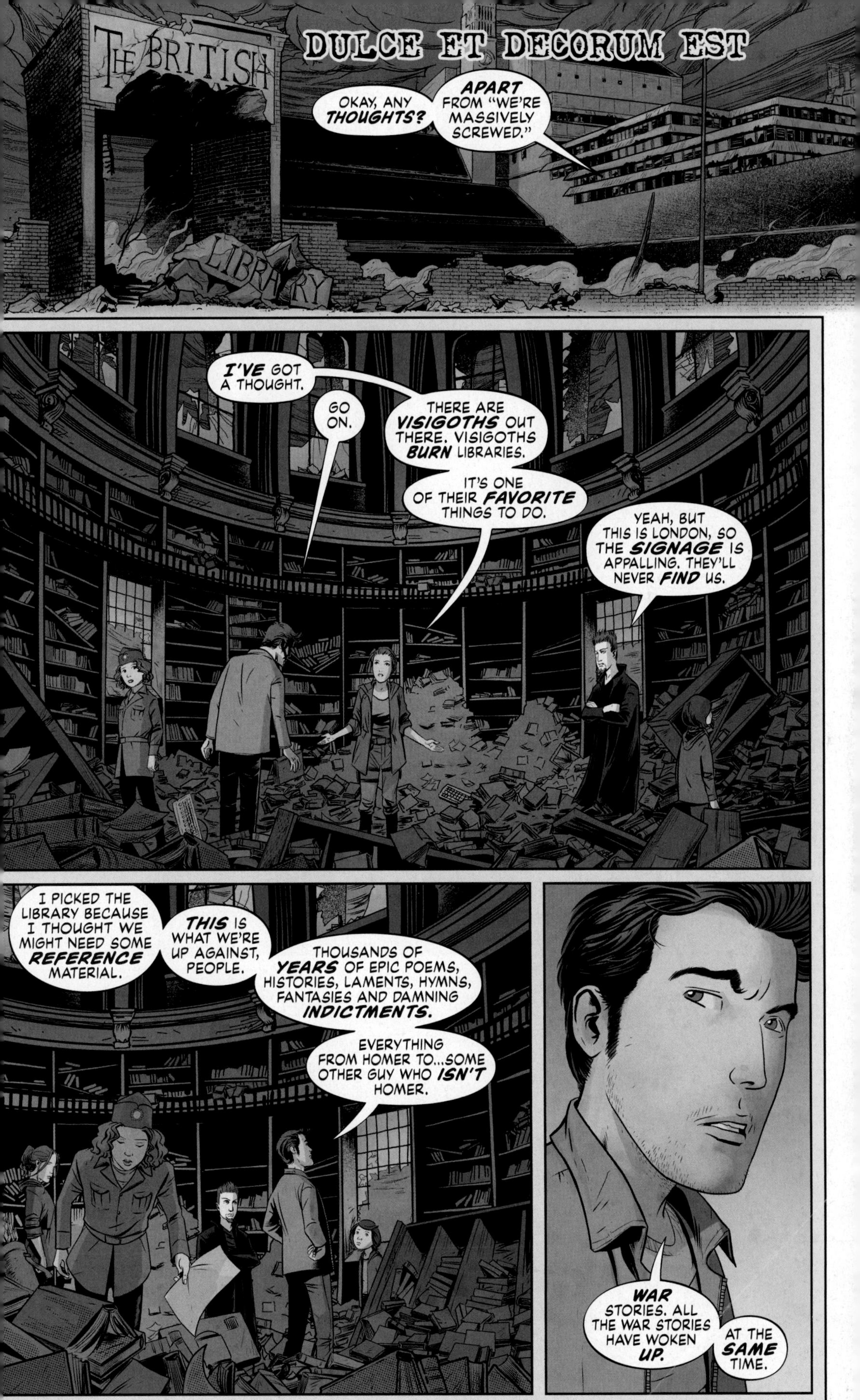
DULCE ET DECORUM EST
THE BRITISH
LIBRARY
OKAY, ANY THOUGHTS?
APART FROM "WE'RE MASSIVELY SCREWED."
I'VE GOT A THOUGHT.
GO ON.
THERE ARE VISIGOTHS OUT THERE. VISIGOTHS BURN LIBRARIES.
IT'S ONE OF THEIR FAVORITE THINGS TO DO.
YEAH, BUT THIS IS LONDON, SO THE SIGNAGE IS APPALLING. THEY'LL NEVER FIND US.
I PICKED THE LIBRARY BECAUSE I THOUGHT WE MIGHT NEED SOME REFERENCE MATERIAL.
THIS IS WHAT WE'RE UP AGAINST, PEOPLE.
THOUSANDS OF YEARS OF EPIC POEMS, HISTORIES, LAMENTS, HYMNS, FANTASIES AND DAMNING INDICTMENTS.
EVERYTHING FROM HOMER TO...SOME OTHER GUY WHO ISN'T HOMER.
WAR STORIES. ALL THE WAR STORIES HAVE WOKEN UP.
AT THE SAME TIME.

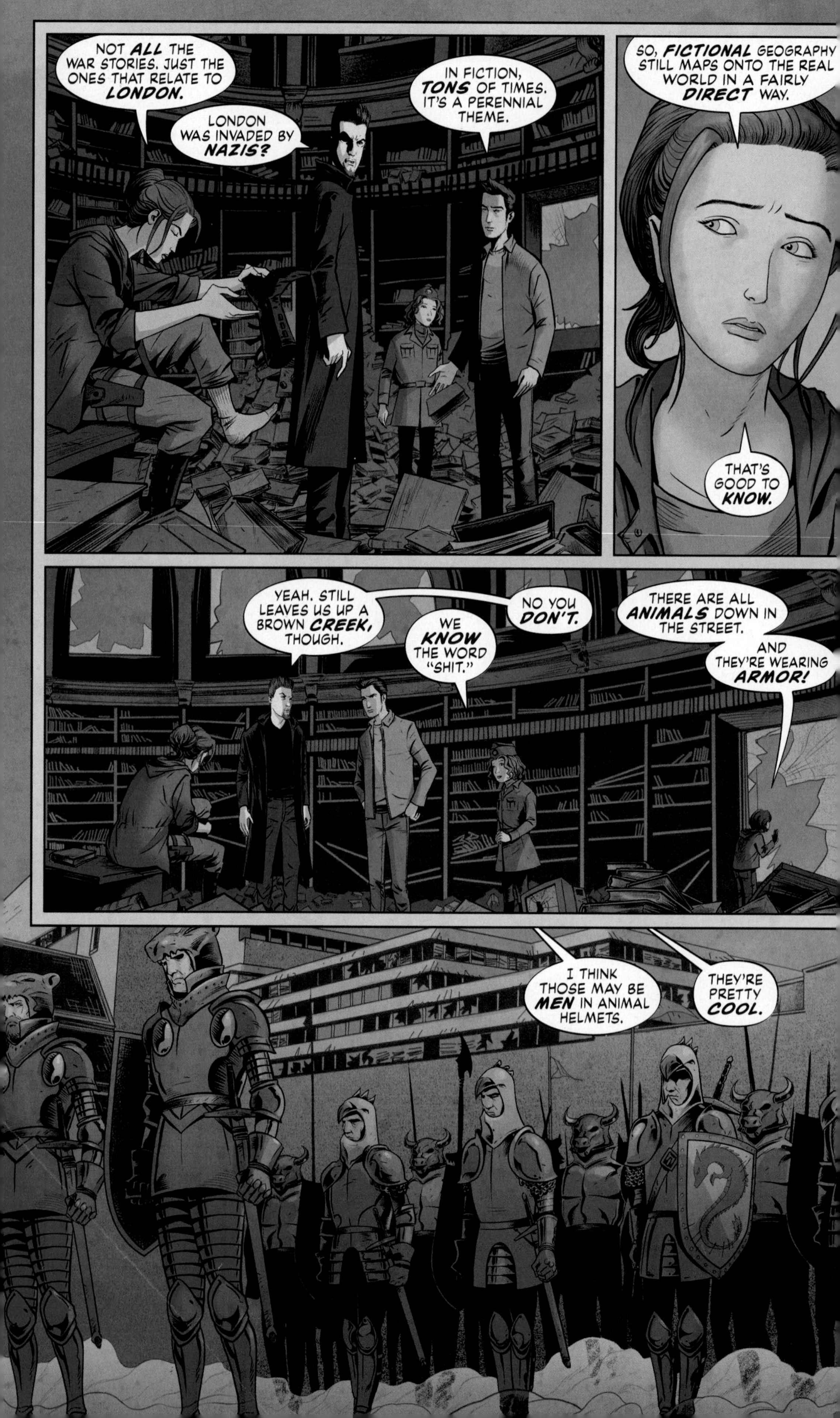
NOT ALL THE WAR STORIES. JUST THE ONES THAT RELATE TO LONDON.
LONDON WAS INVADED BY NAZIS?
IN FICTION, TONS OF TIMES. IT'S A PERENNIAL THEME.
SO, FICTIONAL GEOGRAPHY STILL MAPS ONTO THE REAL WORLD IN A FAIRLY DIRECT WAY.
THAT'S GOOD TO KNOW.
YEAH. STILL LEAVES US UP A BROWN CREEK, THOUGH.
NO YOU DON'T.
WE KNOW THE WORD "SHIT."
THERE ARE ALL ANIMALS DOWN IN THE STREET.
AND THEY'RE WEARING ARMOR!
I THINK THOSE MAY BE MEN IN ANIMAL HELMETS.
THEY'RE PRETTY COOL.

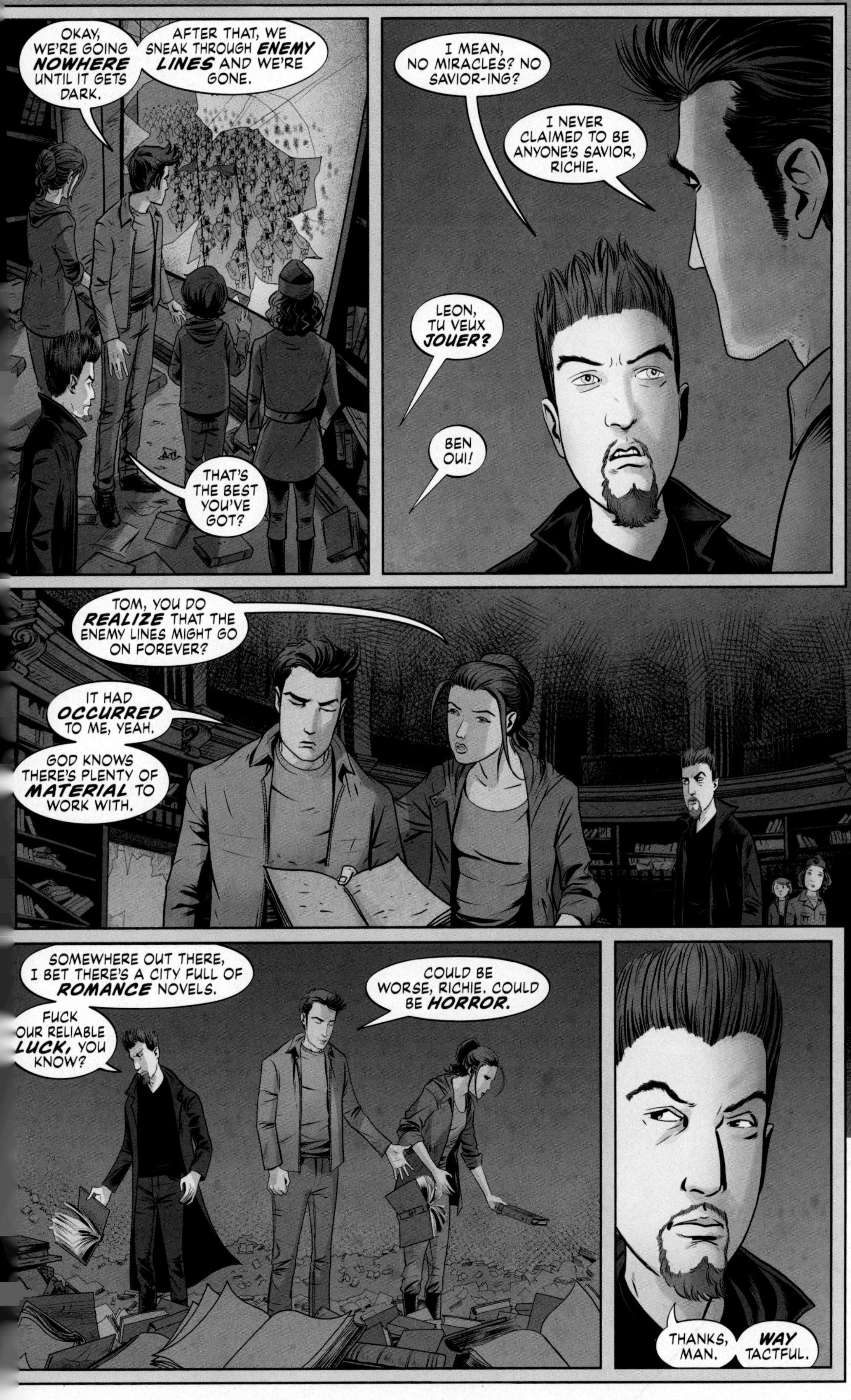
OKAY, WE'RE GOING NOWHERE UNTIL IT GETS DARK.
AFTER THAT, WE SNEAK THROUGH ENEMY LINES AND WE'RE GONE.
THAT'S THE BEST YOU'VE GOT?
I MEAN, NO MIRACLES? NO SAVIOR-ING?
I NEVER CLAIMED TO BE ANYONE'S SAVIOR, RICHIE.
LEON, TU VEUX JOUER?
BEN OUI!
TOM, YOU DO REALIZE THAT THE ENEMY LINES MIGHT GO ON FOREVER?
IT HAD OCCURRED TO ME, YEAH.
GOD KNOWS THERE'S PLENTY OF MATERIAL TO WORK WITH.
SOMEWHERE OUT THERE, I BET THERE'S A CITY FULL OF ROMANCE NOVELS.
FUCK OUR RELIABLE LUCK, YOU KNOW?
COULD BE WORSE, RICHIE. COULD BE HORROR.
THANKS, MAN.
WAY TACTFUL.

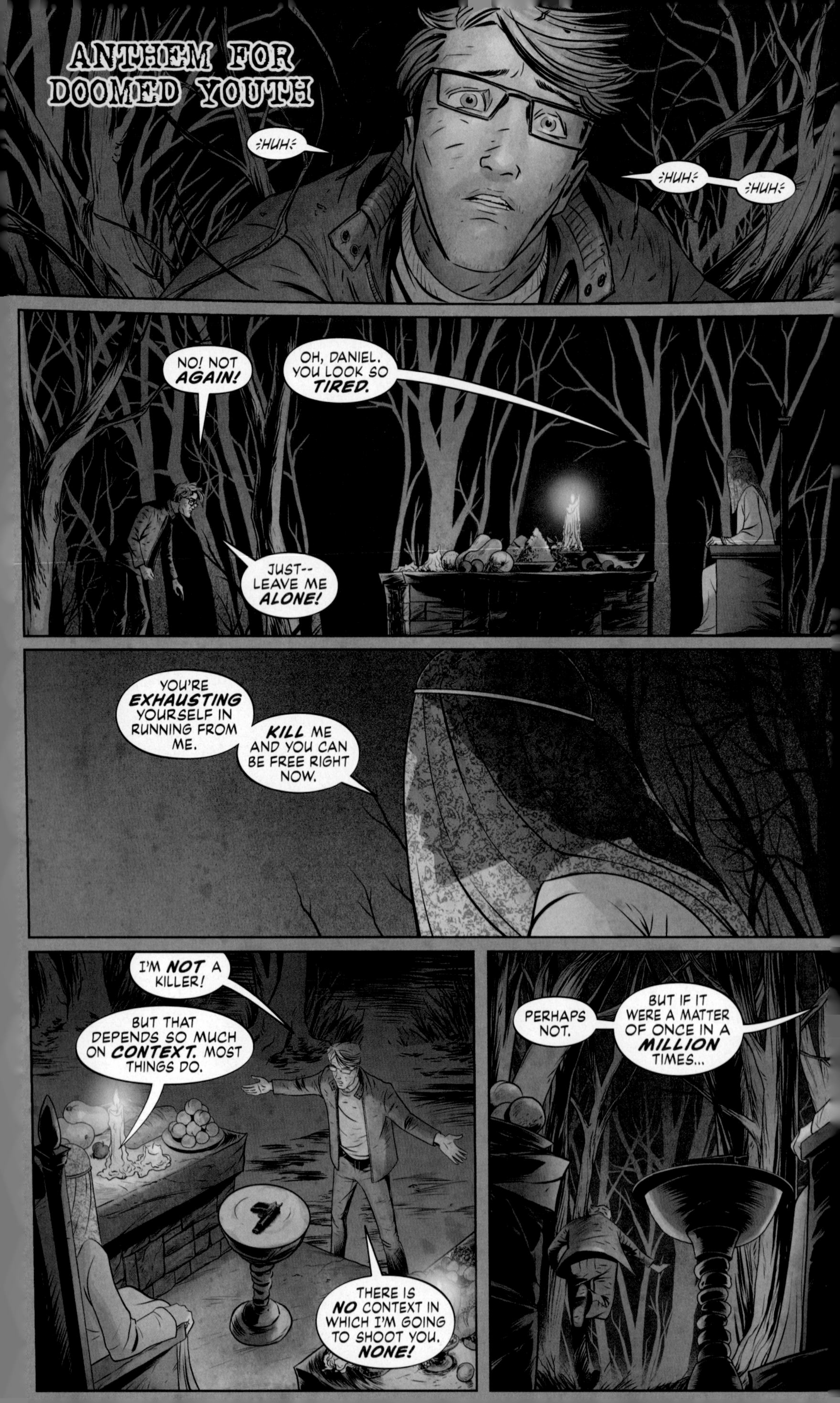

ANTHEM FOR DOOMED YOUTH
HUH
HUH
HUH
NO! NOT AGAIN!
OH, DANIEL. YOU LOOK SO TIRED.
JUST-- LEAVE ME ALONE!
YOU'RE EXHAUSTING YOURSELF IN RUNNING FROM ME.
KILL ME AND YOU CAN BE FREE RIGHT NOW.
I'M NOT A KILLER!
BUT THAT DEPENDS SO MUCH ON CONTEXT. MOST THINGS DO.
THERE IS NO CONTEXT IN WHICH I'M GOING TO SHOOT YOU. NONE!
PERHAPS NOT.
BUT IF IT WERE A MATTER OF ONCE IN A MILLION TIMES...

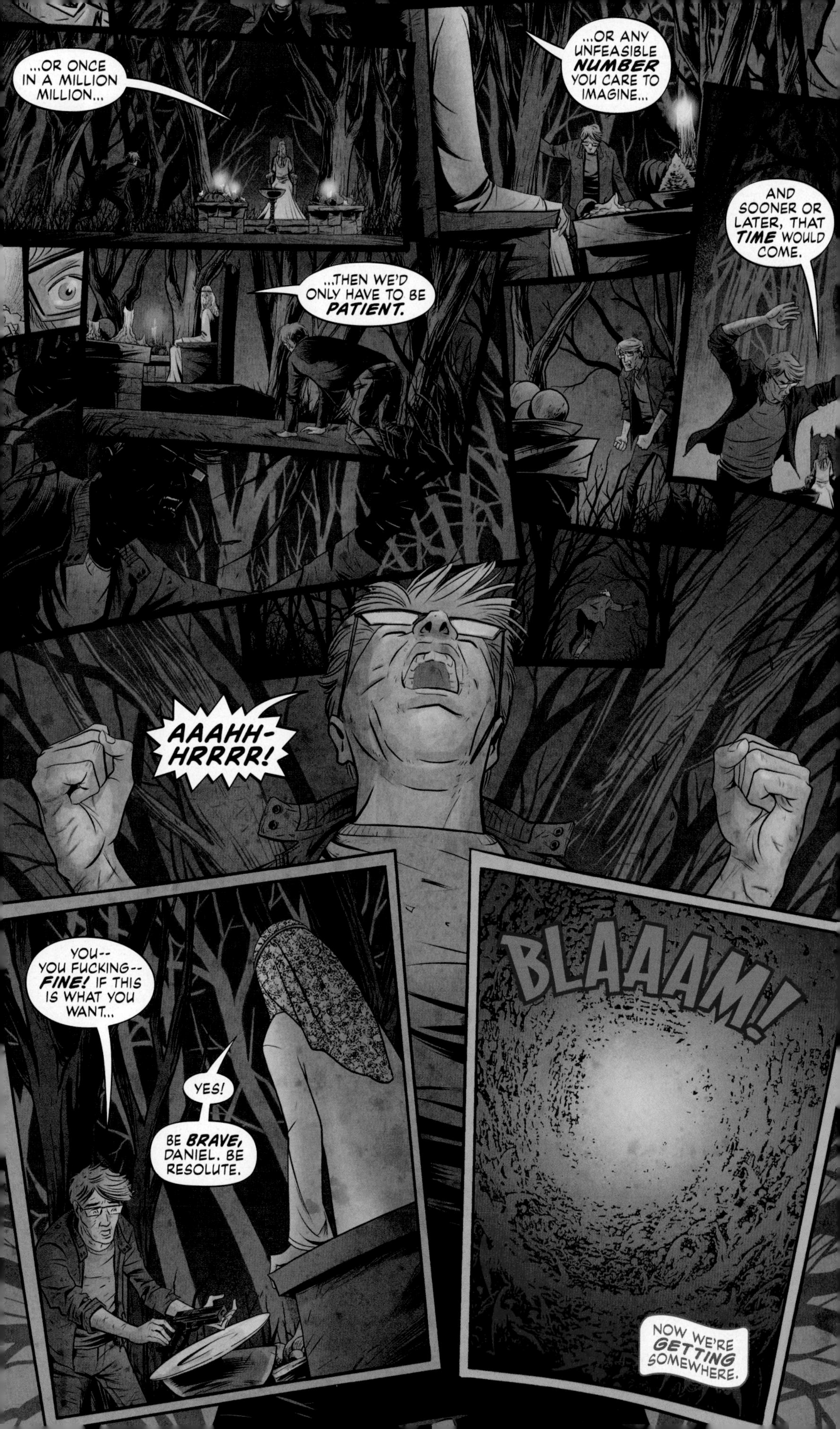
...OR ONCE IN A MILLION MILLION...
...OR ANY UNFEASIBLE NUMBER YOU CARE TO IMAGINE...
...THEN WE'D ONLY HAVE TO BE PATIENT.
AND SOONER OR LATER, THAT TIME WOULD COME.
AAAHH-HRRRR!
YOU-- YOU FUCKING-- FINE! IF THIS IS WHAT YOU WANT...
YES!
BE BRAVE, DANIEL. BE RESOLUTE.
BLAAAM!
NOW WE'RE GETTING SOMEWHERE.

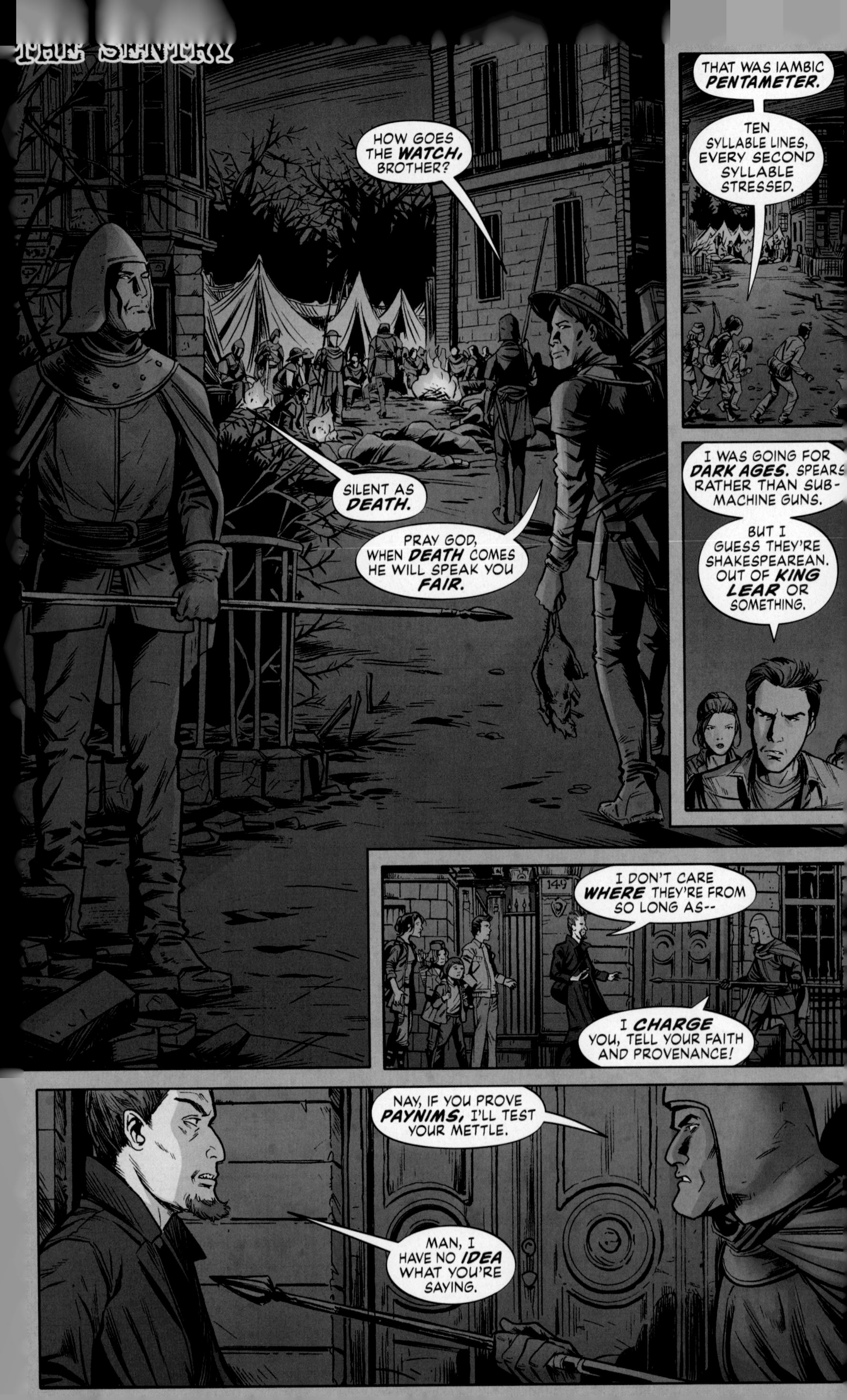
THE SENTRY
HOW GOES THE WATCH, BROTHER?
SILENT AS DEATH.
PRAY GOD, WHEN DEATH COMES HE WILL SPEAK YOU FAIR.
THAT WAS IAMBIC PENTAMETER.
TEN SYLLABLE LINES, EVERY SECOND SYLLABLE STRESSED.
I WAS GOING FOR DARK AGES. SPEARS RATHER THAN SUB-MACHINE GUNS.
BUT I GUESS THEY'RE SHAKESPEAREAN. OUT OF KING LEAR OR SOMETHING.
149
I DON'T CARE WHERE THEY'RE FROM SO LONG AS--
I CHARGE YOU, TELL YOUR FAITH AND PROVENANCE!
NAY, IF YOU PROVE PAYNIMS, I'LL TEST YOUR METTLE.
MAN, I HAVE NO IDEA WHAT YOU'RE SAYING.

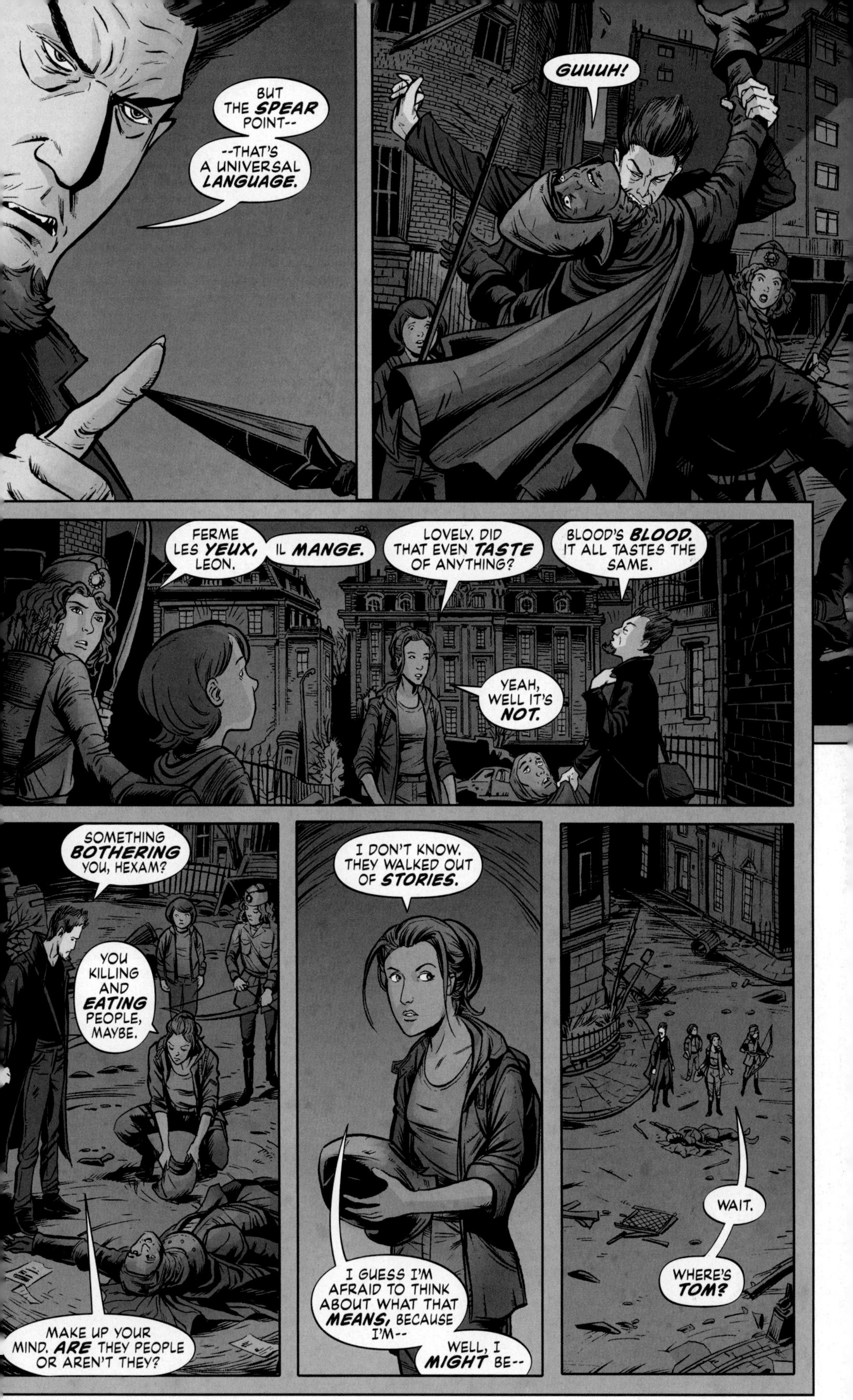
BUT THE SPEAR POINT--
--THAT'S A UNIVERSAL LANGUAGE.
GUUUH!
FERME LES YEUX, LEON.
IL MANGE.
LOVELY. DID THAT EVEN TASTE OF ANYTHING?
BLOOD'S BLOOD. IT ALL TASTES THE SAME.
YEAH, WELL IT'S NOT.
SOMETHING BOTHERING YOU, HEXAM?
YOU KILLING AND EATING PEOPLE, MAYBE.
MAKE UP YOUR MIND. ARE THEY PEOPLE OR AREN'T THEY?
I DON'T KNOW. THEY WALKED OUT OF STORIES.
I GUESS I'M AFRAID TO THINK ABOUT WHAT THAT MEANS, BECAUSE I'M--
WELL, I MIGHT BE--
WAIT.
WHERE'S TOM?

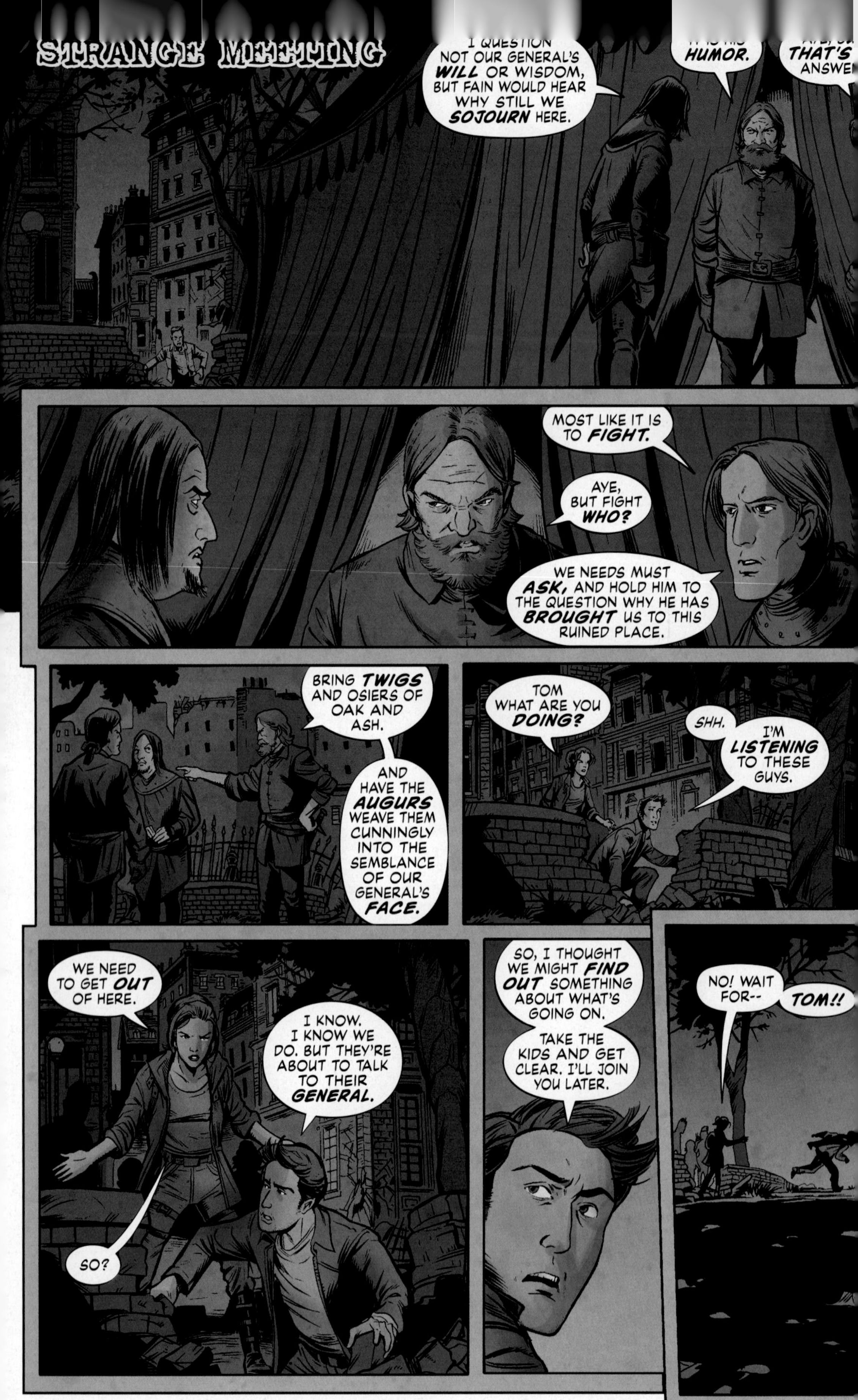
I QUESTION NOT OUR GENERAL'S WILL OR WISDOM, BUT FAIN WOULD HEAR WHY STILL WE SOJOURN HERE.
HUMOR.
THAT'S
MOST LIKE IT IS TO FIGHT.
AYE, BUT FIGHT WHO?
WE NEEDS MUST ASK, AND HOLD HIM TO THE QUESTION WHY HE HAS BROUGHT US TO THIS RUINED PLACE.
BRING TWIGS AND OSIERS OF OAK AND ASH.
AND HAVE THE AUGURS WEAVE THEM CUNNINGLY INTO THE SEMBLANCE OF OUR GENERAL'S FACE.
TOM WHAT ARE YOU DOING?
SHH.
I'M LISTENING TO THESE GUYS.
WE NEED TO GET OUT OF HERE.
I KNOW. I KNOW WE DO. BUT THEY'RE ABOUT TO TALK TO THEIR GENERAL.
SO?
SO, I THOUGHT WE MIGHT FIND OUT SOMETHING ABOUT WHAT'S GOING ON.
TAKE THE KIDS AND GET CLEAR. I'LL JOIN YOU LATER.
NO! WAIT FOR--
TOM!!

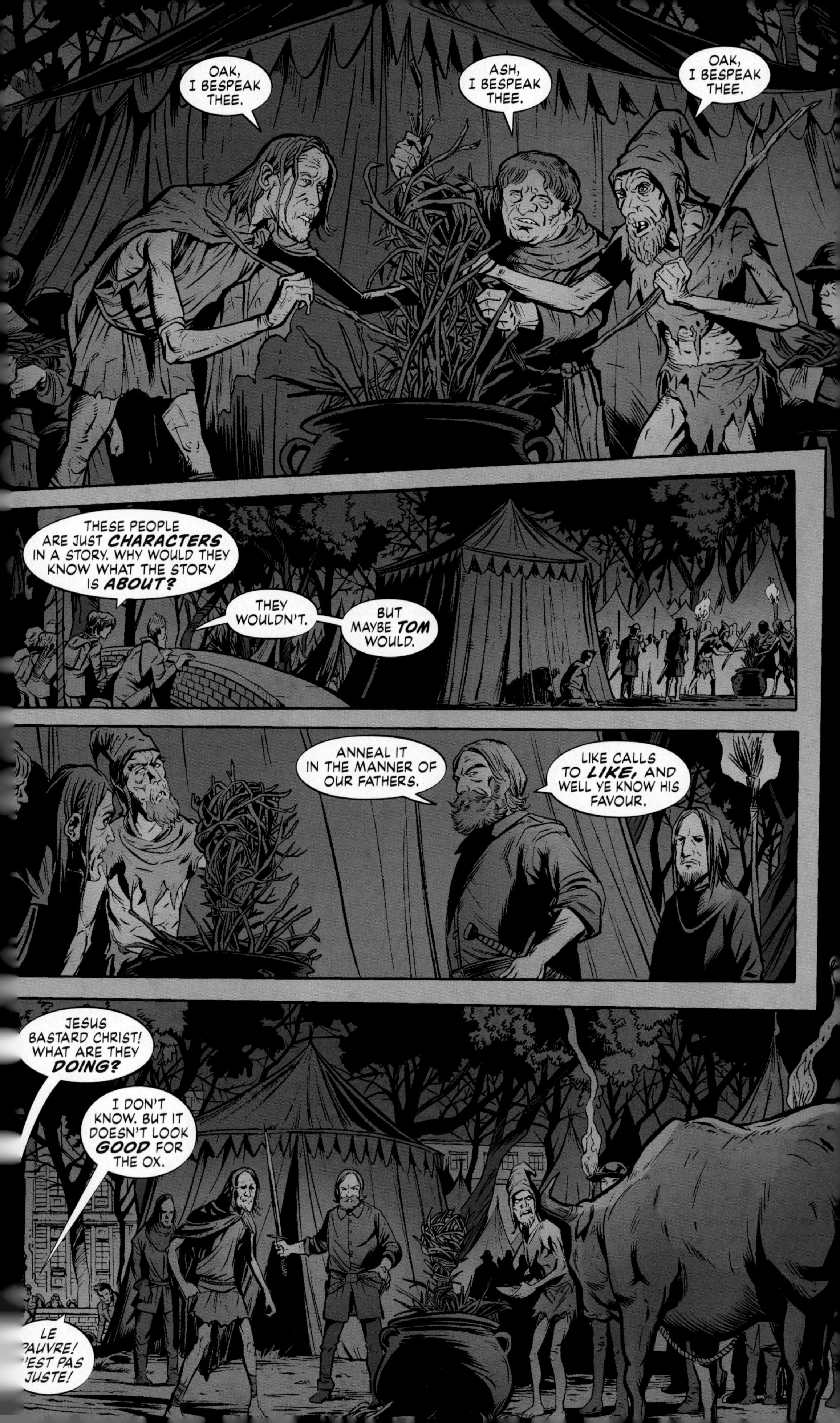
OAK, I BESPEAK THEE.
ASH, I BESPEAK THEE.
OAK, I BESPEAK THEE.
THESE PEOPLE ARE JUST CHARACTERS IN A STORY. WHY WOULD THEY KNOW WHAT THE STORY IS ABOUT?
THEY WOULDN'T.
BUT MAYBE TOM WOULD.
ANNEAL IT IN THE MANNER OF OUR FATHERS.
LIKE CALLS TO LIKE, AND WELL YE KNOW HIS FAVOUR.
JESUS BASTARD CHRIST! WHAT ARE THEY DOING?
I DON'T KNOW. BUT IT DOESN'T LOOK GOOD FOR THE OX.
LE PAUVRE! C'EST PAS JUSTE!

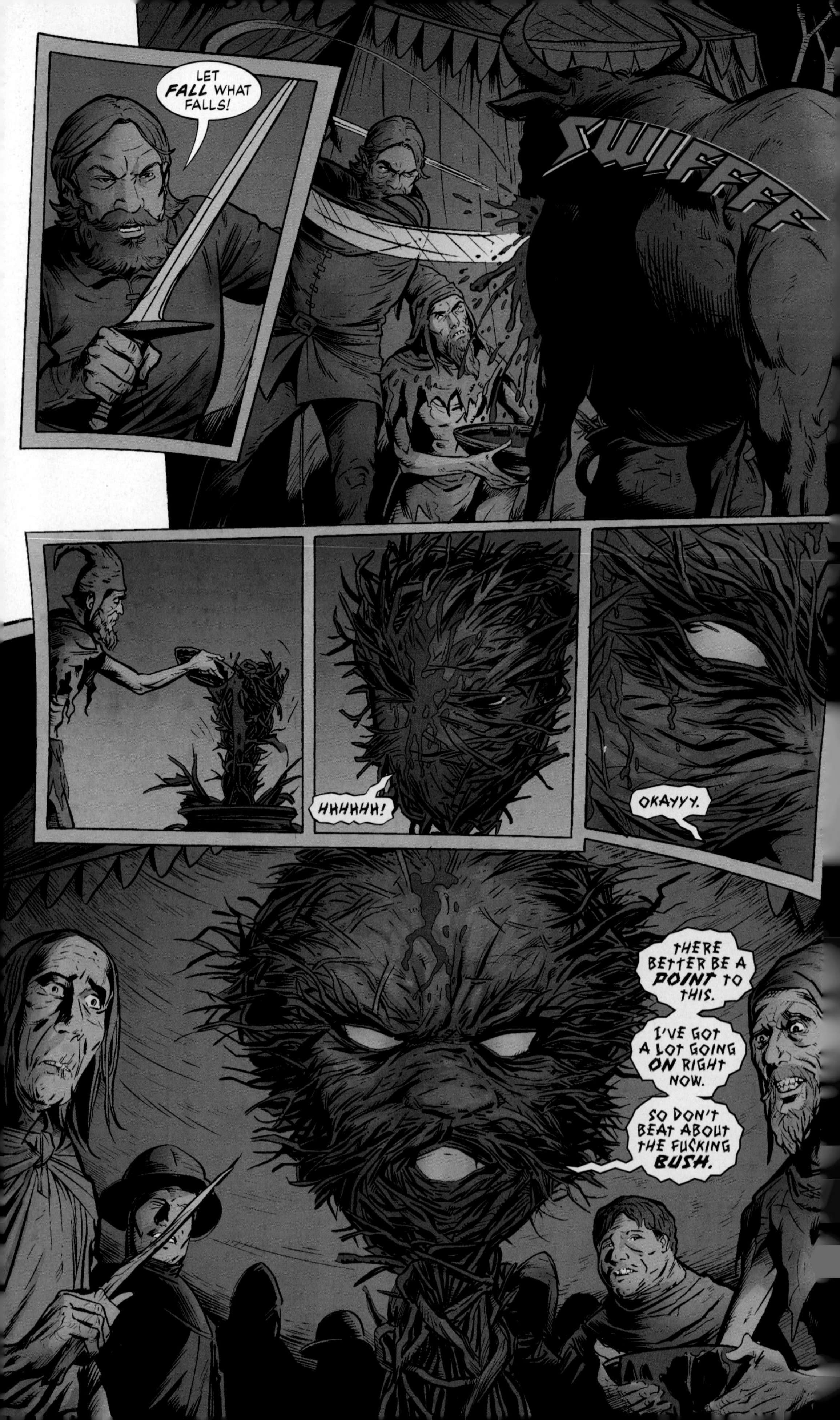
LET FALL WHAT FALLS!
SWIFFFF
HHHHHH!
OKAYYY.
THERE BETTER BE A POINT TO THIS.
I'VE GOT A LOT GOING ON RIGHT NOW.
SO DON'T BEAT ABOUT THE FUCKING BUSH.

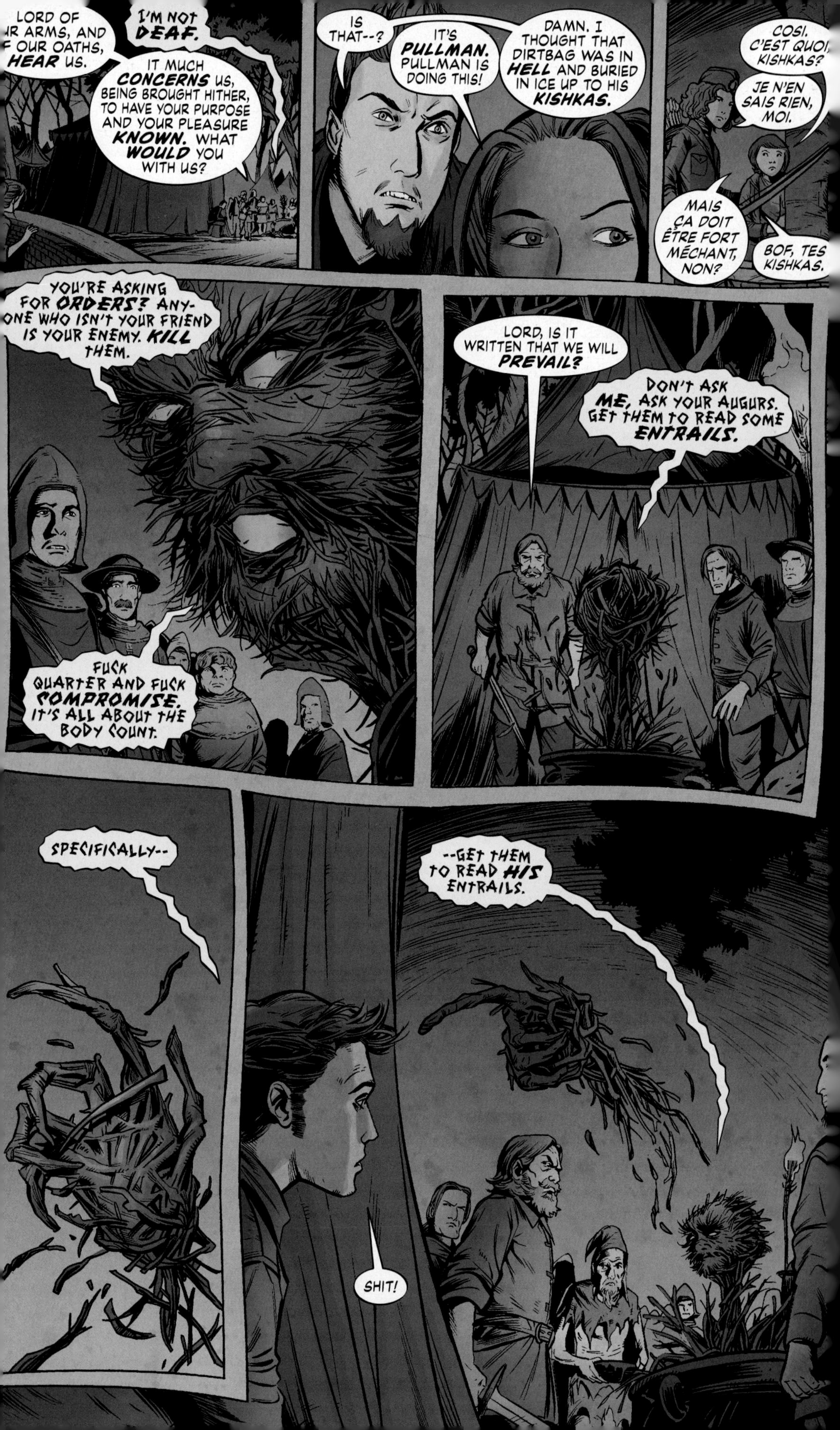

LORD OF ...R ARMS, AND ...F OUR OATHS, HEAR US.
I'M NOT DEAF.
IT MUCH CONCERNS US, BEING BROUGHT HITHER, TO HAVE YOUR PURPOSE AND YOUR PLEASURE KNOWN. WHAT WOULD YOU WITH US?
IS THAT--?
IT'S PULLMAN. PULLMAN IS DOING THIS!
DAMN. I THOUGHT THAT DIRTBAG WAS IN HELL AND BURIED IN ICE UP TO HIS KISHKAS.
COSI. C'EST QUOI, KISHKAS?
JE N'EN SAIS RIEN, MOI.
MAIS ÇA DOIT ÊTRE FORT MÉCHANT, NON?
BOF, TES KISHKAS.
YOU'RE ASKING FOR ORDERS? ANYONE WHO ISN'T YOUR FRIEND IS YOUR ENEMY. KILL THEM.
FUCK QUARTER AND FUCK COMPROMISE. IT'S ALL ABOUT THE BODY COUNT.
LORD, IS IT WRITTEN THAT WE WILL PREVAIL?
DON'T ASK ME, ASK YOUR AUGURS. GET THEM TO READ SOME ENTRAILS.
SPECIFICALLY--
--GET THEM TO READ HIS ENTRAILS.
SHIT!

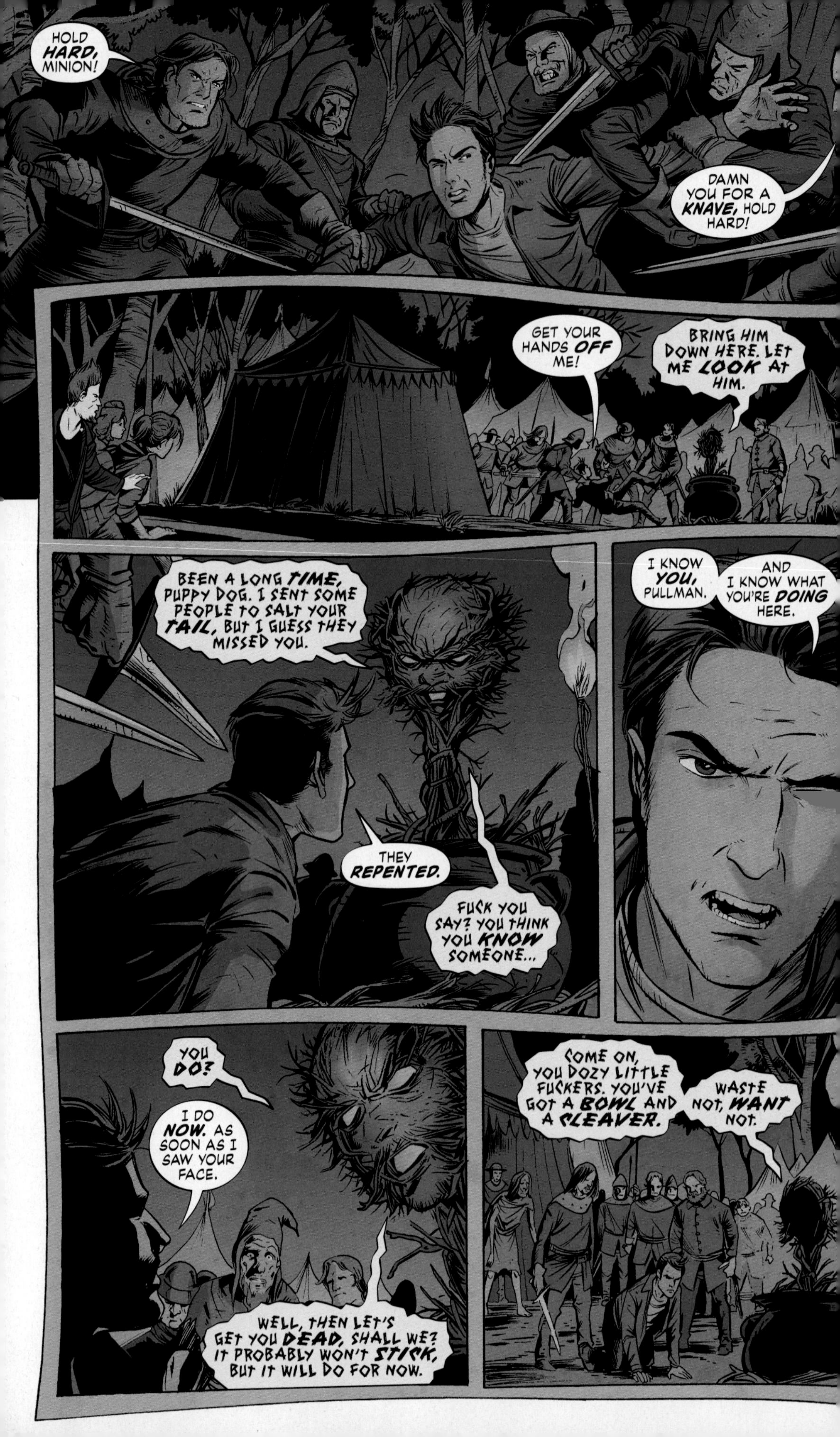
HOLD HARD, MINION!
DAMN YOU FOR A KNAVE, HOLD HARD!
GET YOUR HANDS OFF ME!
BRING HIM DOWN HERE. LET ME LOOK AT HIM.
BEEN A LONG TIME, PUPPY DOG. I SENT SOME PEOPLE TO SALT YOUR TAIL, BUT I GUESS THEY MISSED YOU.
THEY REPENTED.
FUCK YOU SAY? YOU THINK YOU KNOW SOMEONE...
I KNOW YOU, PULLMAN.
AND I KNOW WHAT YOU'RE DOING HERE.
YOU DO?
I DO NOW. AS SOON AS I SAW YOUR FACE.
WELL, THEN LET'S GET YOU DEAD, SHALL WE? IT PROBABLY WON'T STICK, BUT IT WILL DO FOR NOW.
COME ON, YOU DOZY LITTLE FUCKERS. YOU'VE GOT A BOWL AND A CLEAVER.
WASTE NOT, WANT NOT.

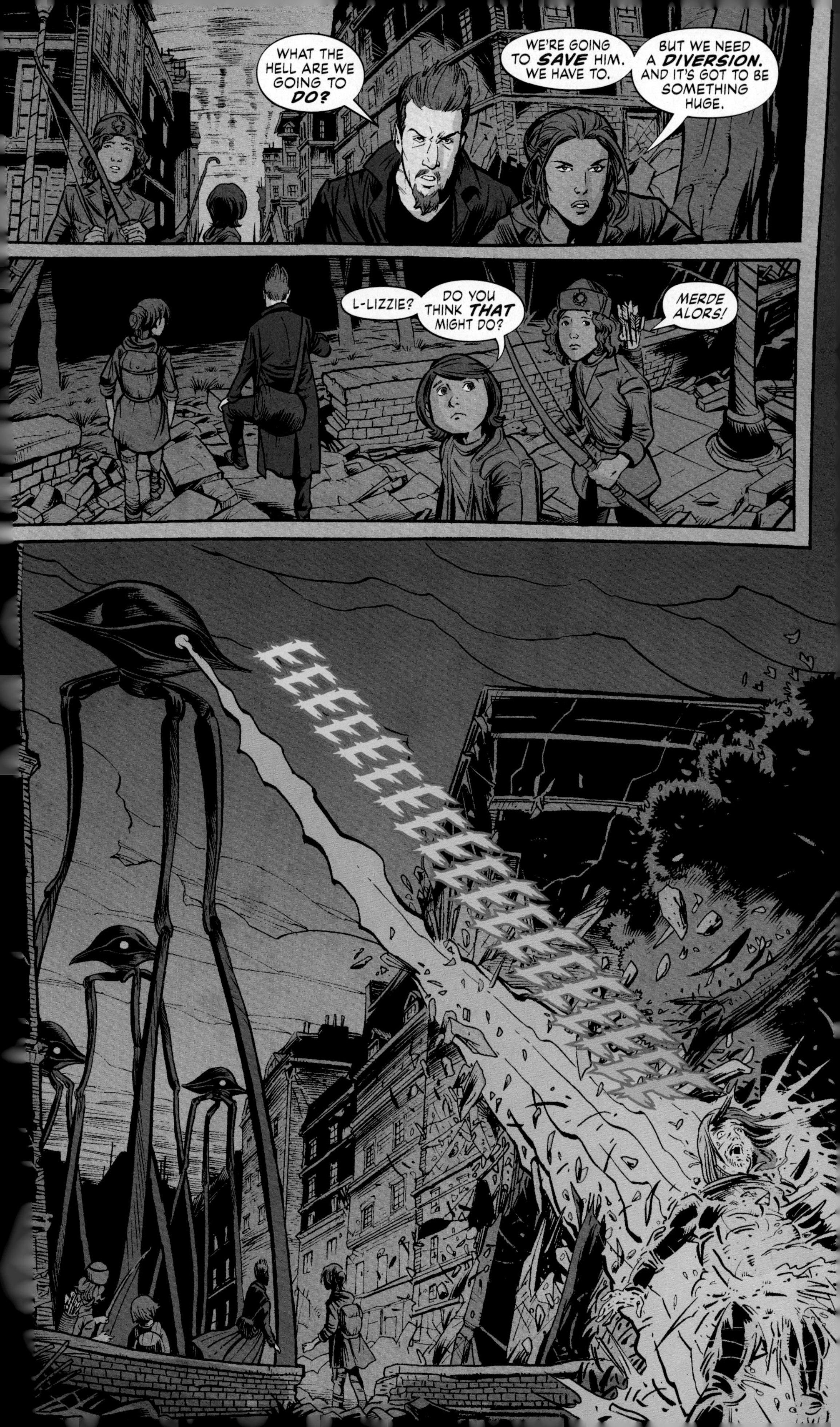

WHAT THE HELL ARE WE GOING TO DO?
WE'RE GOING TO SAVE HIM. WE HAVE TO.
BUT WE NEED A DIVERSION. AND IT'S GOT TO BE SOMETHING HUGE.
L-LIZZIE?
DO YOU THINK THAT MIGHT DO?
MERDE ALORS!
EEEEEEEEEEEEEEEEEE

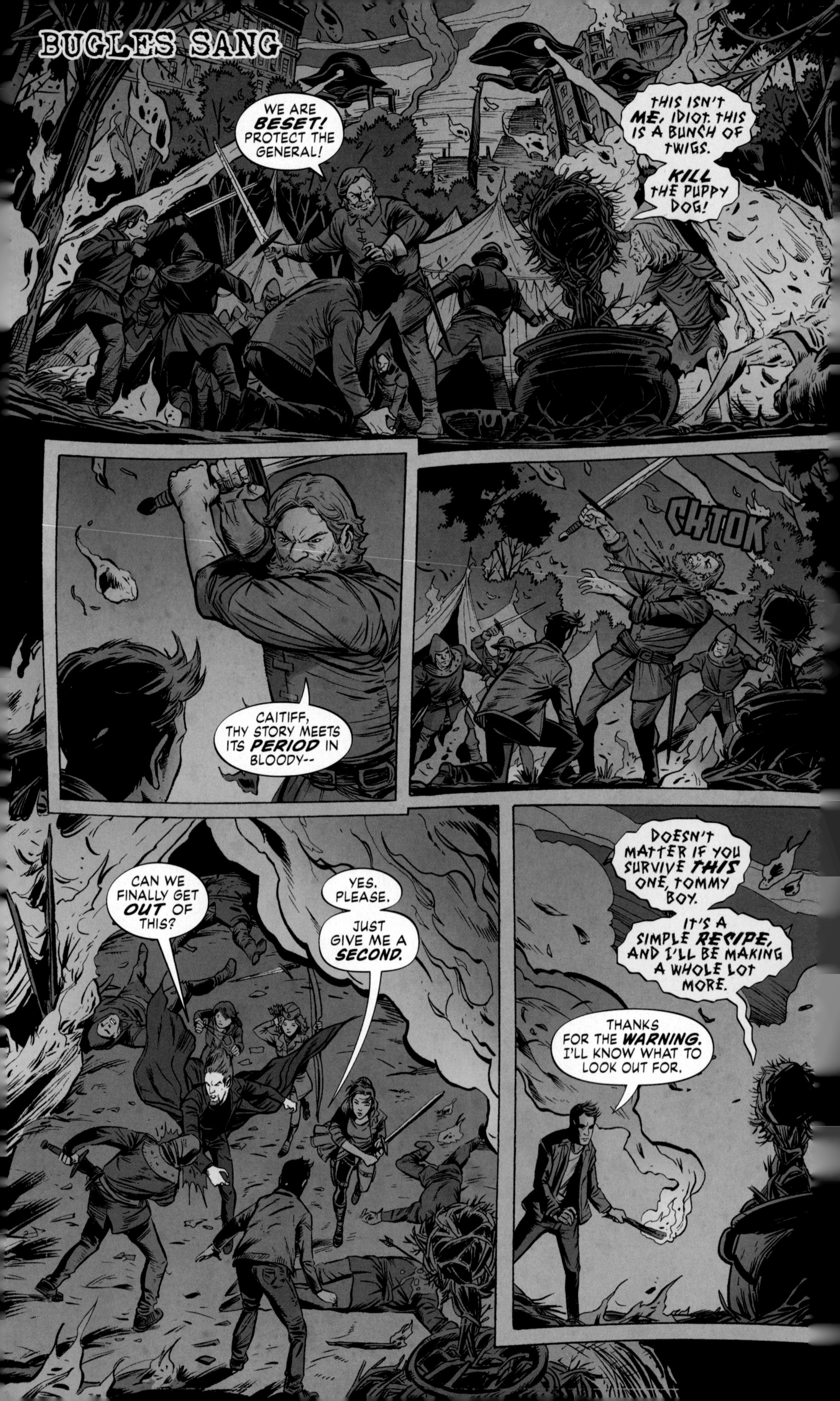

BUGLES SANG
WE ARE BESET! PROTECT THE GENERAL!
THIS ISN'T ME, IDIOT. THIS IS A BUNCH OF TWIGS.
KILL THE PUPPY DOG!
CAITIFF, THY STORY MEETS ITS PERIOD IN BLOODY--
CHTOK
CAN WE FINALLY GET OUT OF THIS?
YES. PLEASE.
JUST GIVE ME A SECOND.
DOESN'T MATTER IF YOU SURVIVE THIS ONE, TOMMY BOY.
IT'S A SIMPLE RECIPE, AND I'LL BE MAKING A WHOLE LOT MORE.
THANKS FOR THE WARNING. I'LL KNOW WHAT TO LOOK OUT FOR.

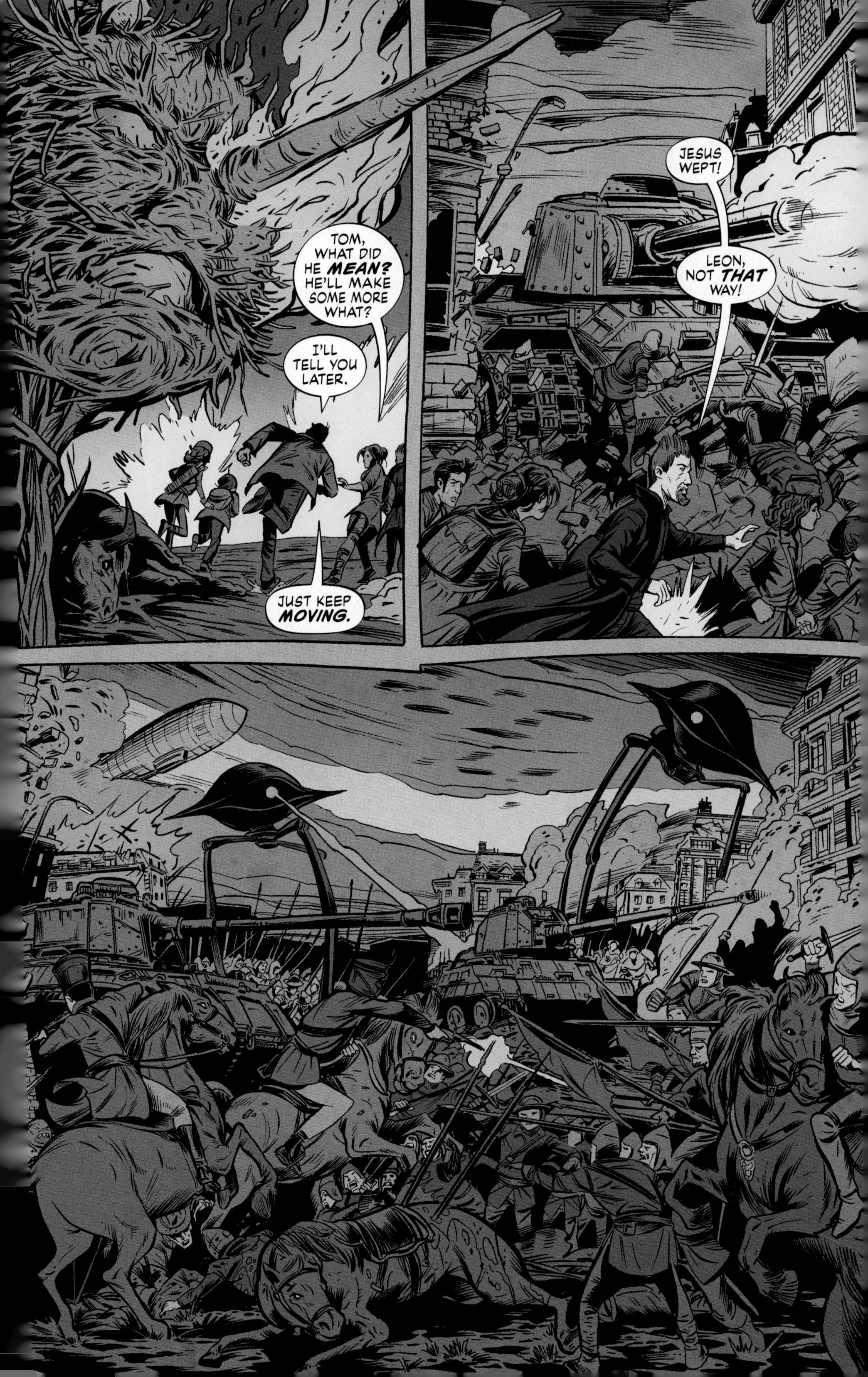
TOM, WHAT DID HE MEAN? HE'LL MAKE SOME MORE WHAT?
I'LL TELL YOU LATER.
JUST KEEP MOVING.
JESUS WEPT!
LEON, NOT THAT WAY!

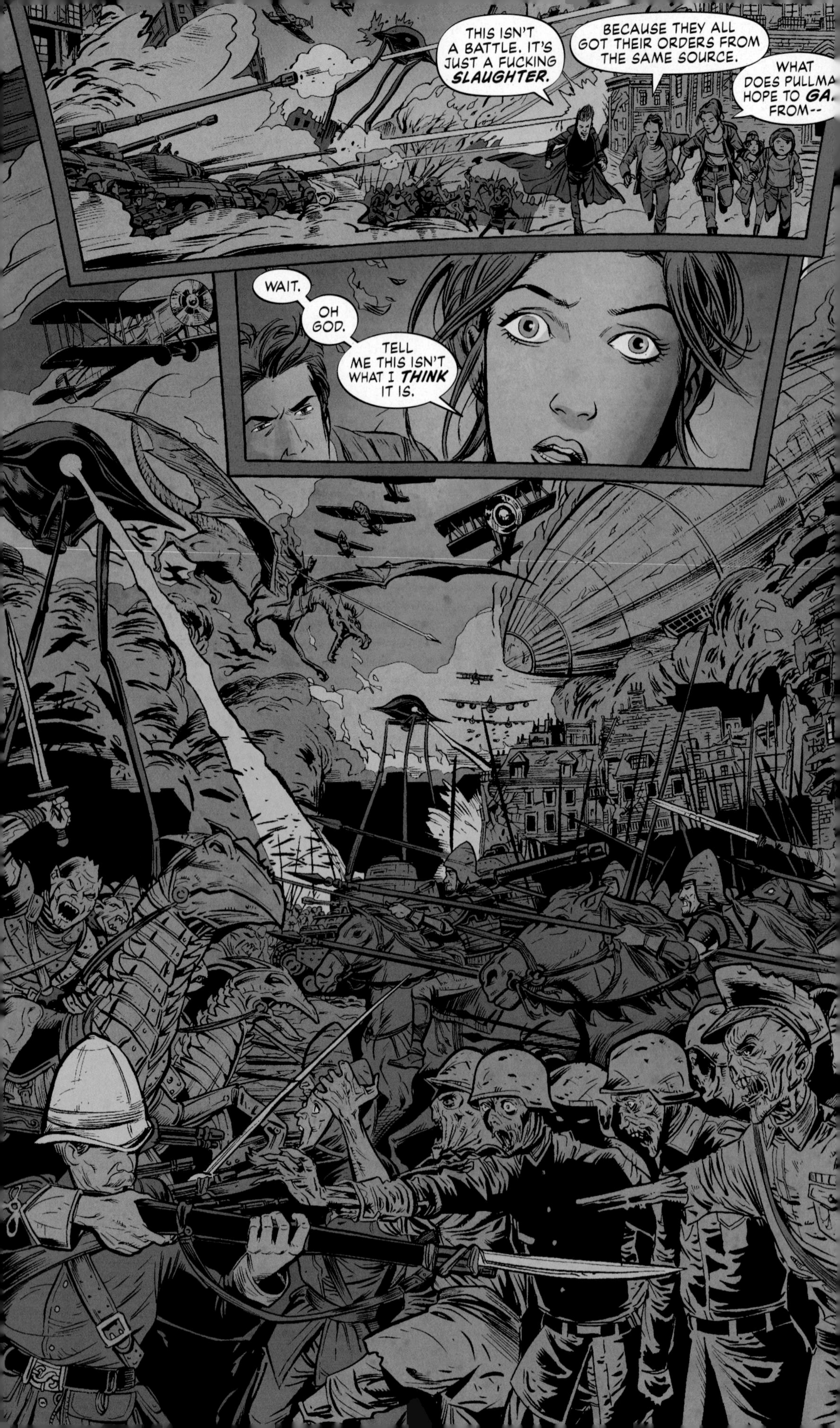
THIS ISN'T A BATTLE. IT'S JUST A FUCKING **SLAUGHTER.**
BECAUSE THEY ALL GOT THEIR ORDERS FROM THE SAME SOURCE.
WHAT DOES PULLMA HOPE TO GA FROM--
WAIT.
OH GOD.
TELL ME THIS ISN'T WHAT I **THINK** IT IS.

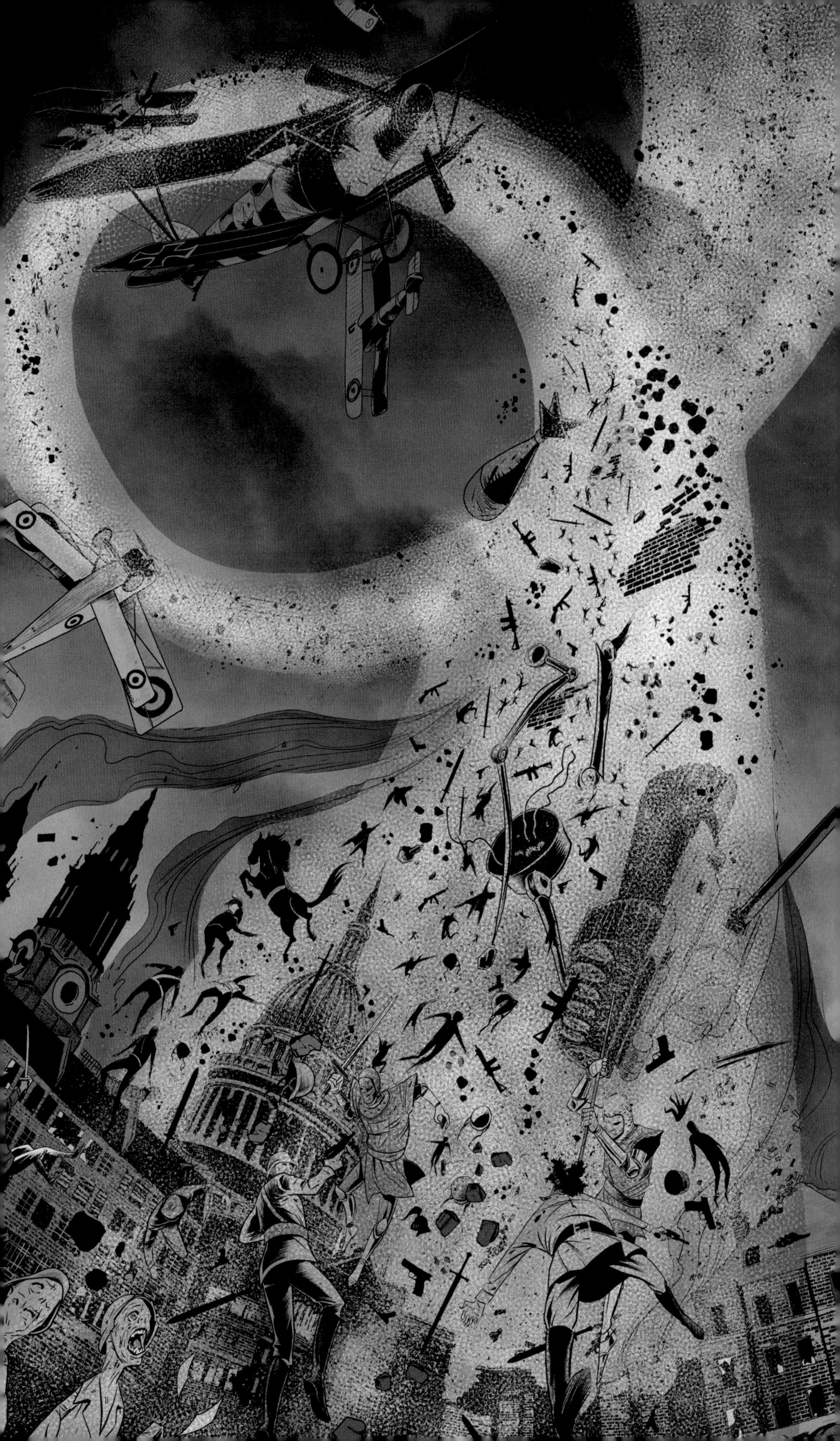

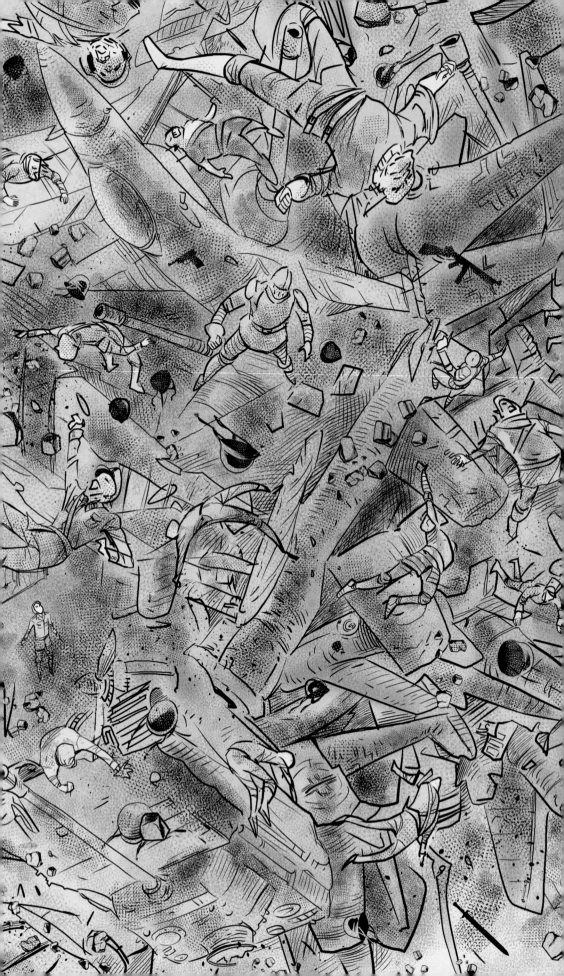

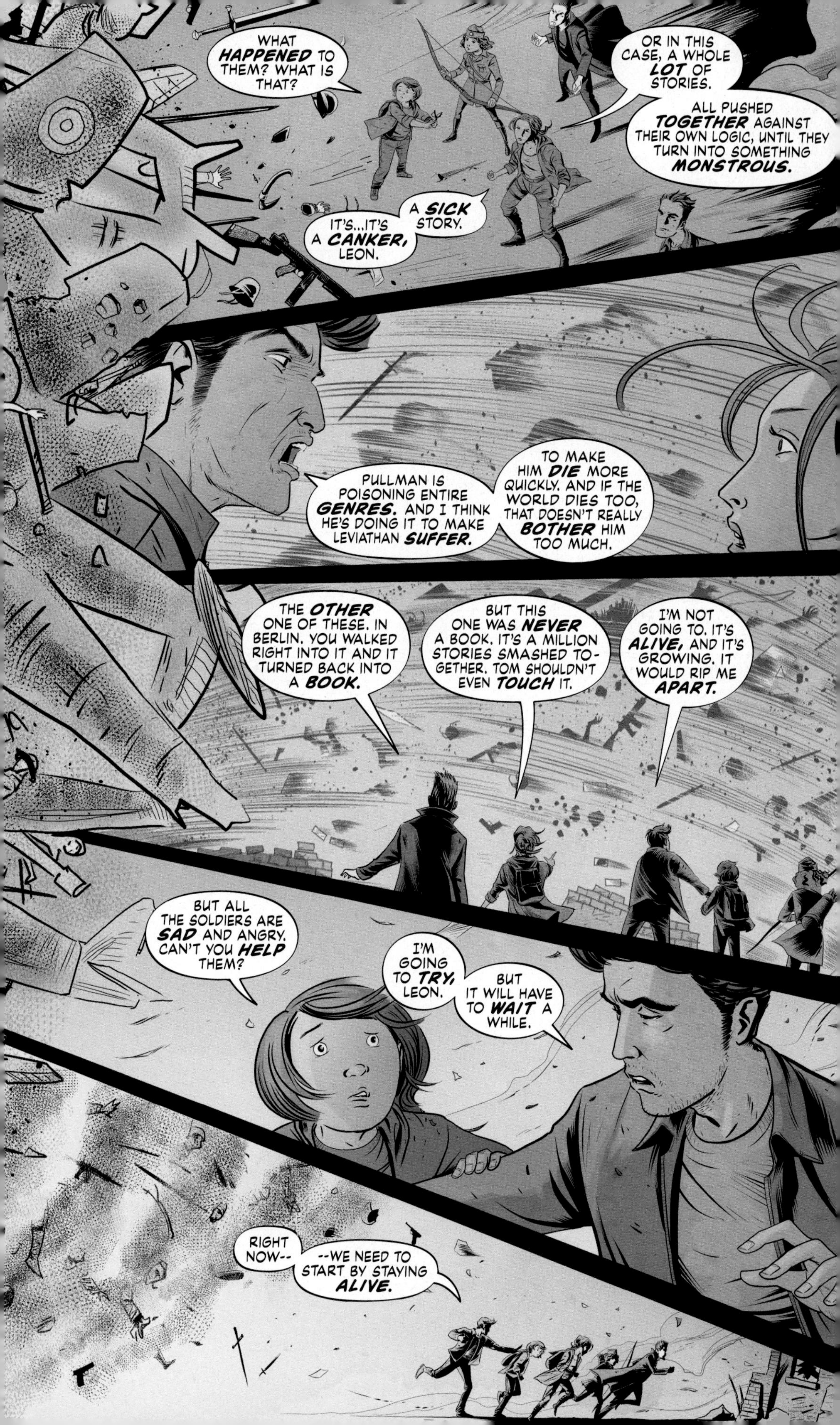
WHAT HAPPENED TO THEM? WHAT IS THAT?
OR IN THIS CASE, A WHOLE LOT OF STORIES.
ALL PUSHED TOGETHER AGAINST THEIR OWN LOGIC, UNTIL THEY TURN INTO SOMETHING MONSTROUS.
IT'S...IT'S A CANKER, LEON.
A SICK STORY.
PULLMAN IS POISONING ENTIRE GENRES. AND I THINK HE'S DOING IT TO MAKE LEVIATHAN SUFFER.
TO MAKE HIM DIE MORE QUICKLY. AND IF THE WORLD DIES TOO, THAT DOESN'T REALLY BOTHER HIM TOO MUCH.
THE OTHER ONE OF THESE. IN BERLIN. YOU WALKED RIGHT INTO IT AND IT TURNED BACK INTO A BOOK.
BUT THIS ONE WAS NEVER A BOOK. IT'S A MILLION STORIES SMASHED TO-GETHER. TOM SHOULDN'T EVEN TOUCH IT.
I'M NOT GOING TO. IT'S ALIVE, AND IT'S GROWING. IT WOULD RIP ME APART.
BUT ALL THE SOLDIERS ARE SAD AND ANGRY. CAN'T YOU HELP THEM?
I'M GOING TO TRY, LEON.
BUT IT WILL HAVE TO WAIT A WHILE.
RIGHT NOW--
--WE NEED TO START BY STAYING ALIVE.

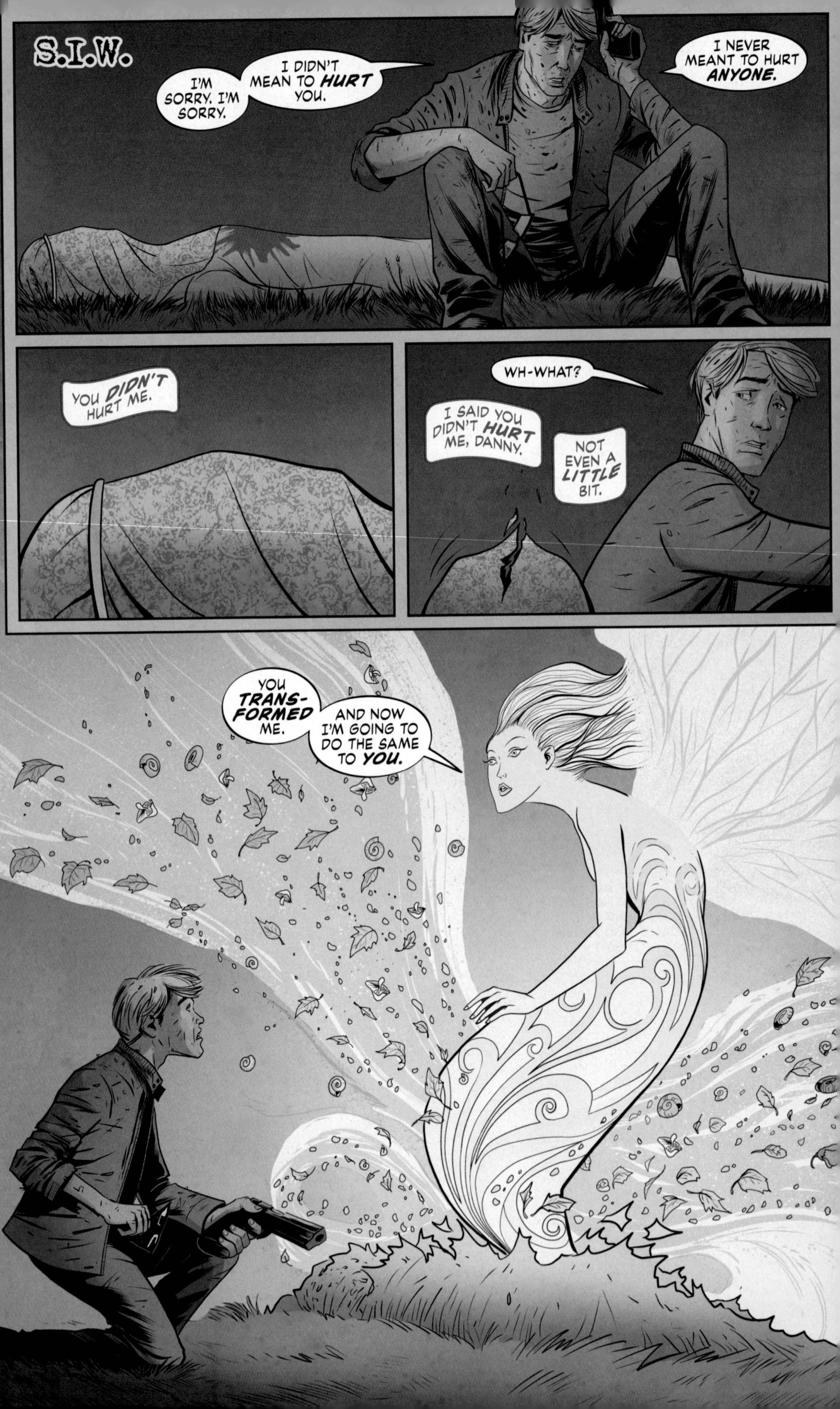
S.I.W.
I'M SORRY. I'M SORRY.
I DIDN'T MEAN TO HURT YOU.
I NEVER MEANT TO HURT ANYONE.
YOU DIDN'T HURT ME.
WH-WHAT?
I SAID YOU DIDN'T HURT ME, DANNY.
NOT EVEN A LITTLE BIT.
YOU TRANSFORMED ME.
AND NOW I'M GOING TO DO THE SAME TO YOU.

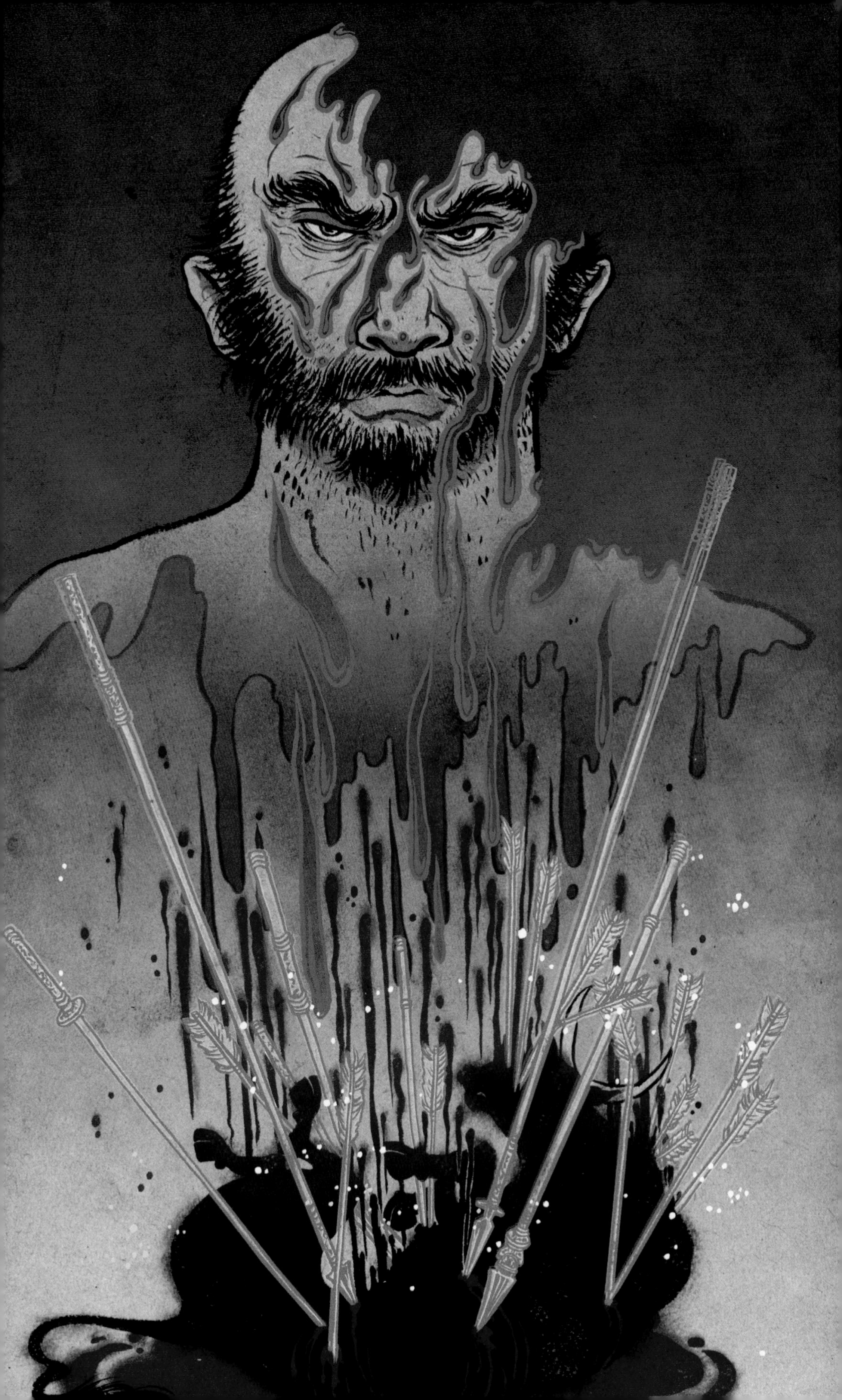

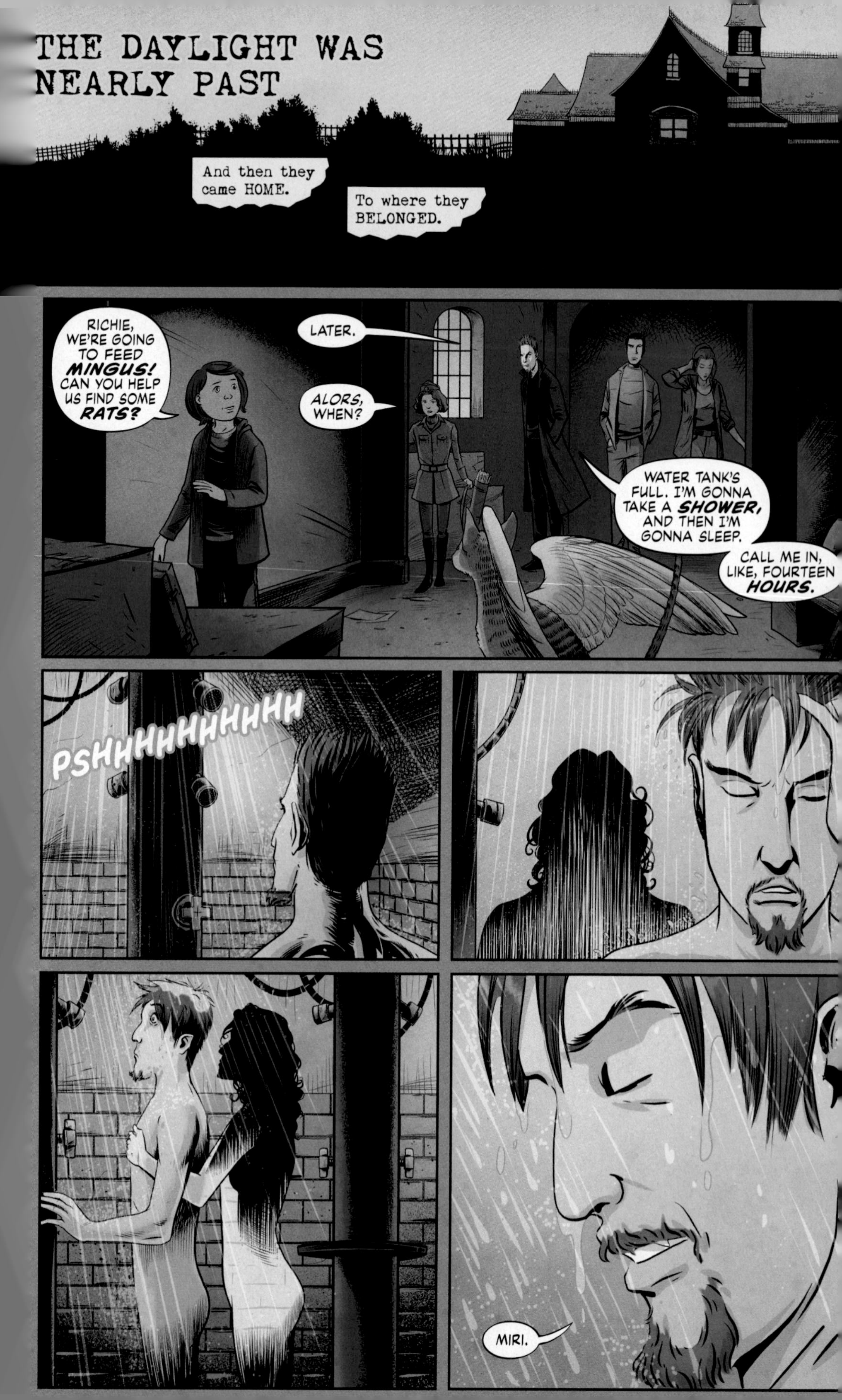
THE DAYLIGHT WAS NEARLY PAST
And then they came HOME.
To where they BELONGED.
RICHIE, WE'RE GOING TO FEED MINGUS! CAN YOU HELP US FIND SOME RATS?
LATER.
ALORS, WHEN?
WATER TANK'S FULL. I'M GONNA TAKE A SHOWER, AND THEN I'M GONNA SLEEP.
CALL ME IN, LIKE, FOURTEEN HOURS.
PSHHHHHHHHHH
MIRI.

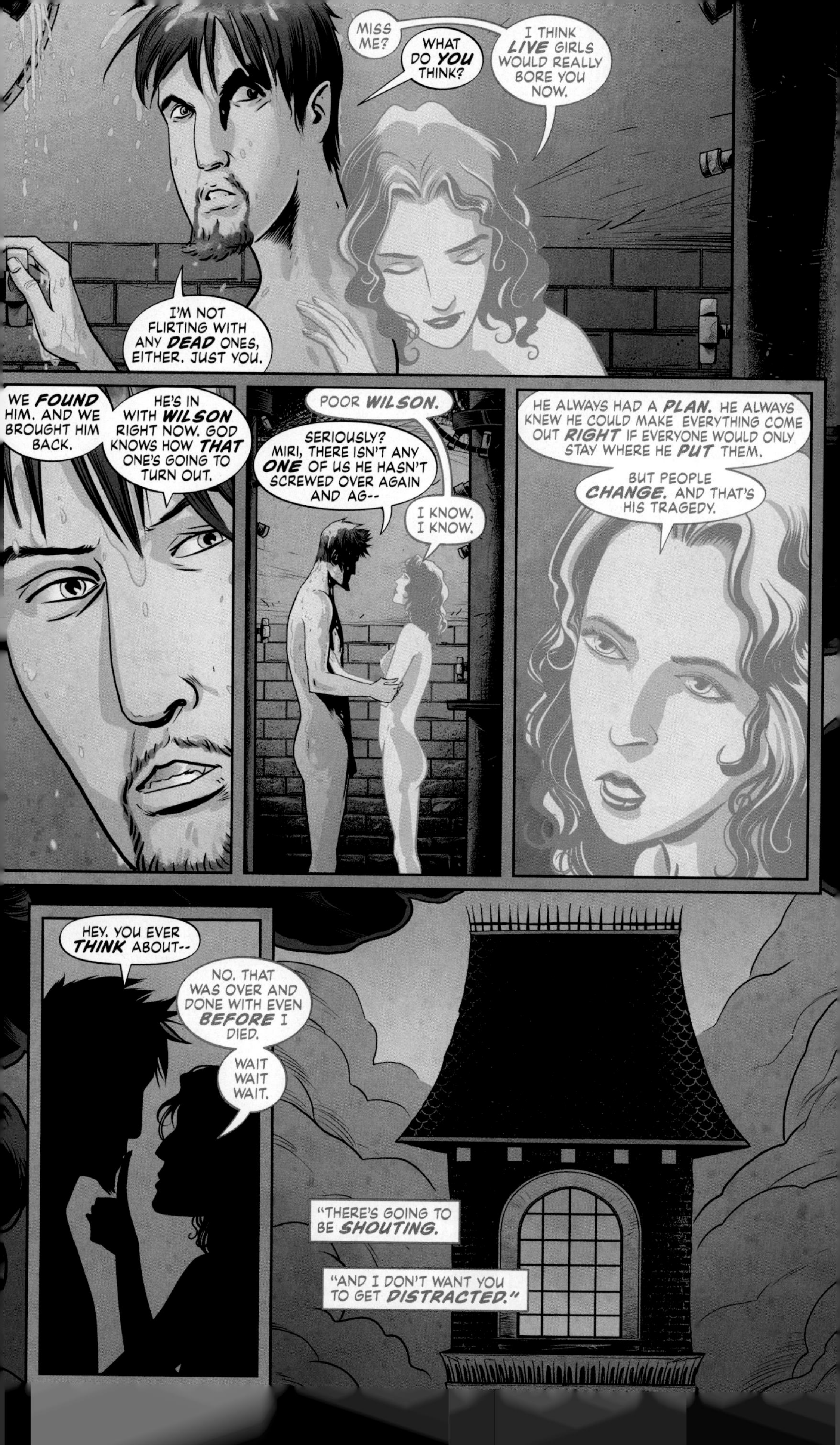
MISS ME?
WHAT DO YOU THINK?
I THINK LIVE GIRLS WOULD REALLY BORE YOU NOW.
I'M NOT FLIRTING WITH ANY DEAD ONES, EITHER. JUST YOU.
WE FOUND HIM. AND WE BROUGHT HIM BACK.
HE'S IN WITH WILSON RIGHT NOW. GOD KNOWS HOW THAT ONE'S GOING TO TURN OUT.
POOR WILSON.
SERIOUSLY? MIRI, THERE ISN'T ANY ONE OF US HE HASN'T SCREWED OVER AGAIN AND AG--
I KNOW. I KNOW.
HE ALWAYS HAD A PLAN. HE ALWAYS KNEW HE COULD MAKE EVERYTHING COME OUT RIGHT IF EVERYONE WOULD ONLY STAY WHERE HE PUT THEM.
BUT PEOPLE CHANGE. AND THAT'S HIS TRAGEDY.
HEY. YOU EVER THINK ABOUT--
NO. THAT WAS OVER AND DONE WITH EVEN BEFORE I DIED.
WAIT WAIT WAIT.
"THERE'S GOING TO BE SHOUTING.
"AND I DON'T WANT YOU TO GET DISTRACTED."

WHAT I TELL YOU THREE-TIMES IS TRUE.

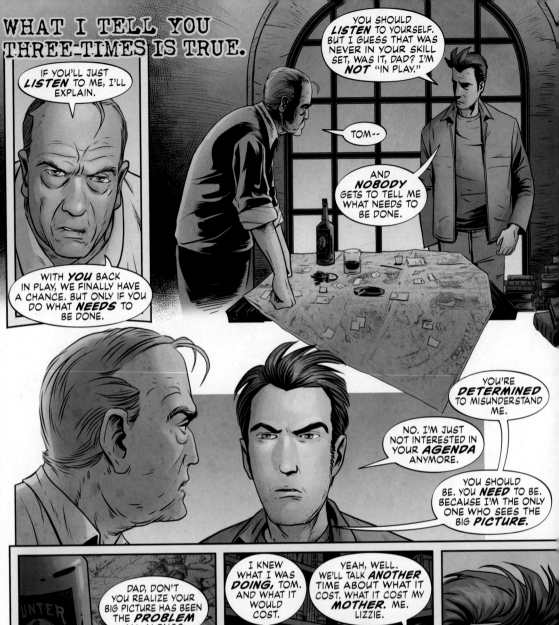

IF YOU'LL JUST *LISTEN* TO ME, I'LL EXPLAIN.

WITH *YOU* BACK IN PLAY, WE FINALLY HAVE A CHANCE. BUT ONLY IF YOU DO WHAT *NEEDS* TO BE DONE.

YOU SHOULD *LISTEN* TO YOURSELF. BUT I GUESS THAT WAS NEVER IN YOUR SKILL SET, WAS IT, DAD? I'M *NOT* "IN PLAY."

TOM--

AND *NOBODY* GETS TO TELL ME WHAT NEEDS TO BE DONE.

YOU'RE *DETERMINED* TO MISUNDERSTAND ME.

NO. I'M JUST NOT INTERESTED IN YOUR *AGENDA* ANYMORE.

YOU SHOULD BE. YOU *NEED* TO BE. BECAUSE I'M THE ONLY ONE WHO SEES THE BIG *PICTURE*.

DAD, DON'T YOU REALIZE YOUR BIG PICTURE HAS BEEN THE *PROBLEM* ALL ALONG?

YOU GOT USED TO SEEING EVERYONE AS JUST *DETAILS*. FIGURES IN THAT FUCKING LANDSCAPE.

YOU ZOOMED *OUT* SO FAR, YOU COULDN'T ZOOM BACK IN AGAIN.

I KNEW WHAT I WAS *DOING*, TOM. AND WHAT IT WOULD COST.

YEAH, WELL. WE'LL TALK *ANOTHER* TIME ABOUT WHAT IT COST. WHAT IT COST MY *MOTHER*. ME. LIZZIE.

LIZZIE IS TO *BLAME* IN THIS, TOO.

SHE--SHE'S *WHAT*?

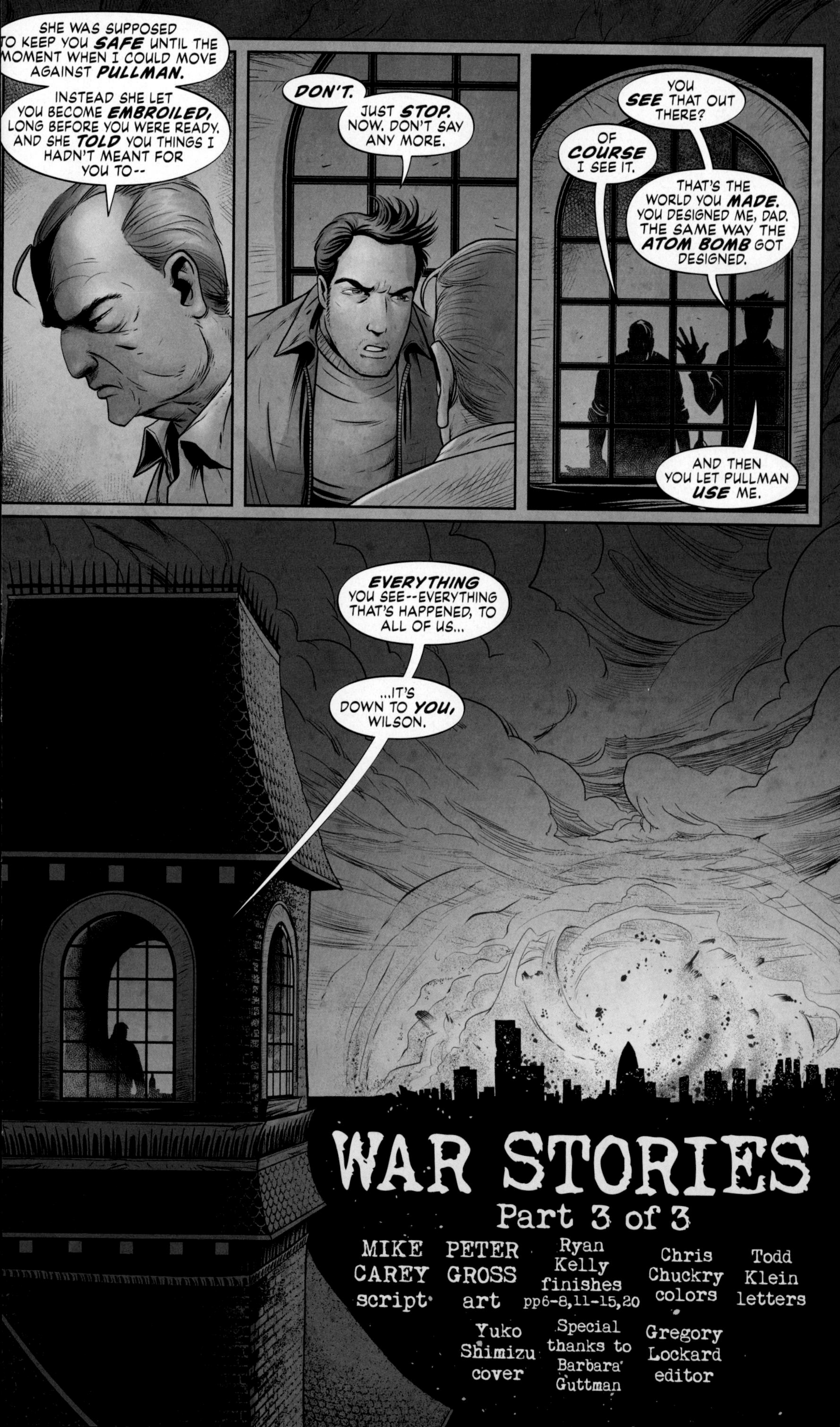
SHE WAS SUPPOSED TO KEEP YOU SAFE UNTIL THE MOMENT WHEN I COULD MOVE AGAINST PULLMAN.
INSTEAD SHE LET YOU BECOME EMBROILED, LONG BEFORE YOU WERE READY. AND SHE TOLD YOU THINGS I HADN'T MEANT FOR YOU TO--
DON'T.
JUST STOP. NOW. DON'T SAY ANY MORE.
YOU SEE THAT OUT THERE?
OF COURSE I SEE IT.
THAT'S THE WORLD YOU MADE. YOU DESIGNED ME, DAD. THE SAME WAY THE ATOM BOMB GOT DESIGNED.
AND THEN YOU LET PULLMAN USE ME.
EVERYTHING YOU SEE--EVERYTHING THAT'S HAPPENED, TO ALL OF US...
...IT'S DOWN TO YOU, WILSON.
WAR STORIES
Part 3 of 3
MIKE CAREY script
PETER GROSS art
Ryan Kelly finishes pp6-8,11-15,20
Chris Chuckry colors
Todd Klein letters
Yuko Shimizu cover
Special thanks to Barbara Guttman
Gregory Lockard editor

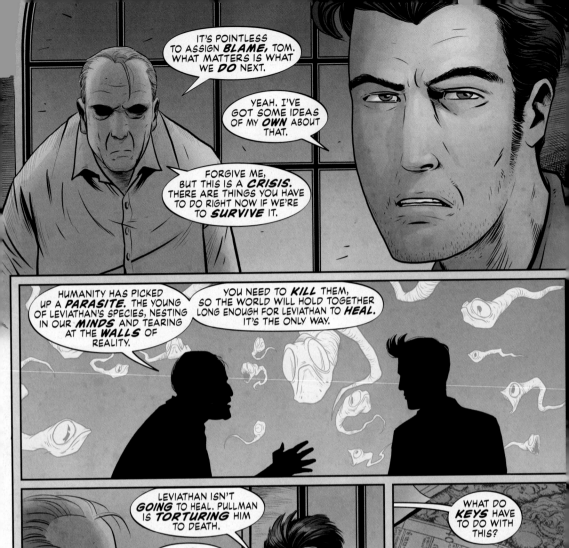

IT'S POINTLESS TO ASSIGN *BLAME,* TOM. WHAT MATTERS IS WHAT WE *DO* NEXT.

YEAH. I'VE GOT SOME IDEAS OF MY *OWN* ABOUT THAT.

FORGIVE ME, BUT THIS IS A *CRISIS.* THERE ARE THINGS YOU HAVE TO DO RIGHT NOW IF WE'RE TO *SURVIVE* IT.

HUMANITY HAS PICKED UP A *PARASITE.* THE YOUNG OF LEVIATHAN'S SPECIES, NESTING IN OUR *MINDS* AND TEARING AT THE *WALLS* OF REALITY.

YOU NEED TO *KILL* THEM, SO THE WORLD WILL HOLD TOGETHER LONG ENOUGH FOR LEVIATHAN TO *HEAL.* IT'S THE ONLY WAY.

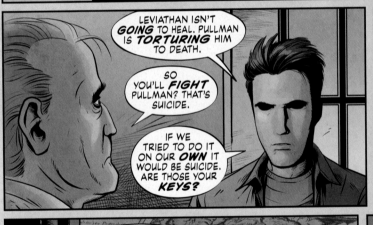

LEVIATHAN ISN'T *GOING* TO HEAL. PULLMAN IS *TORTURING* HIM TO DEATH.

SO YOU'LL *FIGHT* PULLMAN? THAT'S SUICIDE.

IF WE TRIED TO DO IT ON OUR *OWN* IT WOULD BE SUICIDE. ARE THOSE YOUR *KEYS?*

WHAT DO *KEYS* HAVE TO DO WITH THIS?

NOT A WHOLE LOT. BUT "WHAT NEEDS TO BE *DONE,*" DAD? IT'S A SLIPPERY CONCEPT, YOU KNOW.

IT DEPENDS HOW FAR BACK YOUR *MEMORY* GOES, OR HOW MUCH YOU CARE ABOUT THE PEOPLE YOU *FUCKED OVER.* SO, TELL ME--

--WHICH ONE OF THESE OPENS *PAULY BRUCKNER'S* ROOM?

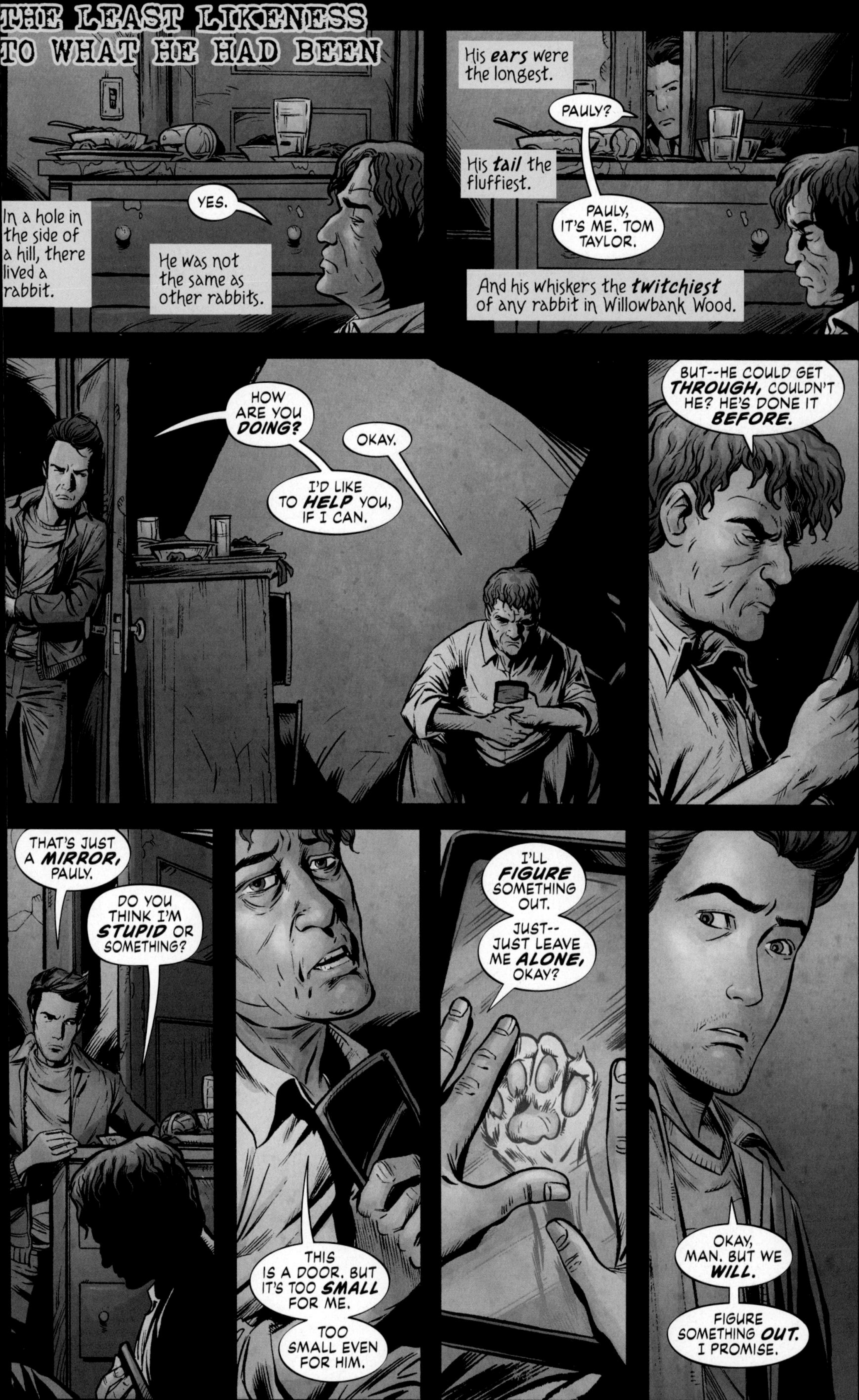

THE LEAST LIKENESS TO WHAT HE HAD BEEN
In a hole in the side of a hill, there lived a rabbit.
YES.
He was not the same as other rabbits.
His ears were the longest.
PAULY?
His tail the fluffiest.
PAULY, IT'S ME. TOM TAYLOR.
And his whiskers the twitchiest of any rabbit in Willowbank Wood.
HOW ARE YOU DOING?
OKAY.
I'D LIKE TO HELP YOU, IF I CAN.
BUT--HE COULD GET THROUGH, COULDN'T HE? HE'S DONE IT BEFORE.
THAT'S JUST A MIRROR, PAULY.
DO YOU THINK I'M STUPID OR SOMETHING?
THIS IS A DOOR. BUT IT'S TOO SMALL FOR ME.
TOO SMALL EVEN FOR HIM.
I'LL FIGURE SOMETHING OUT.
JUST-- JUST LEAVE ME ALONE, OKAY?
OKAY, MAN. BUT WE WILL.
FIGURE SOMETHING OUT. I PROMISE.

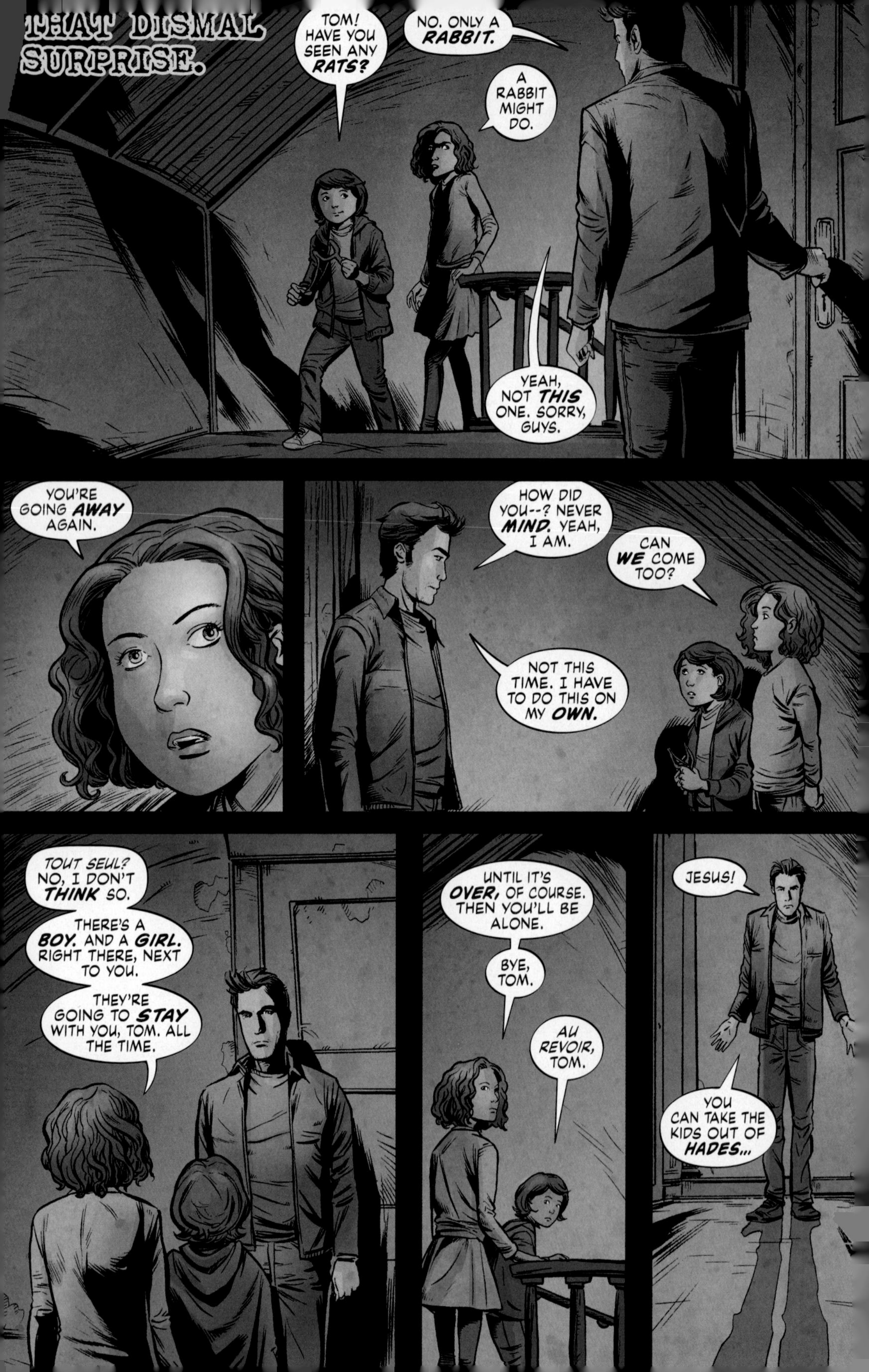
THAT DISMAL SURPRISE.
TOM! HAVE YOU SEEN ANY RATS?
NO. ONLY A RABBIT.
A RABBIT MIGHT DO.
YEAH, NOT THIS ONE. SORRY, GUYS.
YOU'RE GOING AWAY AGAIN.
HOW DID YOU--? NEVER MIND. YEAH, I AM.
CAN WE COME TOO?
NOT THIS TIME. I HAVE TO DO THIS ON MY OWN.
TOUT SEUL? NO, I DON'T THINK SO.
THERE'S A BOY. AND A GIRL. RIGHT THERE, NEXT TO YOU.
THEY'RE GOING TO STAY WITH YOU, TOM. ALL THE TIME.
UNTIL IT'S OVER, OF COURSE. THEN YOU'LL BE ALONE.
BYE, TOM.
AU REVOIR, TOM.
JESUS!
YOU CAN TAKE THE KIDS OUT OF HADES...

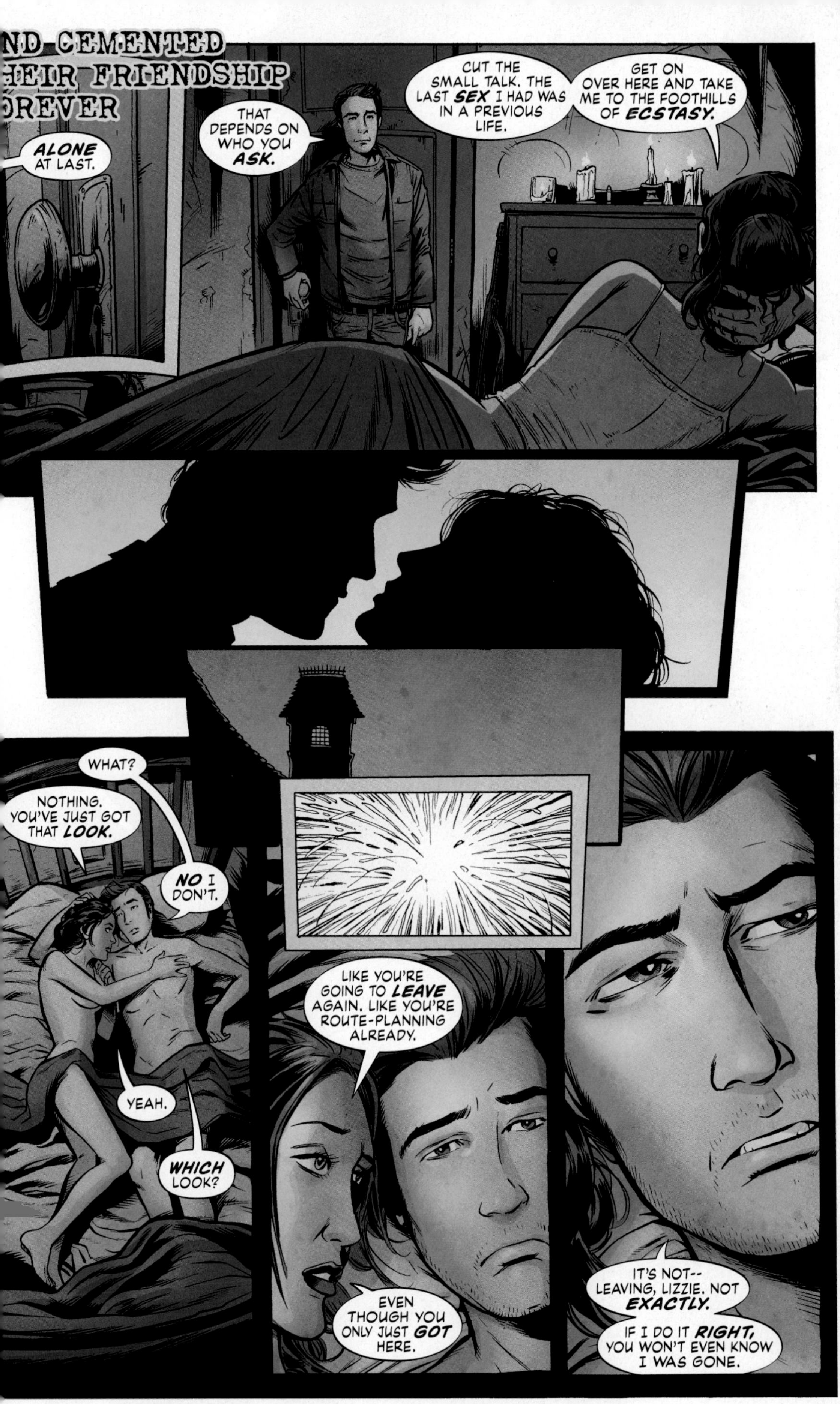
ND CEMENTED
HEIR FRIENDSHIP
OREVER
ALONE AT LAST.
THAT DEPENDS ON WHO YOU ASK.
CUT THE SMALL TALK. THE LAST SEX I HAD WAS IN A PREVIOUS LIFE.
GET ON OVER HERE AND TAKE ME TO THE FOOTHILLS OF ECSTASY.
WHAT?
NOTHING. YOU'VE JUST GOT THAT LOOK.
NO I DON'T.
YEAH.
WHICH LOOK?
LIKE YOU'RE GOING TO LEAVE AGAIN. LIKE YOU'RE ROUTE-PLANNING ALREADY.
EVEN THOUGH YOU ONLY JUST GOT HERE.
IT'S NOT-- LEAVING, LIZZIE. NOT EXACTLY.
IF I DO IT RIGHT, YOU WON'T EVEN KNOW I WAS GONE.

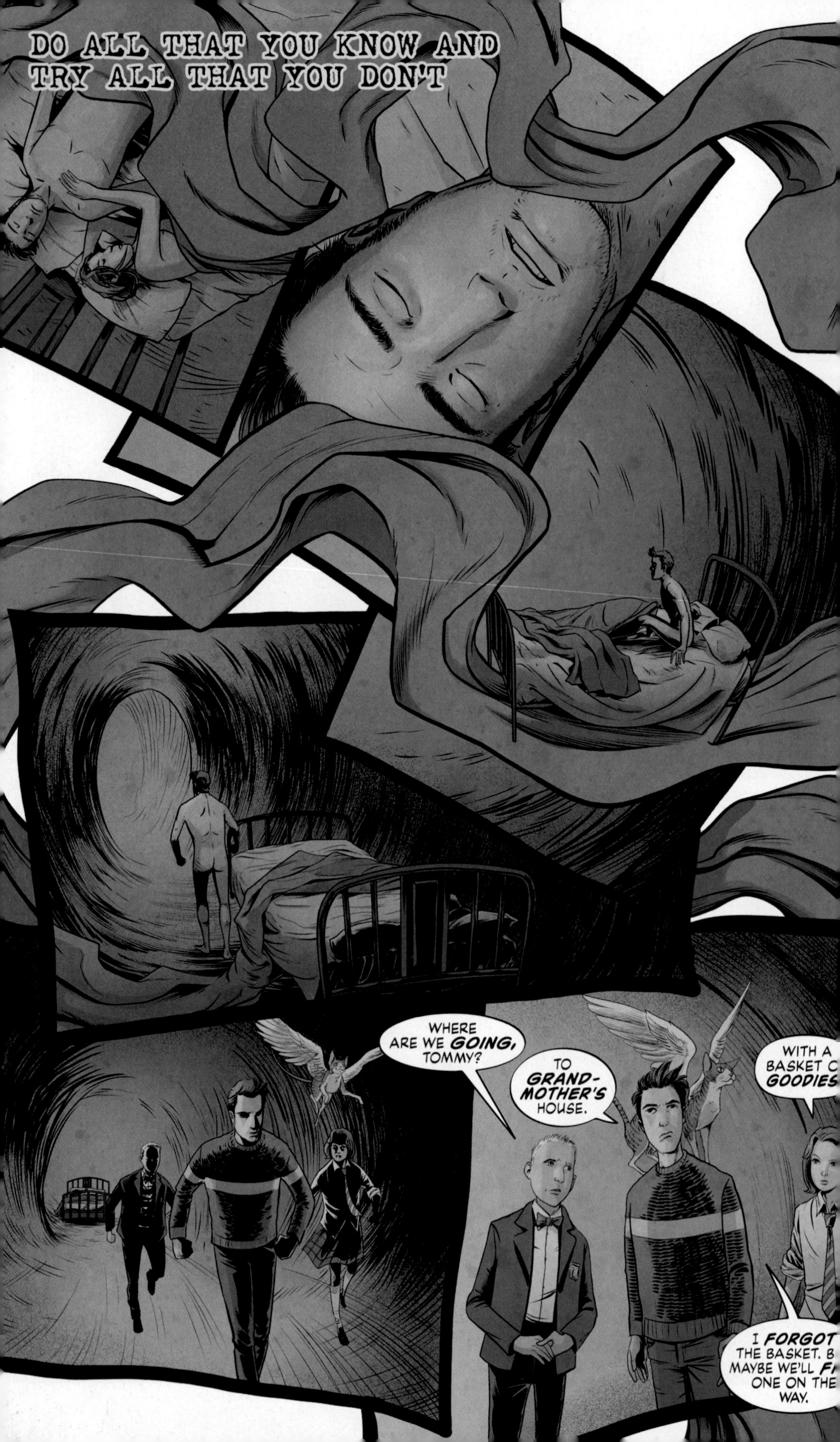
DO ALL THAT YOU KNOW AND TRY ALL THAT YOU DON'T
WHERE ARE WE GOING, TOMMY?
TO GRAND-MOTHER'S HOUSE.
WITH A BASKET O GOODIES
I FORGOT THE BASKET. B MAYBE WE'LL F ONE ON THE WAY.

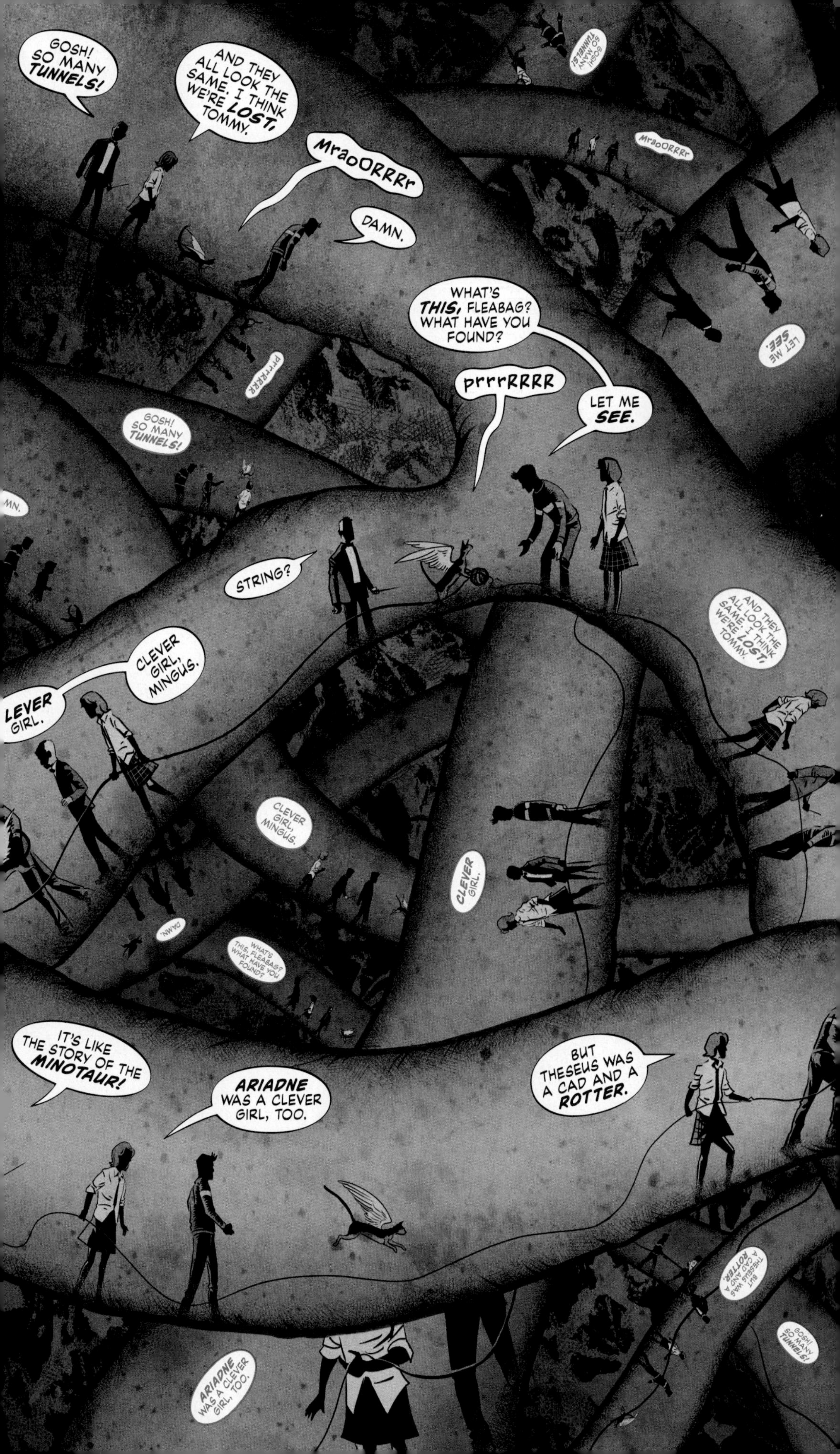
GOSH! SO MANY TUNNELS!
AND THEY ALL LOOK THE SAME. I THINK WE'RE LOST, TOMMY.
MraoORRRr
DAMN.
GOSH! SO MANY TUNNELS!
MraoORRRr
WHAT'S THIS, FLEABAG? WHAT HAVE YOU FOUND?
prrrRRRR
LET ME SEE.
LET ME SEE.
prrrRRRR
GOSH! SO MANY TUNNELS!
MN.
STRING?
CLEVER GIRL, MINGUS.
LEVER GIRL.
AND THEY ALL LOOK THE SAME. I THINK WE'RE LOST, TOMMY.
CLEVER GIRL, MINGUS.
CLEVER GIRL.
DAMN.
WHAT'S THIS, FLEABAG? WHAT HAVE YOU FOUND?
IT'S LIKE THE STORY OF THE MINOTAUR!
ARIADNE WAS A CLEVER GIRL, TOO.
BUT THESEUS WAS A CAD AND A ROTTER.
BUT THESEUS WAS A CAD AND A ROTTER.
GOSH! SO MANY TUNNELS!
ARIADNE WAS A CLEVER GIRL, TOO.

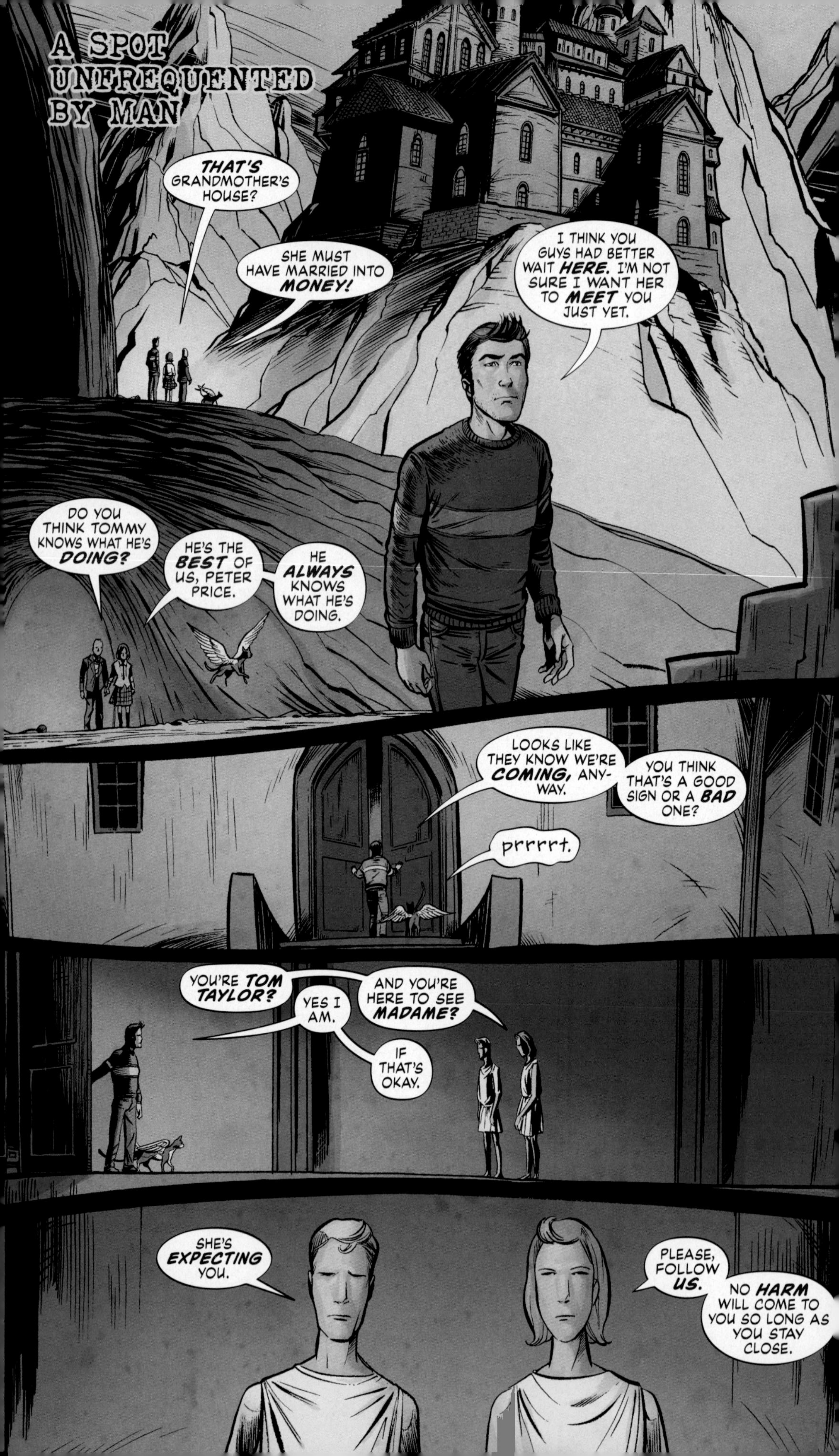
A SPOT UNFREQUENTED BY MAN
THAT'S GRANDMOTHER'S HOUSE?
SHE MUST HAVE MARRIED INTO MONEY!
I THINK YOU GUYS HAD BETTER WAIT HERE. I'M NOT SURE I WANT HER TO MEET YOU JUST YET.
DO YOU THINK TOMMY KNOWS WHAT HE'S DOING?
HE'S THE BEST OF US, PETER PRICE.
HE ALWAYS KNOWS WHAT HE'S DOING.
LOOKS LIKE THEY KNOW WE'RE COMING, ANYWAY.
YOU THINK THAT'S A GOOD SIGN OR A BAD ONE?
prrrrt.
YOU'RE TOM TAYLOR?
YES I AM.
AND YOU'RE HERE TO SEE MADAME?
IF THAT'S OKAY.
SHE'S EXPECTING YOU.
PLEASE, FOLLOW US.
NO HARM WILL COME TO YOU SO LONG AS YOU STAY CLOSE.

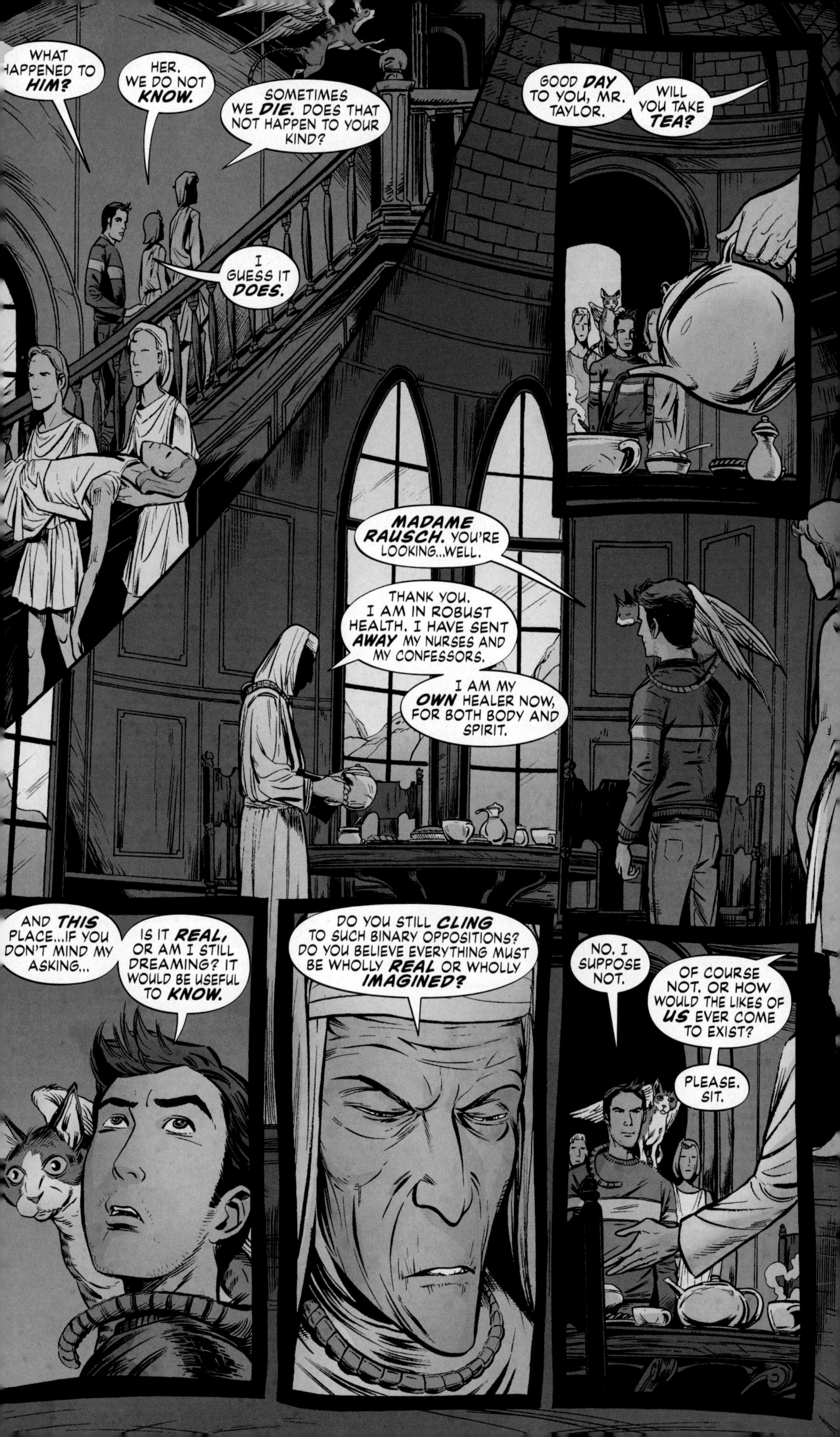
WHAT HAPPENED TO HIM?
HER. WE DO NOT KNOW.
SOMETIMES WE DIE. DOES THAT NOT HAPPEN TO YOUR KIND?
I GUESS IT DOES.
GOOD DAY TO YOU, MR. TAYLOR.
WILL YOU TAKE TEA?
MADAME RAUSCH. YOU'RE LOOKING...WELL.
THANK YOU. I AM IN ROBUST HEALTH. I HAVE SENT AWAY MY NURSES AND MY CONFESSORS.
I AM MY OWN HEALER NOW, FOR BOTH BODY AND SPIRIT.
AND THIS PLACE...IF YOU DON'T MIND MY ASKING...
IS IT REAL, OR AM I STILL DREAMING? IT WOULD BE USEFUL TO KNOW.
DO YOU STILL CLING TO SUCH BINARY OPPOSITIONS? DO YOU BELIEVE EVERYTHING MUST BE WHOLLY REAL OR WHOLLY IMAGINED?
NO. I SUPPOSE NOT.
OF COURSE NOT. OR HOW WOULD THE LIKES OF US EVER COME TO EXIST?
PLEASE. SIT.

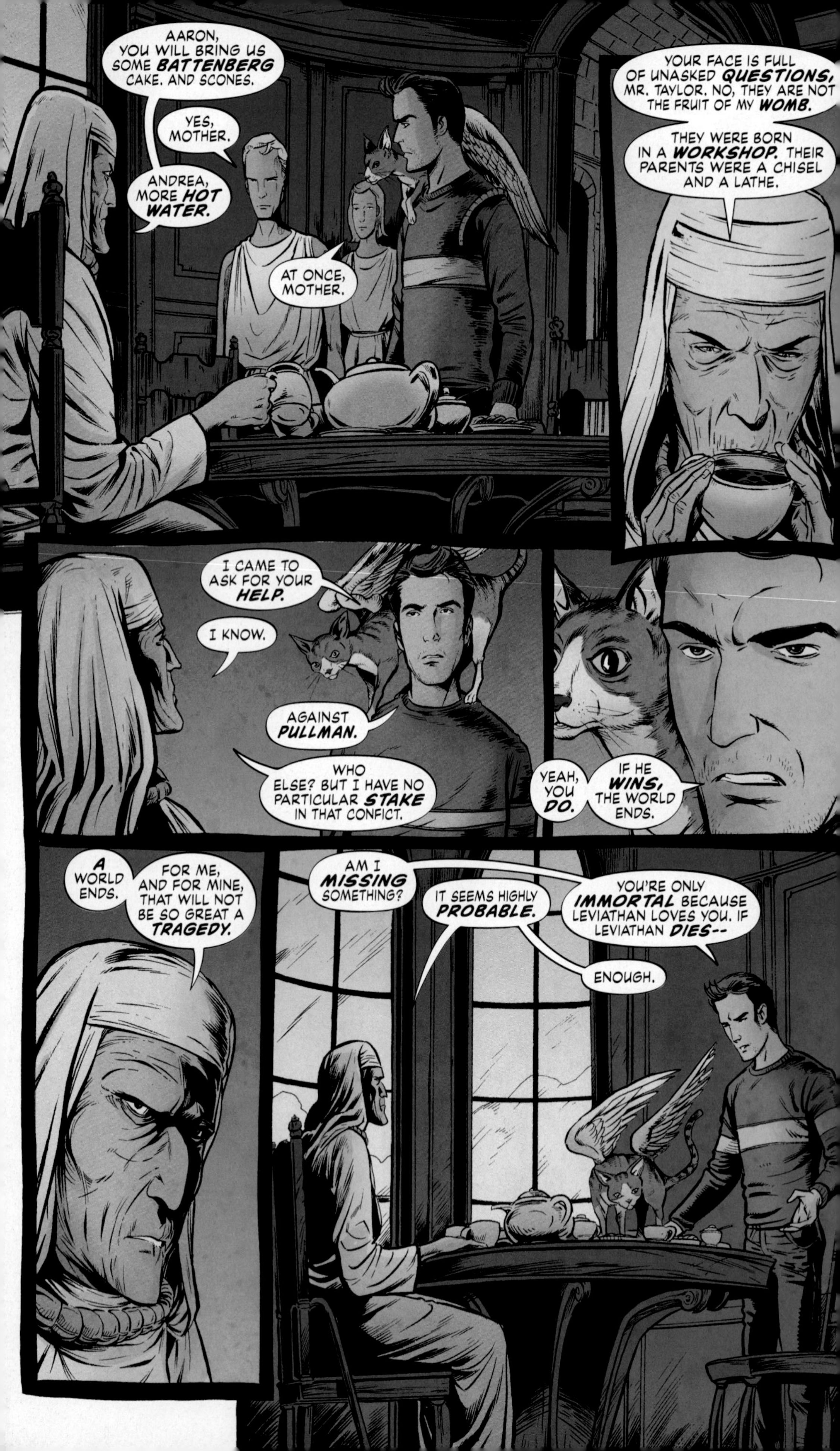
AARON, YOU WILL BRING US SOME BATTENBERG CAKE. AND SCONES.
YES, MOTHER.
ANDREA, MORE HOT WATER.
AT ONCE, MOTHER.
YOUR FACE IS FULL OF UNASKED QUESTIONS, MR. TAYLOR. NO, THEY ARE NOT THE FRUIT OF MY WOMB.
THEY WERE BORN IN A WORKSHOP. THEIR PARENTS WERE A CHISEL AND A LATHE.
I CAME TO ASK FOR YOUR HELP.
I KNOW.
AGAINST PULLMAN.
WHO ELSE? BUT I HAVE NO PARTICULAR STAKE IN THAT CONFICT.
YEAH, YOU DO.
IF HE WINS, THE WORLD ENDS.
A WORLD ENDS.
FOR ME, AND FOR MINE, THAT WILL NOT BE SO GREAT A TRAGEDY.
AM I MISSING SOMETHING?
IT SEEMS HIGHLY PROBABLE.
YOU'RE ONLY IMMORTAL BECAUSE LEVIATHAN LOVES YOU. IF LEVIATHAN DIES--
ENOUGH.

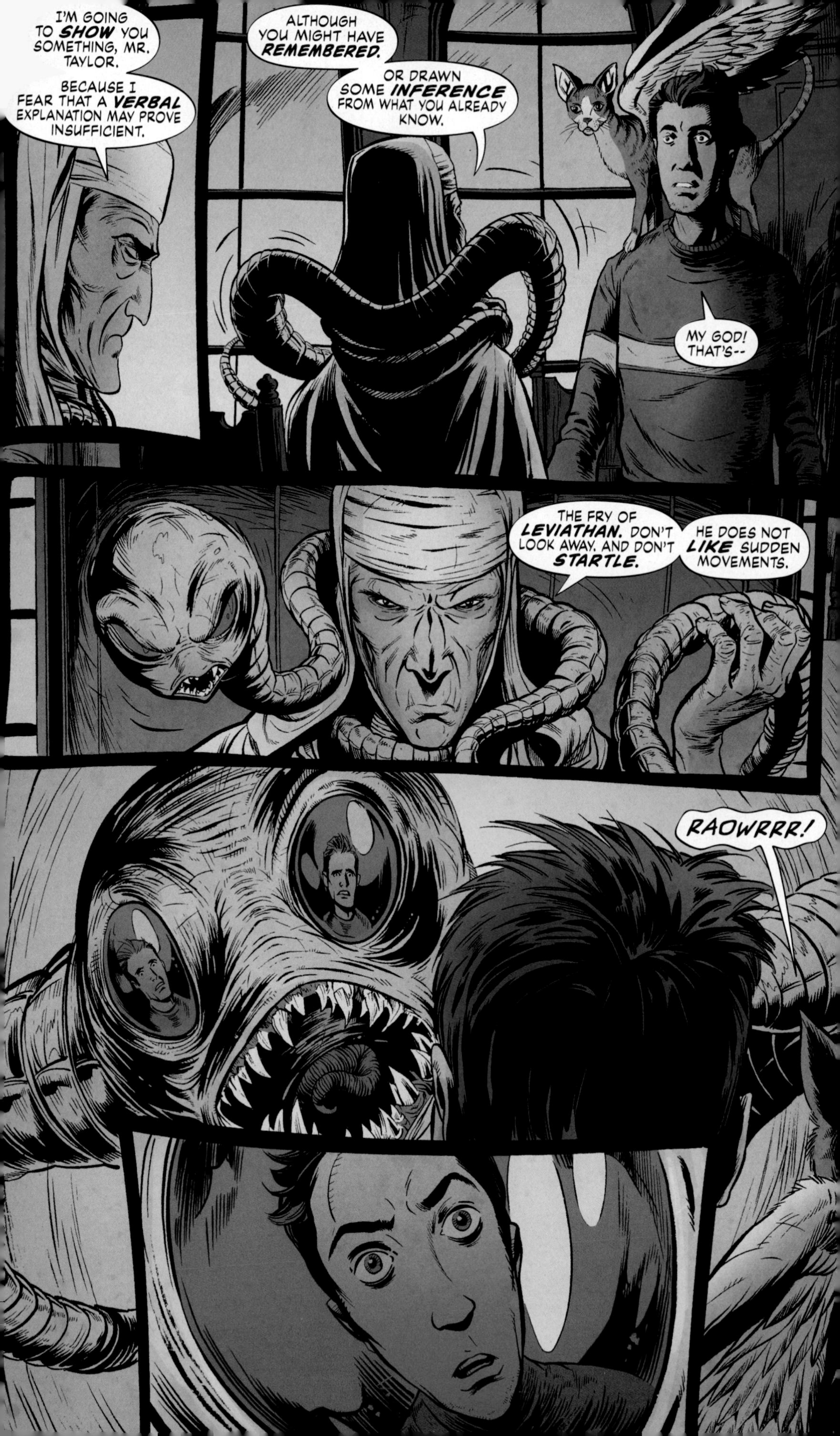
I'M GOING TO SHOW YOU SOMETHING, MR. TAYLOR.
BECAUSE I FEAR THAT A VERBAL EXPLANATION MAY PROVE INSUFFICIENT.
ALTHOUGH YOU MIGHT HAVE REMEMBERED.
OR DRAWN SOME INFERENCE FROM WHAT YOU ALREADY KNOW.
MY GOD! THAT'S--
THE FRY OF LEVIATHAN. DON'T LOOK AWAY. AND DON'T STARTLE.
HE DOES NOT LIKE SUDDEN MOVEMENTS.
RAOWRRR!

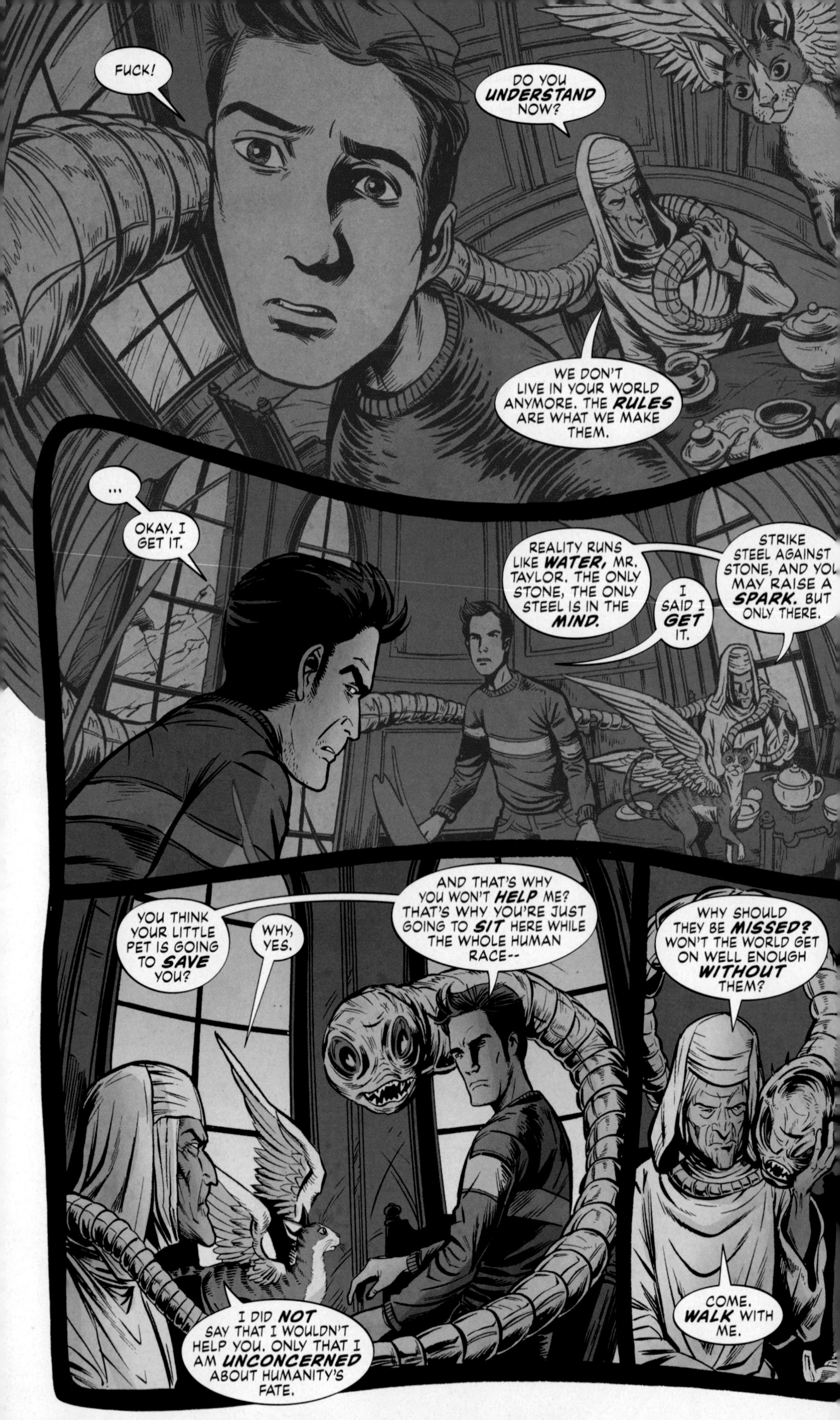
FUCK!
DO YOU UNDERSTAND NOW?
WE DON'T LIVE IN YOUR WORLD ANYMORE. THE RULES ARE WHAT WE MAKE THEM.
...
OKAY. I GET IT.
REALITY RUNS LIKE WATER, MR. TAYLOR. THE ONLY STONE, THE ONLY STEEL IS IN THE MIND.
I SAID I GET IT.
STRIKE STEEL AGAINST STONE, AND YOU MAY RAISE A SPARK. BUT ONLY THERE.
YOU THINK YOUR LITTLE PET IS GOING TO SAVE YOU?
WHY, YES.
AND THAT'S WHY YOU WON'T HELP ME? THAT'S WHY YOU'RE JUST GOING TO SIT HERE WHILE THE WHOLE HUMAN RACE--
I DID NOT SAY THAT I WOULDN'T HELP YOU. ONLY THAT I AM UNCONCERNED ABOUT HUMANITY'S FATE.
WHY SHOULD THEY BE MISSED? WON'T THE WORLD GET ON WELL ENOUGH WITHOUT THEM?
COME. WALK WITH ME.

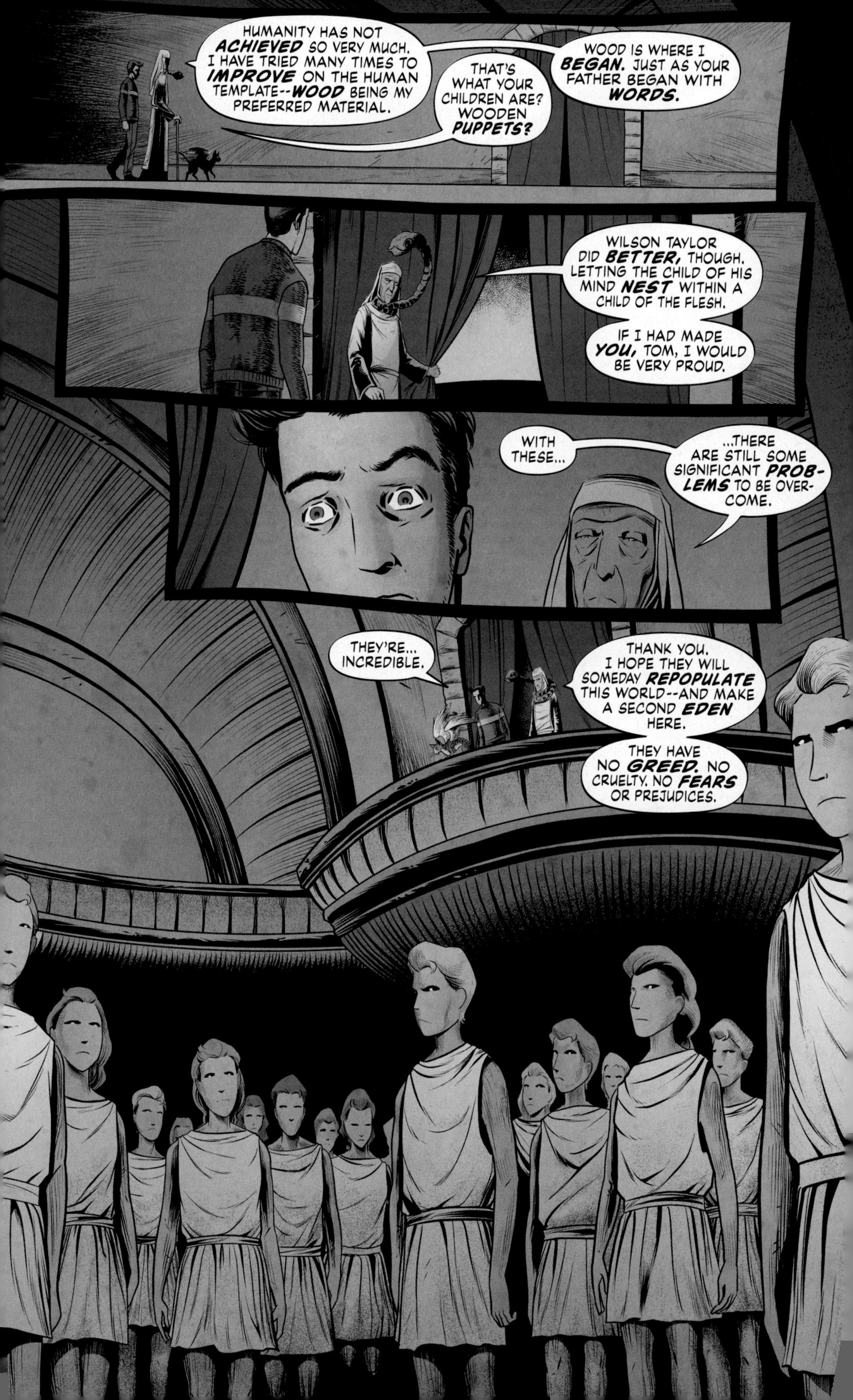
HUMANITY HAS NOT ACHIEVED SO VERY MUCH. I HAVE TRIED MANY TIMES TO IMPROVE ON THE HUMAN TEMPLATE--WOOD BEING MY PREFERRED MATERIAL.
THAT'S WHAT YOUR CHILDREN ARE? WOODEN PUPPETS?
WOOD IS WHERE I BEGAN. JUST AS YOUR FATHER BEGAN WITH WORDS.
WILSON TAYLOR DID BETTER, THOUGH. LETTING THE CHILD OF HIS MIND NEST WITHIN A CHILD OF THE FLESH.
IF I HAD MADE YOU, TOM, I WOULD BE VERY PROUD.
WITH THESE...
...THERE ARE STILL SOME SIGNIFICANT PROBLEMS TO BE OVERCOME.
THEY'RE... INCREDIBLE.
THANK YOU. I HOPE THEY WILL SOMEDAY REPOPULATE THIS WORLD--AND MAKE A SECOND EDEN HERE.
THEY HAVE NO GREED. NO CRUELTY. NO FEARS OR PREJUDICES.

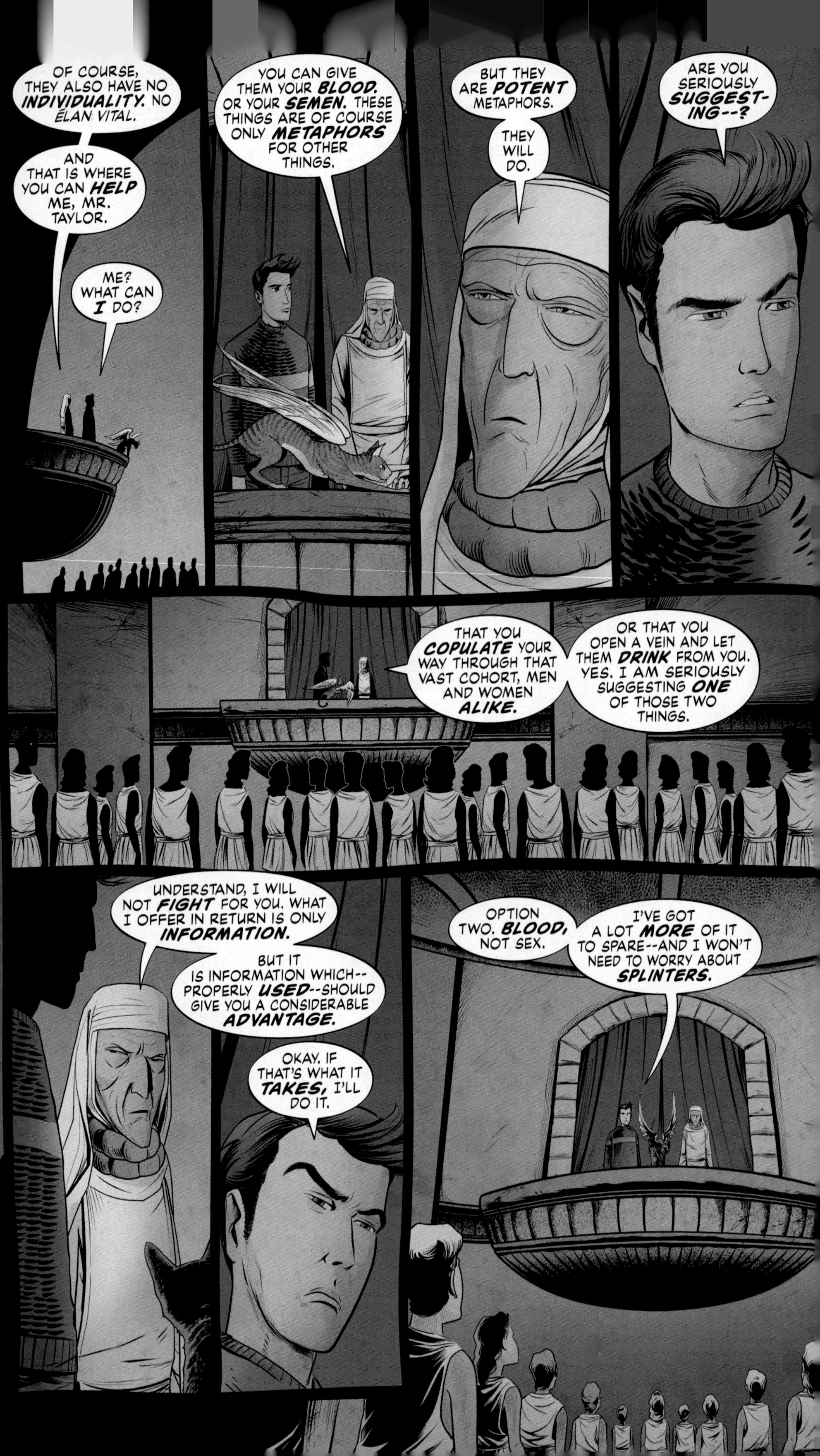

OF COURSE, THEY ALSO HAVE NO INDIVIDUALITY. NO ÉLAN VITAL.
AND THAT IS WHERE YOU CAN HELP ME, MR. TAYLOR.
ME? WHAT CAN I DO?
YOU CAN GIVE THEM YOUR BLOOD. OR YOUR SEMEN. THESE THINGS ARE OF COURSE ONLY METAPHORS FOR OTHER THINGS.
BUT THEY ARE POTENT METAPHORS.
THEY WILL DO.
ARE YOU SERIOUSLY SUGGEST-ING--?
THAT YOU COPULATE YOUR WAY THROUGH THAT VAST COHORT, MEN AND WOMEN ALIKE.
OR THAT YOU OPEN A VEIN AND LET THEM DRINK FROM YOU. YES. I AM SERIOUSLY SUGGESTING ONE OF THOSE TWO THINGS.
UNDERSTAND, I WILL NOT FIGHT FOR YOU. WHAT I OFFER IN RETURN IS ONLY INFORMATION.
BUT IT IS INFORMATION WHICH--PROPERLY USED--SHOULD GIVE YOU A CONSIDERABLE ADVANTAGE.
OKAY. IF THAT'S WHAT IT TAKES, I'LL DO IT.
OPTION TWO. BLOOD, NOT SEX.
I'VE GOT A LOT MORE OF IT TO SPARE--AND I WON'T NEED TO WORRY ABOUT SPLINTERS.

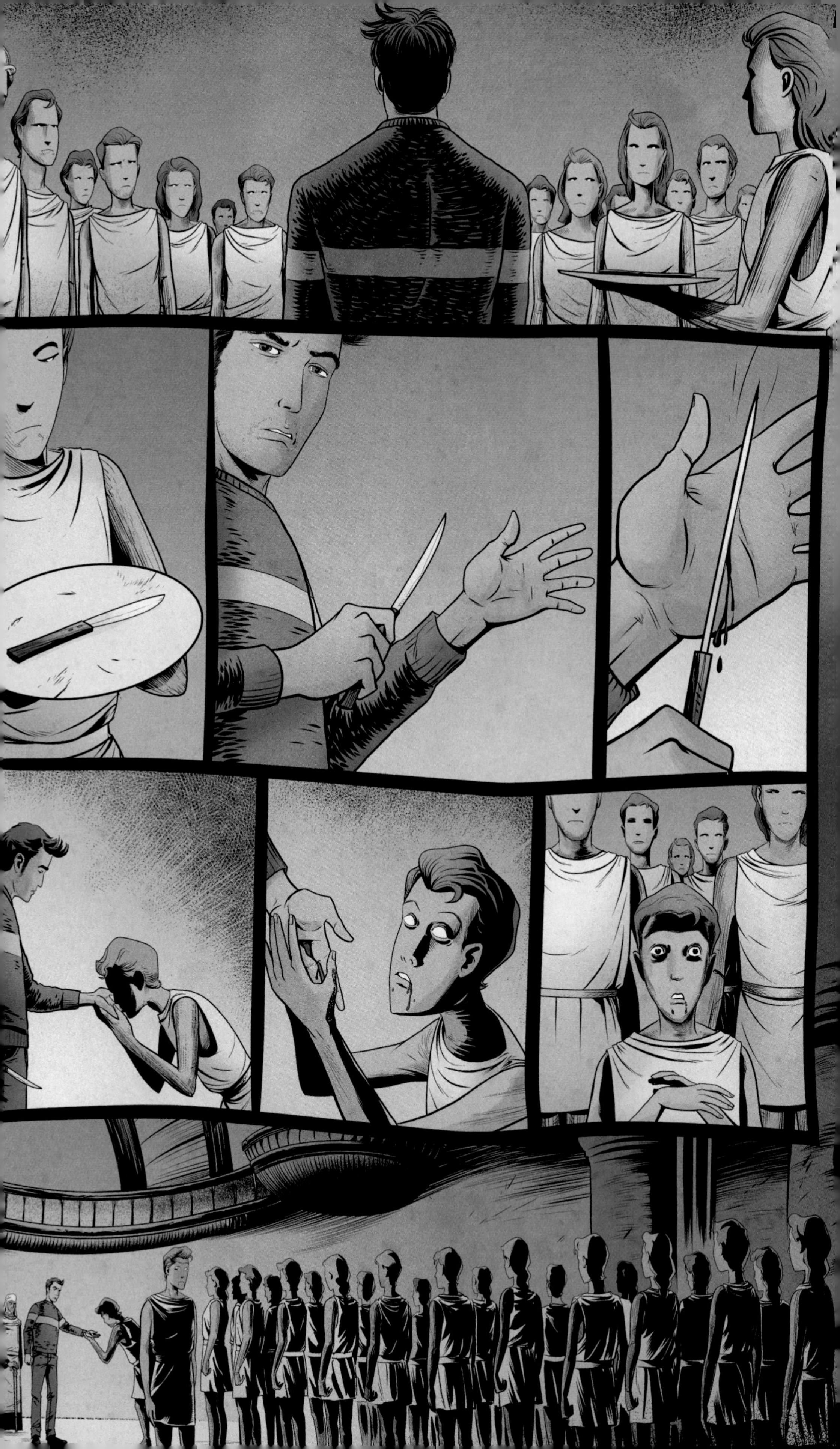

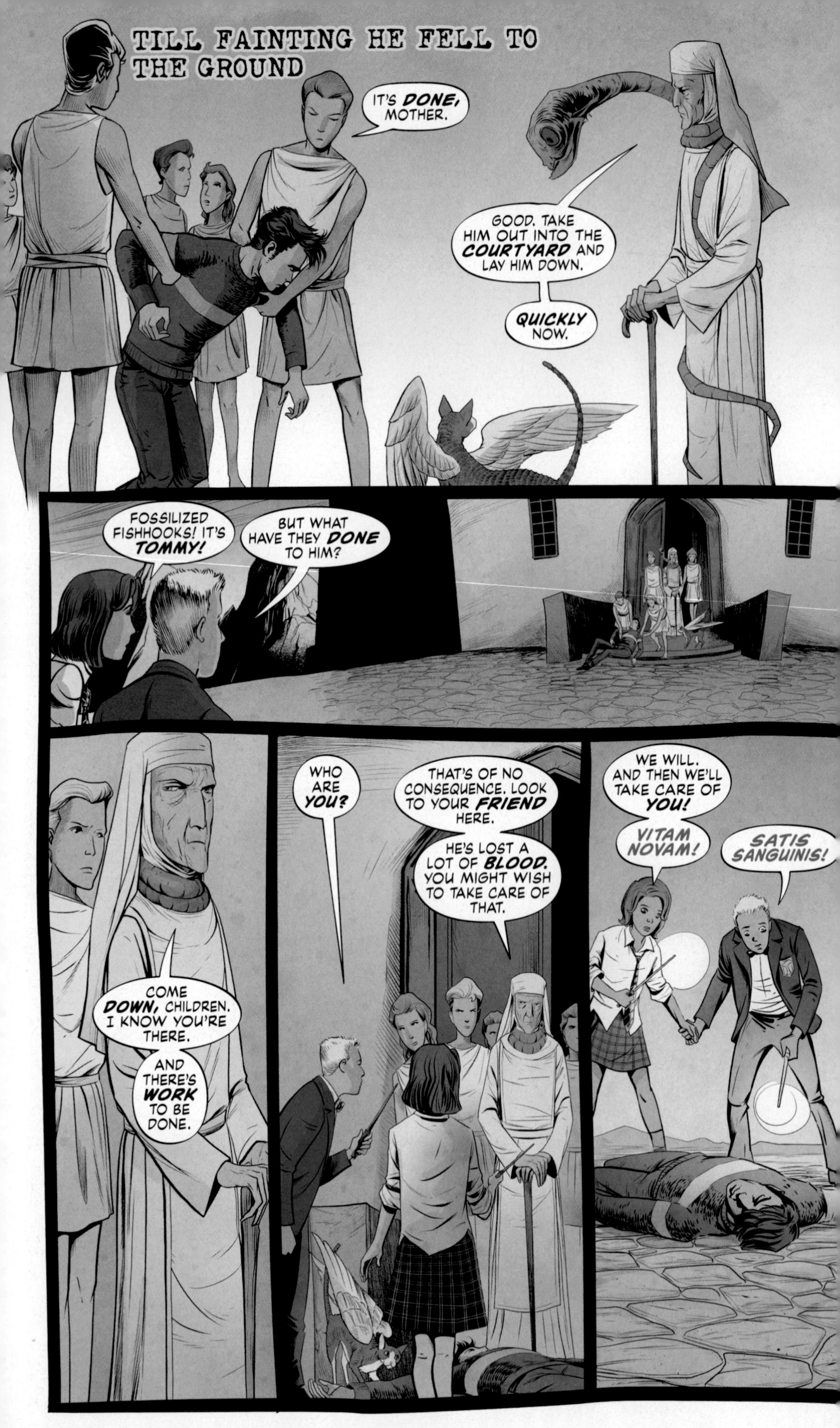
TILL FAINTING HE FELL TO THE GROUND
IT'S DONE, MOTHER.
GOOD. TAKE HIM OUT INTO THE COURTYARD AND LAY HIM DOWN.
QUICKLY NOW.
FOSSILIZED FISHHOOKS! IT'S TOMMY!
BUT WHAT HAVE THEY DONE TO HIM?
COME DOWN, CHILDREN. I KNOW YOU'RE THERE.
AND THERE'S WORK TO BE DONE.
WHO ARE YOU?
THAT'S OF NO CONSEQUENCE. LOOK TO YOUR FRIEND HERE.
HE'S LOST A LOT OF BLOOD. YOU MIGHT WISH TO TAKE CARE OF THAT.
WE WILL. AND THEN WE'LL TAKE CARE OF YOU!
VITAM NOVAM!
SATIS SANGUINIS!

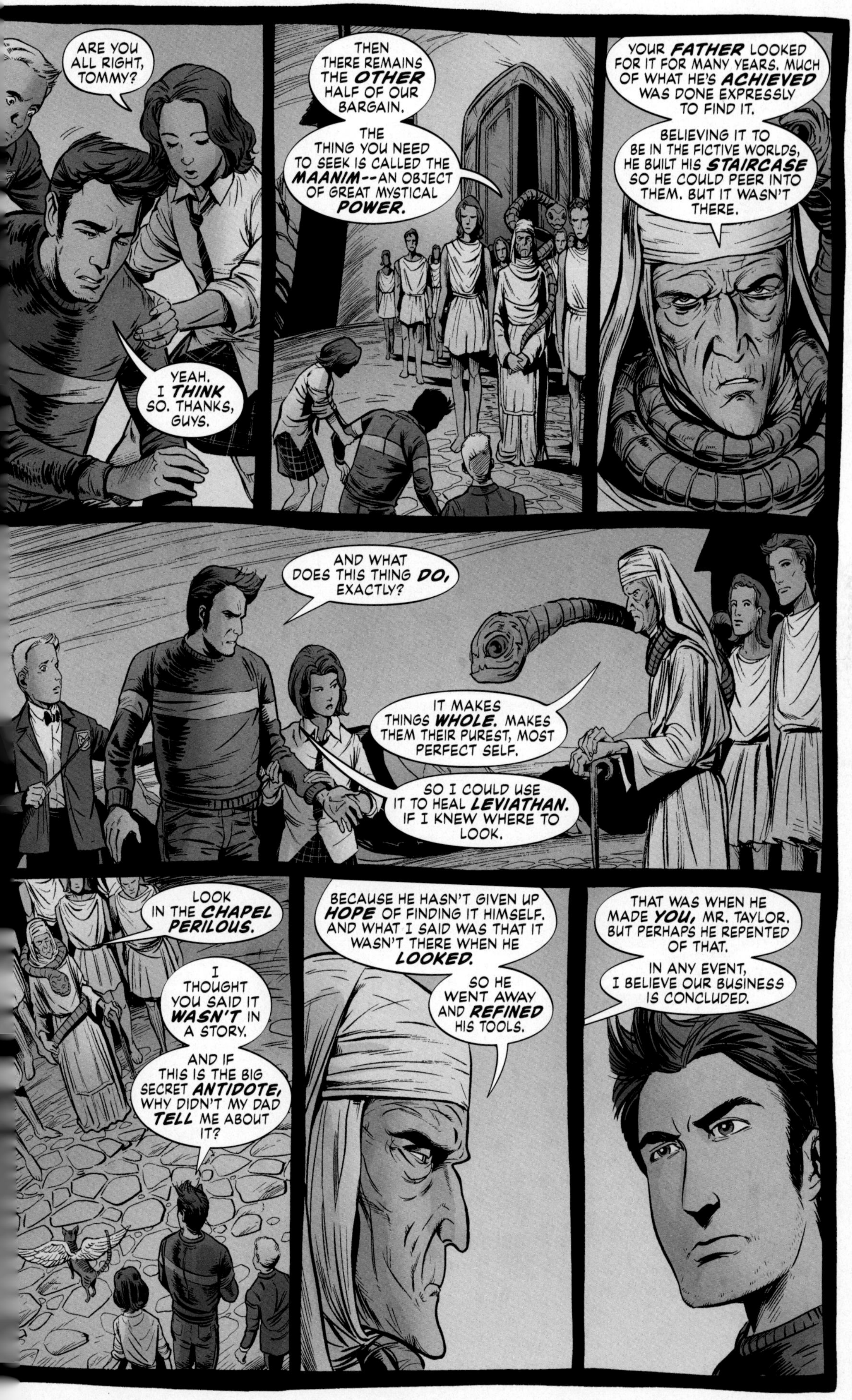
ARE YOU ALL RIGHT, TOMMY?
YEAH. I THINK SO. THANKS, GUYS.
THEN THERE REMAINS THE OTHER HALF OF OUR BARGAIN.
THE THING YOU NEED TO SEEK IS CALLED THE MAANIM--AN OBJECT OF GREAT MYSTICAL POWER.
YOUR FATHER LOOKED FOR IT FOR MANY YEARS. MUCH OF WHAT HE'S ACHIEVED WAS DONE EXPRESSLY TO FIND IT.
BELIEVING IT TO BE IN THE FICTIVE WORLDS, HE BUILT HIS STAIRCASE SO HE COULD PEER INTO THEM. BUT IT WASN'T THERE.
AND WHAT DOES THIS THING DO, EXACTLY?
IT MAKES THINGS WHOLE. MAKES THEM THEIR PUREST, MOST PERFECT SELF.
SO I COULD USE IT TO HEAL LEVIATHAN. IF I KNEW WHERE TO LOOK.
LOOK IN THE CHAPEL PERILOUS.
I THOUGHT YOU SAID IT WASN'T IN A STORY.
AND IF THIS IS THE BIG SECRET ANTIDOTE, WHY DIDN'T MY DAD TELL ME ABOUT IT?
BECAUSE HE HASN'T GIVEN UP HOPE OF FINDING IT HIMSELF. AND WHAT I SAID WAS THAT IT WASN'T THERE WHEN HE LOOKED.
SO HE WENT AWAY AND REFINED HIS TOOLS.
THAT WAS WHEN HE MADE YOU, MR. TAYLOR. BUT PERHAPS HE REPENTED OF THAT.
IN ANY EVENT, I BELIEVE OUR BUSINESS IS CONCLUDED.

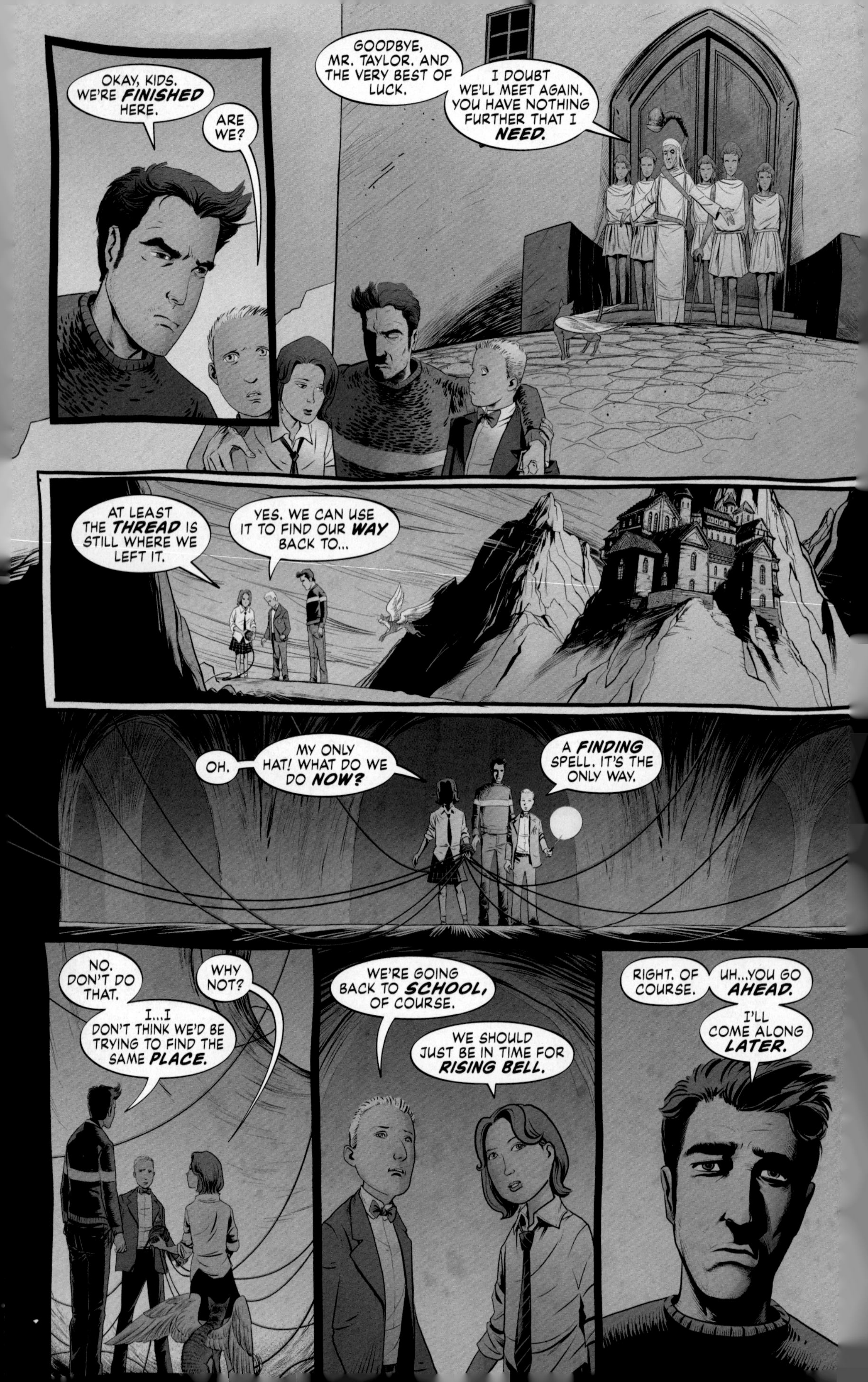
OKAY, KIDS. WE'RE FINISHED HERE.
ARE WE?
GOODBYE, MR. TAYLOR. AND THE VERY BEST OF LUCK.
I DOUBT WE'LL MEET AGAIN. YOU HAVE NOTHING FURTHER THAT I NEED.
AT LEAST THE THREAD IS STILL WHERE WE LEFT IT.
YES. WE CAN USE IT TO FIND OUR WAY BACK TO...
OH.
MY ONLY HAT! WHAT DO WE DO NOW?
A FINDING SPELL. IT'S THE ONLY WAY.
NO. DON'T DO THAT.
WHY NOT?
I...I DON'T THINK WE'D BE TRYING TO FIND THE SAME PLACE.
WE'RE GOING BACK TO SCHOOL, OF COURSE.
WE SHOULD JUST BE IN TIME FOR RISING BELL.
RIGHT. OF COURSE.
UH...YOU GO AHEAD.
I'LL COME ALONG LATER.

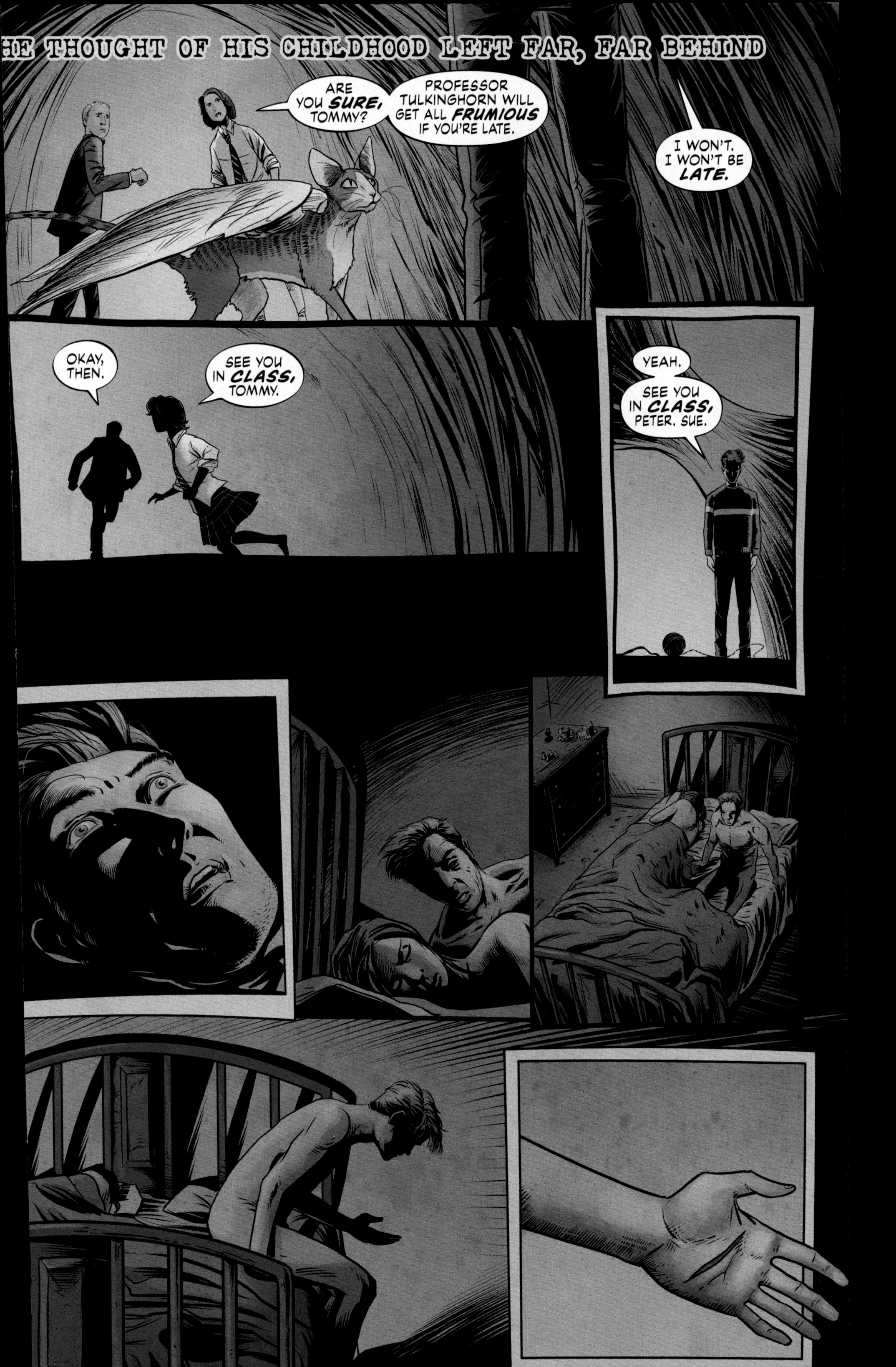
HE THOUGHT OF HIS CHILDHOOD LEFT FAR, FAR BEHIND
ARE YOU SURE, TOMMY?
PROFESSOR TULKINGHORN WILL GET ALL FRUMIOUS IF YOU'RE LATE.
I WON'T. I WON'T BE LATE.
OKAY, THEN.
SEE YOU IN CLASS, TOMMY.
YEAH.
SEE YOU IN CLASS, PETER. SUE.

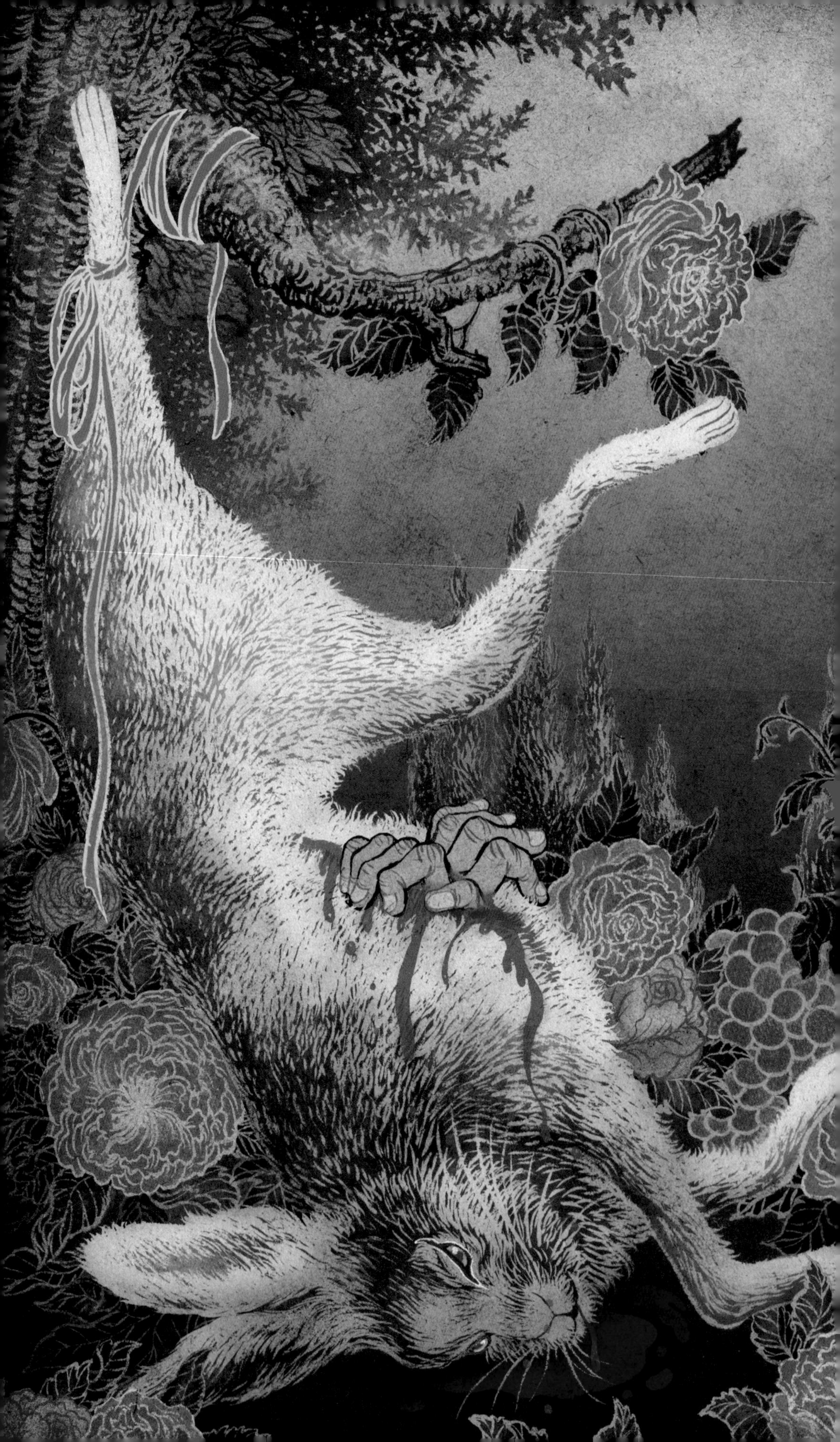

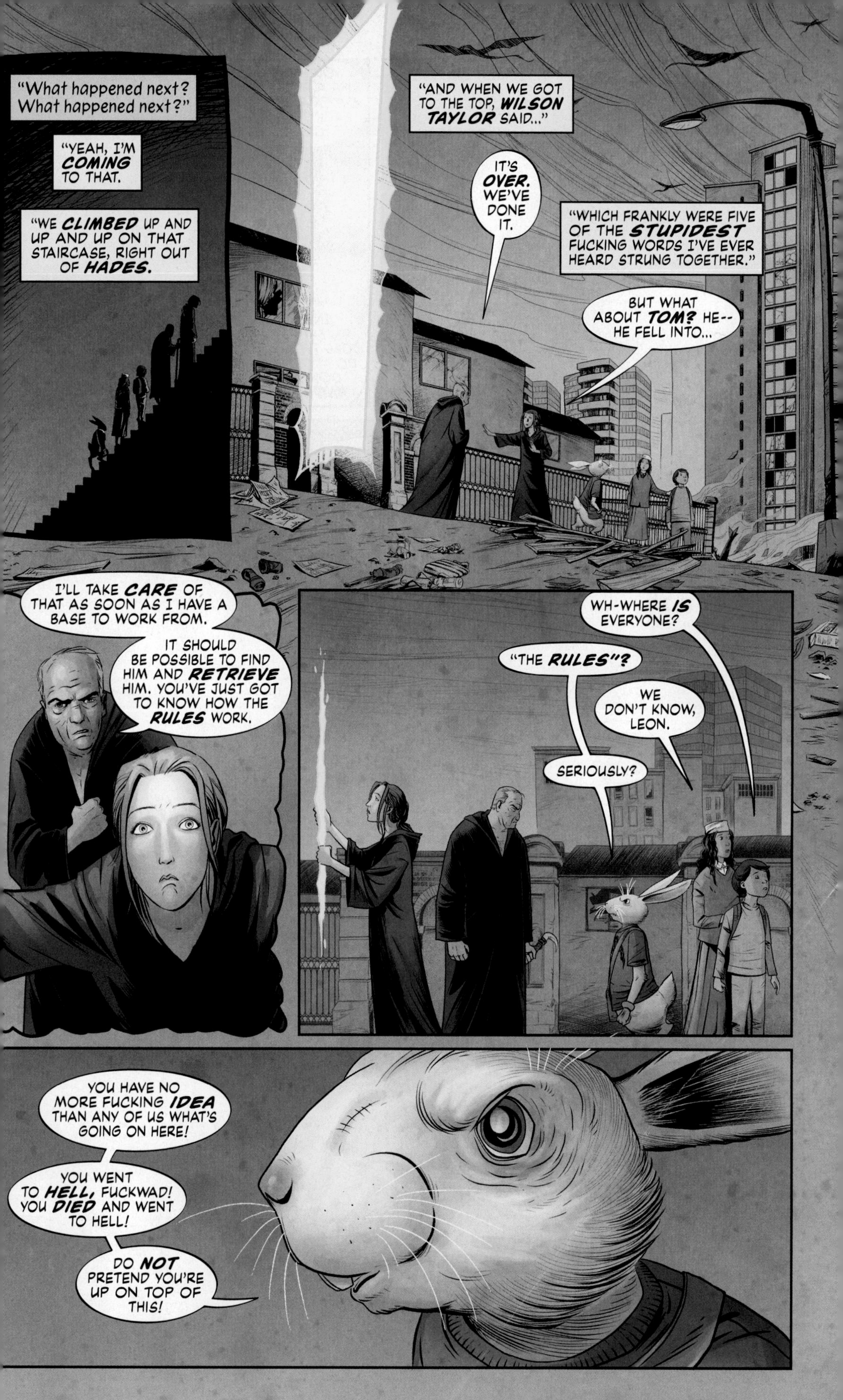
"What happened next? What happened next?"
"YEAH, I'M COMING TO THAT.
"WE CLIMBED UP AND UP AND UP ON THAT STAIRCASE, RIGHT OUT OF HADES.
"AND WHEN WE GOT TO THE TOP, WILSON TAYLOR SAID..."
IT'S OVER. WE'VE DONE IT.
"WHICH FRANKLY WERE FIVE OF THE STUPIDEST FUCKING WORDS I'VE EVER HEARD STRUNG TOGETHER."
BUT WHAT ABOUT TOM? HE-- HE FELL INTO...
I'LL TAKE CARE OF THAT AS SOON AS I HAVE A BASE TO WORK FROM.
IT SHOULD BE POSSIBLE TO FIND HIM AND RETRIEVE HIM. YOU'VE JUST GOT TO KNOW HOW THE RULES WORK.
WH-WHERE IS EVERYONE?
"THE RULES"?
WE DON'T KNOW, LEON.
SERIOUSLY?
YOU HAVE NO MORE FUCKING IDEA THAN ANY OF US WHAT'S GOING ON HERE!
YOU WENT TO HELL, FUCKWAD! YOU DIED AND WENT TO HELL!
DO NOT PRETEND YOU'RE UP ON TOP OF THIS!

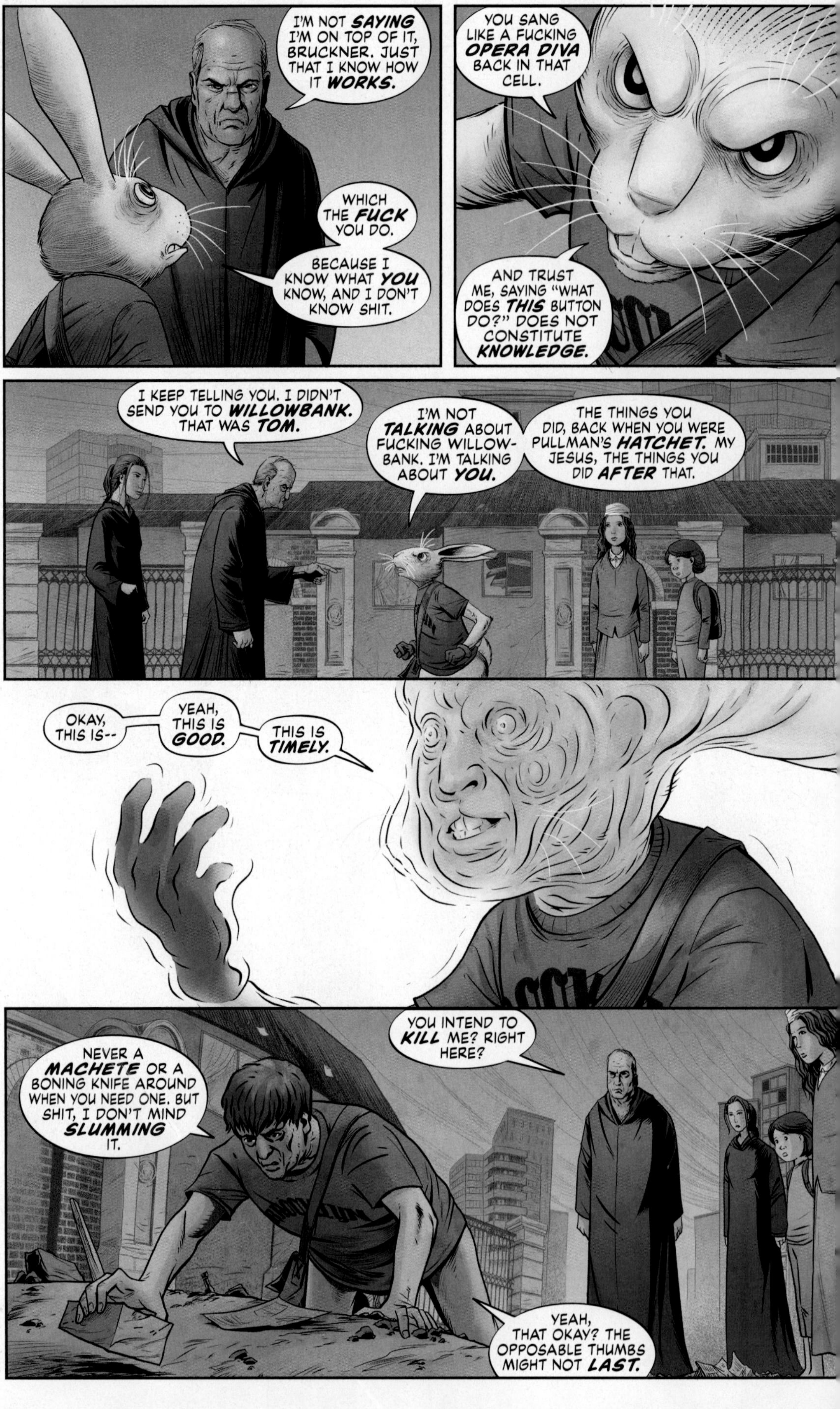
I'M NOT SAYING I'M ON TOP OF IT, BRUCKNER. JUST THAT I KNOW HOW IT WORKS.
WHICH THE FUCK YOU DO.
BECAUSE I KNOW WHAT YOU KNOW, AND I DON'T KNOW SHIT.
YOU SANG LIKE A FUCKING OPERA DIVA BACK IN THAT CELL.
AND TRUST ME, SAYING "WHAT DOES THIS BUTTON DO?" DOES NOT CONSTITUTE KNOWLEDGE.
I KEEP TELLING YOU. I DIDN'T SEND YOU TO WILLOWBANK. THAT WAS TOM.
I'M NOT TALKING ABOUT FUCKING WILLOW-BANK. I'M TALKING ABOUT YOU.
THE THINGS YOU DID, BACK WHEN YOU WERE PULLMAN'S HATCHET. MY JESUS, THE THINGS YOU DID AFTER THAT.
OKAY, THIS IS--
YEAH, THIS IS GOOD.
THIS IS TIMELY.
NEVER A MACHETE OR A BONING KNIFE AROUND WHEN YOU NEED ONE. BUT SHIT, I DON'T MIND SLUMMING IT.
YOU INTEND TO KILL ME? RIGHT HERE?
YEAH, THAT OKAY? THE OPPOSABLE THUMBS MIGHT NOT LAST.

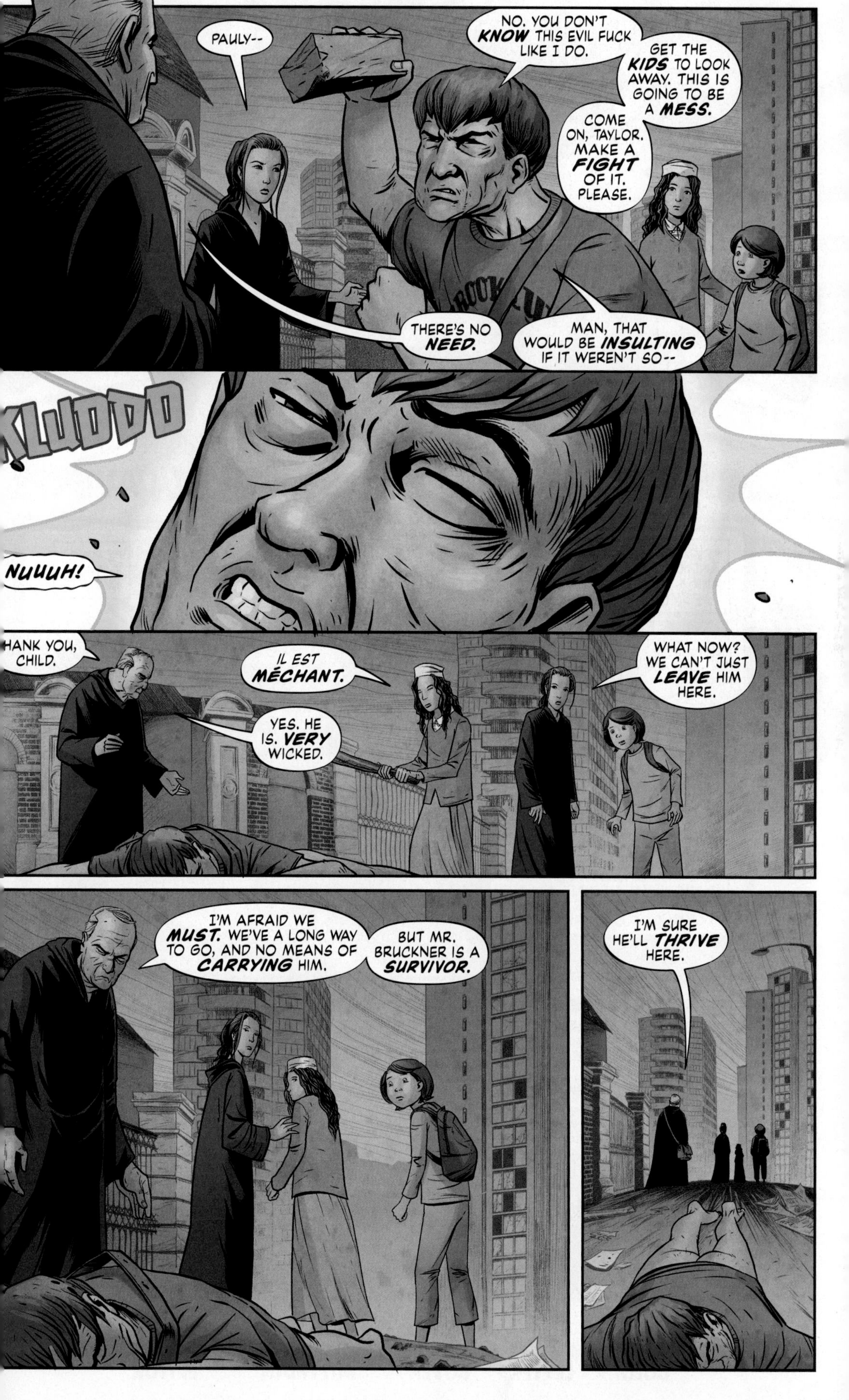
PAULY--
NO. YOU DON'T KNOW THIS EVIL FUCK LIKE I DO.
GET THE KIDS TO LOOK AWAY. THIS IS GOING TO BE A MESS.
COME ON, TAYLOR. MAKE A FIGHT OF IT. PLEASE.
THERE'S NO NEED.
MAN, THAT WOULD BE INSULTING IF IT WEREN'T SO--
KLUDDD
NUUUH!
HANK YOU, CHILD.
IL EST MÉCHANT.
YES. HE IS. VERY WICKED.
WHAT NOW? WE CAN'T JUST LEAVE HIM HERE.
I'M AFRAID WE MUST. WE'VE A LONG WAY TO GO, AND NO MEANS OF CARRYING HIM.
BUT MR. BRUCKNER IS A SURVIVOR.
I'M SURE HE'LL THRIVE HERE.

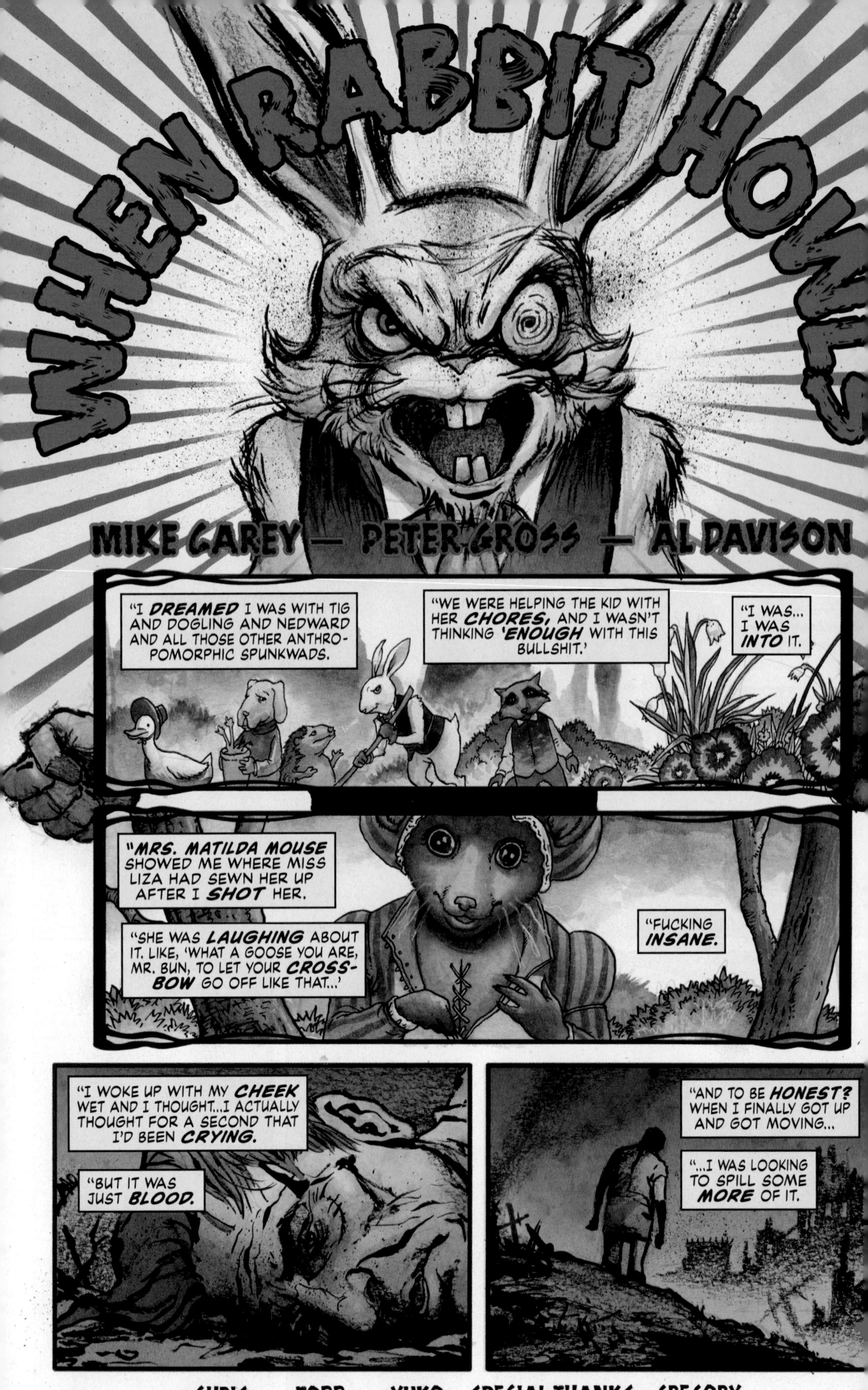
WHEN RABBIT HOWLS
MIKE CAREY — PETER GROSS — AL DAVISON
"I DREAMED I WAS WITH TIG AND DOGLING AND NEDWARD AND ALL THOSE OTHER ANTHRO-POMORPHIC SPUNKWADS.
"WE WERE HELPING THE KID WITH HER CHORES, AND I WASN'T THINKING 'ENOUGH WITH THIS BULLSHIT.'
"I WAS... I WAS INTO IT.
"MRS. MATILDA MOUSE SHOWED ME WHERE MISS LIZA HAD SEWN HER UP AFTER I SHOT HER.
"SHE WAS LAUGHING ABOUT IT. LIKE, 'WHAT A GOOSE YOU ARE, MR. BUN, TO LET YOUR CROSS-BOW GO OFF LIKE THAT...'
"FUCKING INSANE.
"I WOKE UP WITH MY CHEEK WET AND I THOUGHT...I ACTUALLY THOUGHT FOR A SECOND THAT I'D BEEN CRYING.
"BUT IT WAS JUST BLOOD.
"AND TO BE HONEST? WHEN I FINALLY GOT UP AND GOT MOVING...
"...I WAS LOOKING TO SPILL SOME MORE OF IT.

CHRIS CHUCKRY COLORS — TODD KLEIN LETTERS — YUKO SHIMIZU COVER — SPECIAL THANKS TO BARBARA GUTTMAN — GREGORY LOCKARD EDITOR

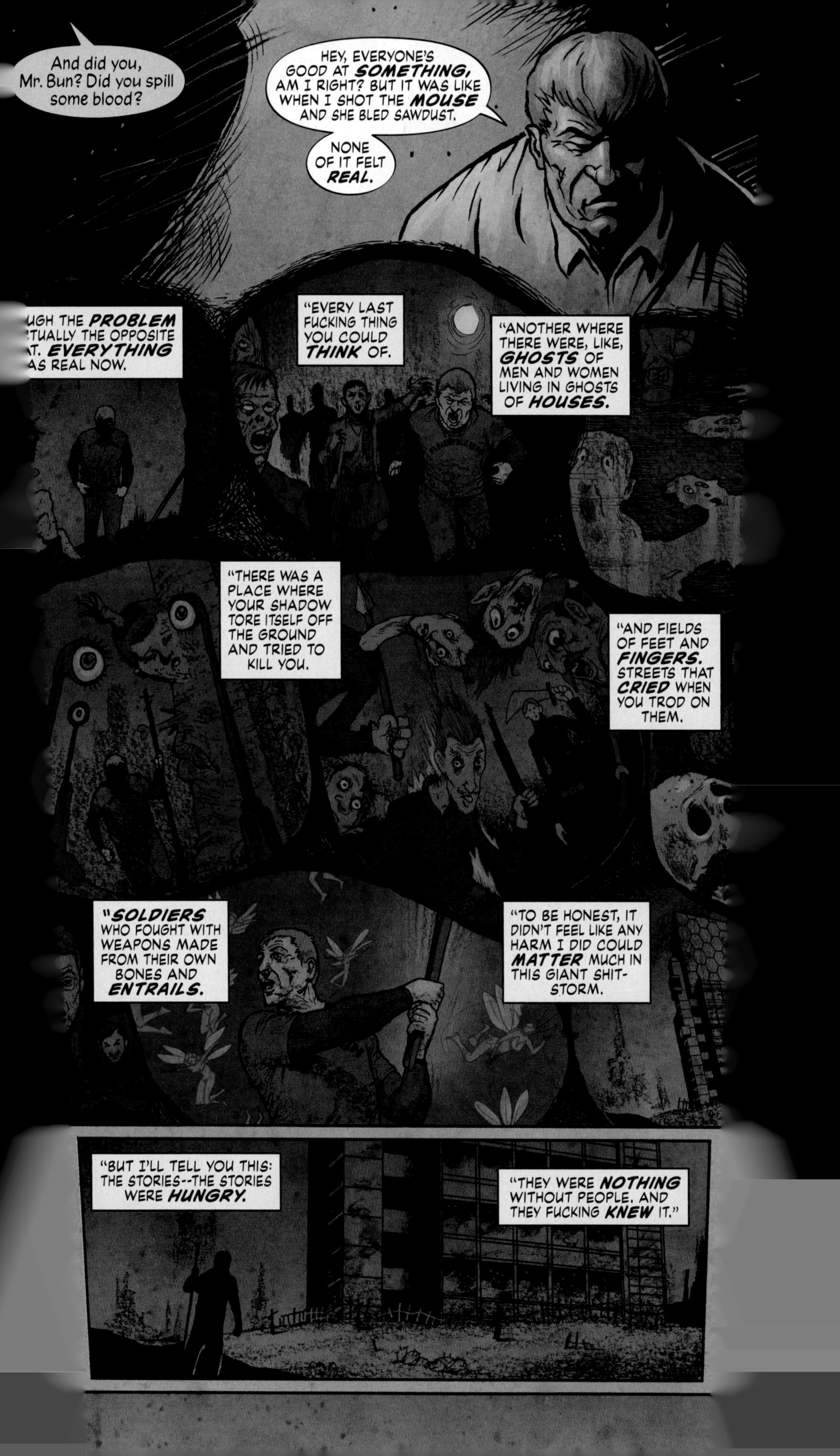
And did you, Mr. Bun? Did you spill some blood?
HEY, EVERYONE'S GOOD AT SOMETHING, AM I RIGHT? BUT IT WAS LIKE WHEN I SHOT THE MOUSE AND SHE BLED SAWDUST.
NONE OF IT FELT REAL.
UGH THE PROBLEM CTUALLY THE OPPOSITE AT. EVERYTHING AS REAL NOW.
"EVERY LAST FUCKING THING YOU COULD THINK OF.
"ANOTHER WHERE THERE WERE, LIKE, GHOSTS OF MEN AND WOMEN LIVING IN GHOSTS OF HOUSES.
"THERE WAS A PLACE WHERE YOUR SHADOW TORE ITSELF OFF THE GROUND AND TRIED TO KILL YOU.
"AND FIELDS OF FEET AND FINGERS. STREETS THAT CRIED WHEN YOU TROD ON THEM.
"SOLDIERS WHO FOUGHT WITH WEAPONS MADE FROM THEIR OWN BONES AND ENTRAILS.
"TO BE HONEST, IT DIDN'T FEEL LIKE ANY HARM I DID COULD MATTER MUCH IN THIS GIANT SHIT-STORM.
"BUT I'LL TELL YOU THIS: THE STORIES--THE STORIES WERE HUNGRY.
"THEY WERE NOTHING WITHOUT PEOPLE. AND THEY FUCKING KNEW IT."

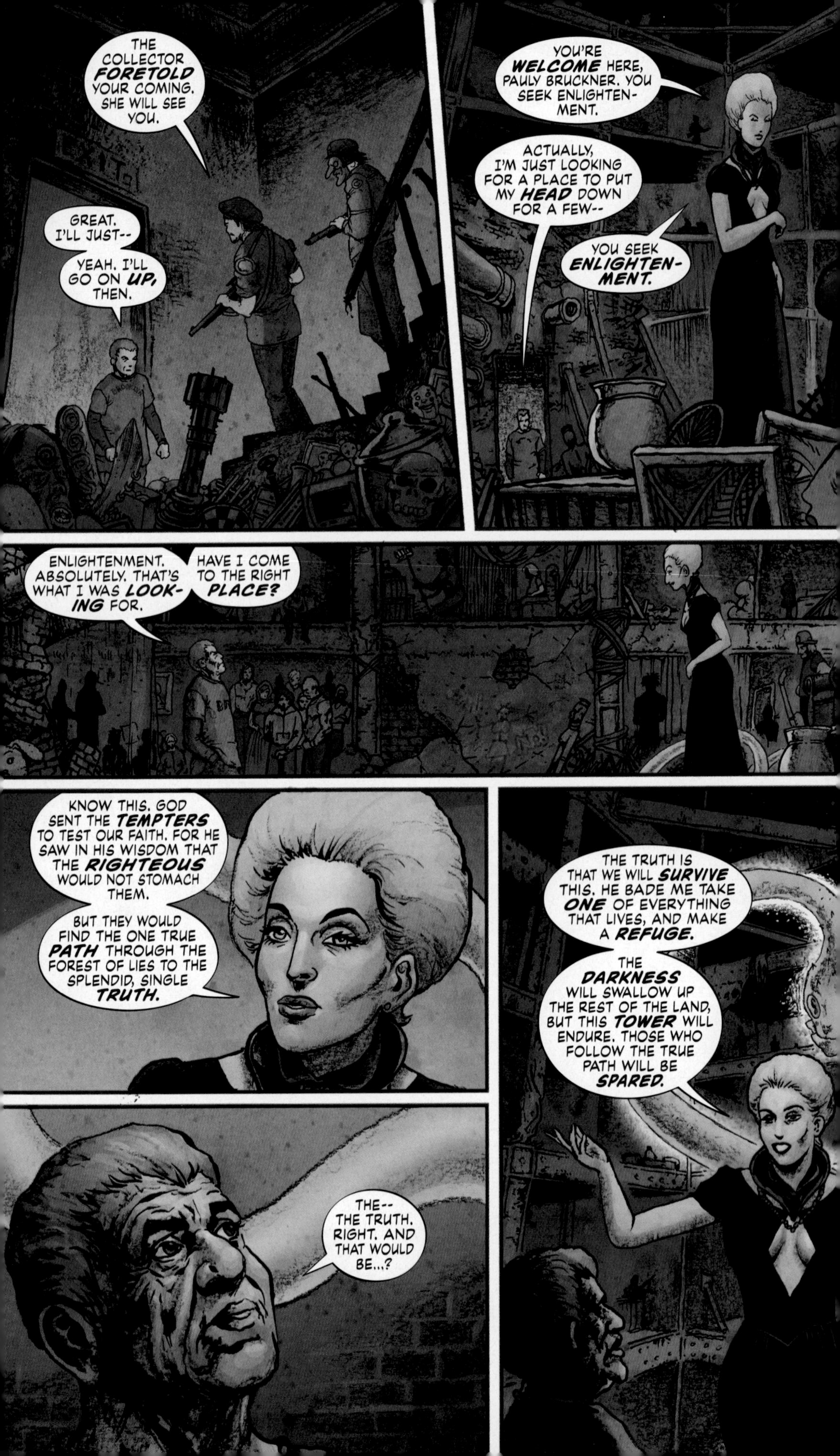
THE COLLECTOR FORETOLD YOUR COMING. SHE WILL SEE YOU.
GREAT. I'LL JUST--
YEAH. I'LL GO ON UP, THEN.
YOU'RE WELCOME HERE, PAULY BRUCKNER. YOU SEEK ENLIGHTENMENT.
ACTUALLY, I'M JUST LOOKING FOR A PLACE TO PUT MY HEAD DOWN FOR A FEW--
YOU SEEK ENLIGHTENMENT.
ENLIGHTENMENT. ABSOLUTELY. THAT'S WHAT I WAS LOOKING FOR.
HAVE I COME TO THE RIGHT PLACE?
KNOW THIS. GOD SENT THE TEMPTERS TO TEST OUR FAITH. FOR HE SAW IN HIS WISDOM THAT THE RIGHTEOUS WOULD NOT STOMACH THEM.
BUT THEY WOULD FIND THE ONE TRUE PATH THROUGH THE FOREST OF LIES TO THE SPLENDID, SINGLE TRUTH.
THE-- THE TRUTH. RIGHT. AND THAT WOULD BE...?
THE TRUTH IS THAT WE WILL SURVIVE THIS. HE BADE ME TAKE ONE OF EVERYTHING THAT LIVES, AND MAKE A REFUGE.
THE DARKNESS WILL SWALLOW UP THE REST OF THE LAND, BUT THIS TOWER WILL ENDURE. THOSE WHO FOLLOW THE TRUE PATH WILL BE SPARED.

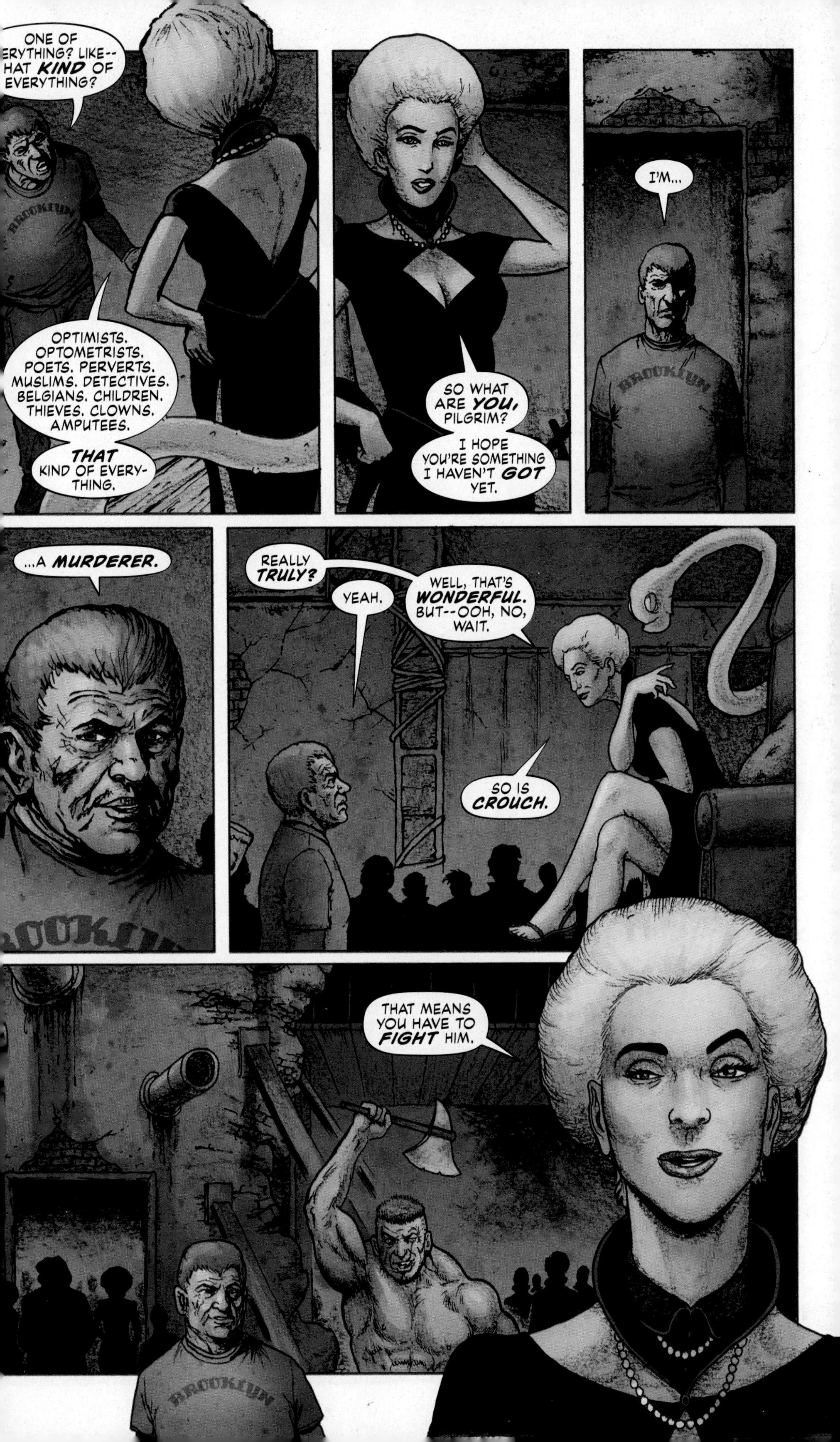

ONE OF
ERYTHING? LIKE--
HAT KIND OF
EVERYTHING?
OPTIMISTS. OPTOMETRISTS. POETS. PERVERTS. MUSLIMS. DETECTIVES. BELGIANS. CHILDREN. THIEVES. CLOWNS. AMPUTEES.
THAT KIND OF EVERY-THING.
SO WHAT ARE YOU, PILGRIM?
I HOPE YOU'RE SOMETHING I HAVEN'T GOT YET.
I'M...
BROOKLYN
...A MURDERER.
REALLY TRULY?
YEAH.
WELL, THAT'S WONDERFUL. BUT--OOH, NO, WAIT.
SO IS CROUCH.
THAT MEANS YOU HAVE TO FIGHT HIM.
BROOKLYN

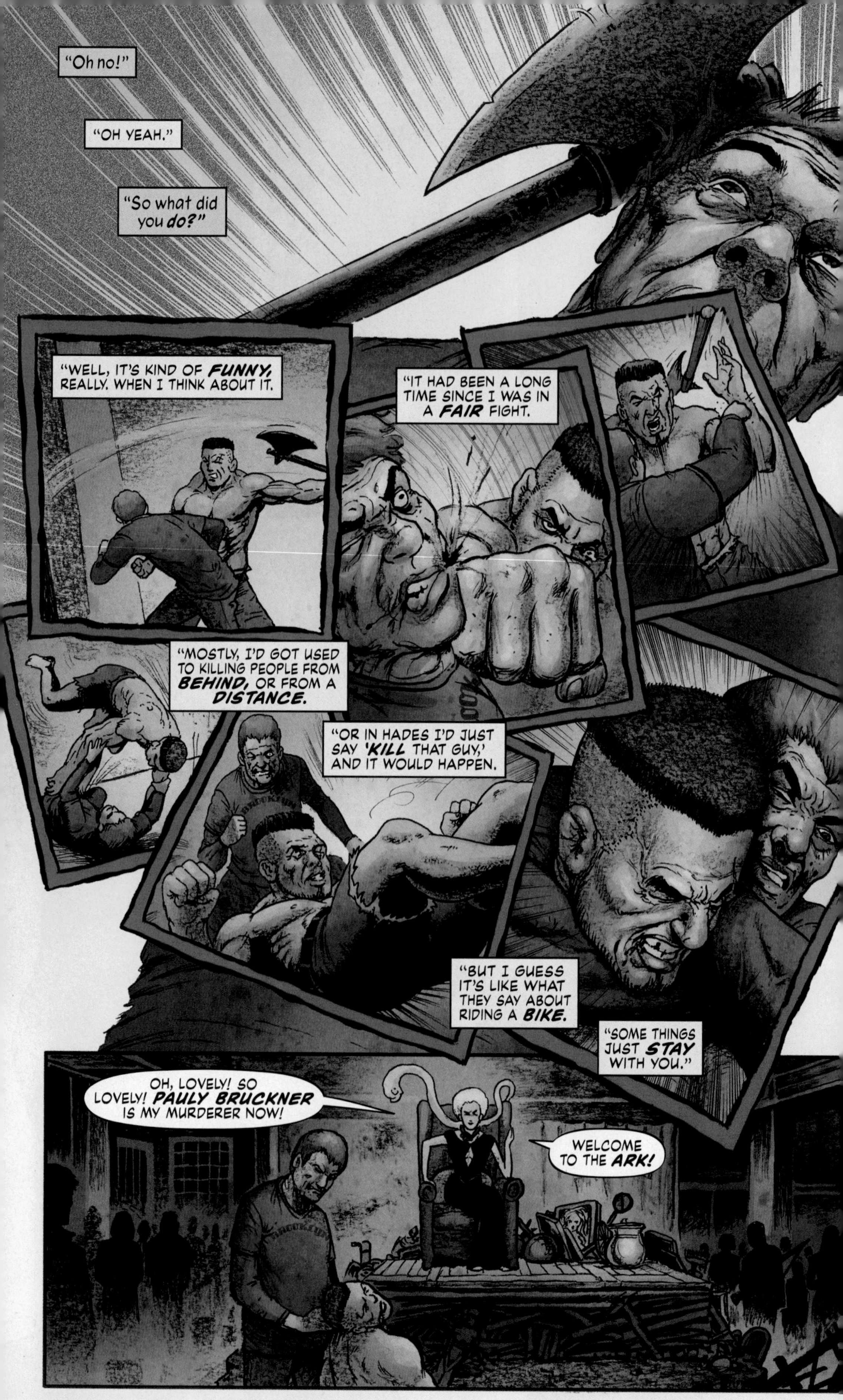
"Oh no!"
"OH YEAH."
"So what did you *do?*"
"WELL, IT'S KIND OF ***FUNNY,*** REALLY. WHEN I THINK ABOUT IT.
"IT HAD BEEN A LONG TIME SINCE I WAS IN A ***FAIR*** FIGHT.
"MOSTLY, I'D GOT USED TO KILLING PEOPLE FROM ***BEHIND,*** OR FROM A ***DISTANCE.***
"OR IN HADES I'D JUST SAY '***KILL*** THAT GUY,' AND IT WOULD HAPPEN.
"BUT I GUESS IT'S LIKE WHAT THEY SAY ABOUT RIDING A ***BIKE.***
"SOME THINGS JUST ***STAY*** WITH YOU."
OH, LOVELY! SO LOVELY! ***PAULY BRUCKNER*** IS MY MURDERER NOW!
WELCOME TO THE ***ARK!***

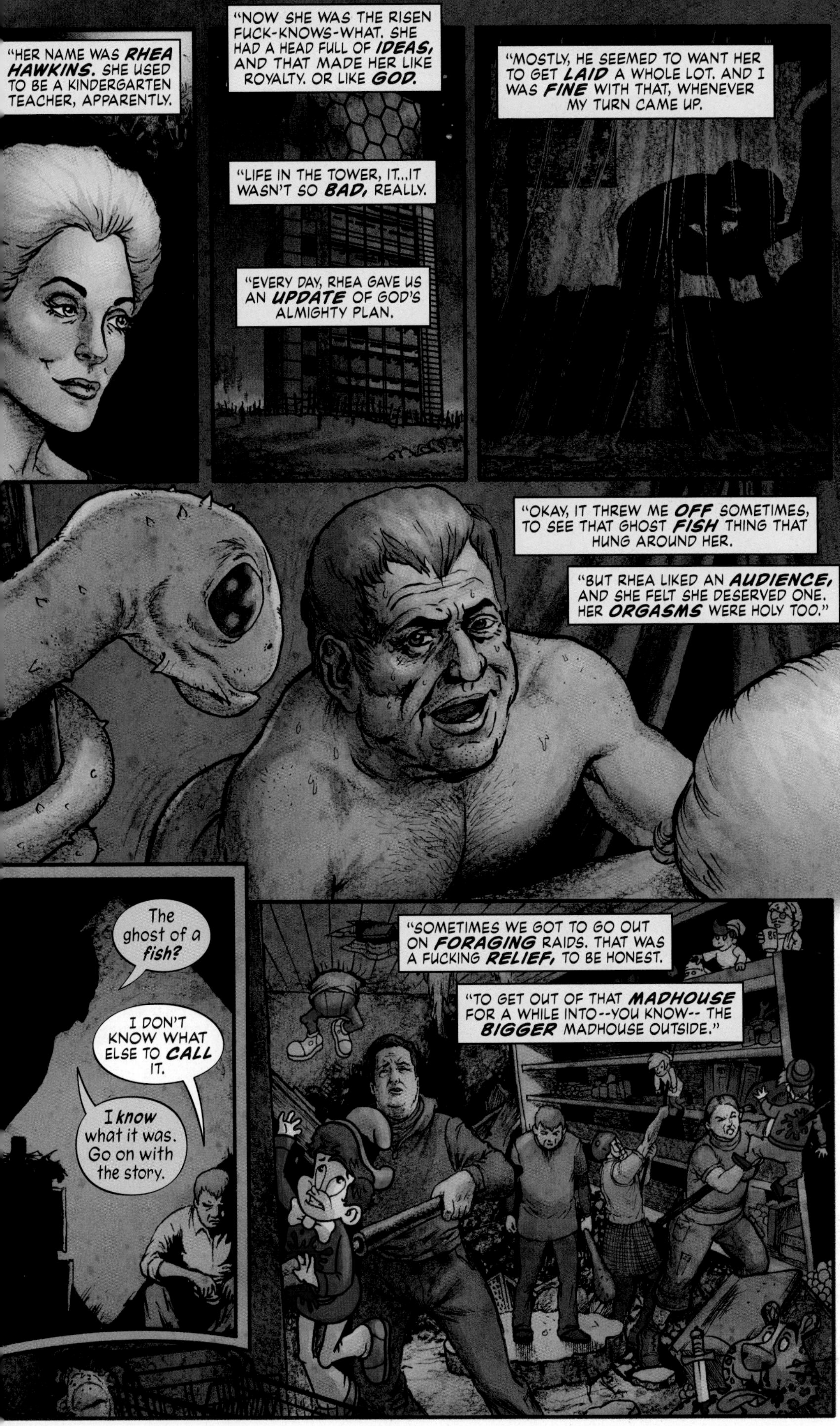
"HER NAME WAS RHEA HAWKINS. SHE USED TO BE A KINDERGARTEN TEACHER, APPARENTLY.
"NOW SHE WAS THE RISEN FUCK-KNOWS-WHAT. SHE HAD A HEAD FULL OF IDEAS, AND THAT MADE HER LIKE ROYALTY. OR LIKE GOD.
"LIFE IN THE TOWER, IT...IT WASN'T SO BAD, REALLY.
"EVERY DAY, RHEA GAVE US AN UPDATE OF GOD'S ALMIGHTY PLAN.
"MOSTLY, HE SEEMED TO WANT HER TO GET LAID A WHOLE LOT. AND I WAS FINE WITH THAT, WHENEVER MY TURN CAME UP.
"OKAY, IT THREW ME OFF SOMETIMES, TO SEE THAT GHOST FISH THING THAT HUNG AROUND HER.
"BUT RHEA LIKED AN AUDIENCE, AND SHE FELT SHE DESERVED ONE. HER ORGASMS WERE HOLY TOO."
The ghost of a fish?
I DON'T KNOW WHAT ELSE TO CALL IT.
I know what it was. Go on with the story.
"SOMETIMES WE GOT TO GO OUT ON FORAGING RAIDS. THAT WAS A FUCKING RELIEF, TO BE HONEST.
"TO GET OUT OF THAT MADHOUSE FOR A WHILE INTO--YOU KNOW-- THE BIGGER MADHOUSE OUTSIDE."

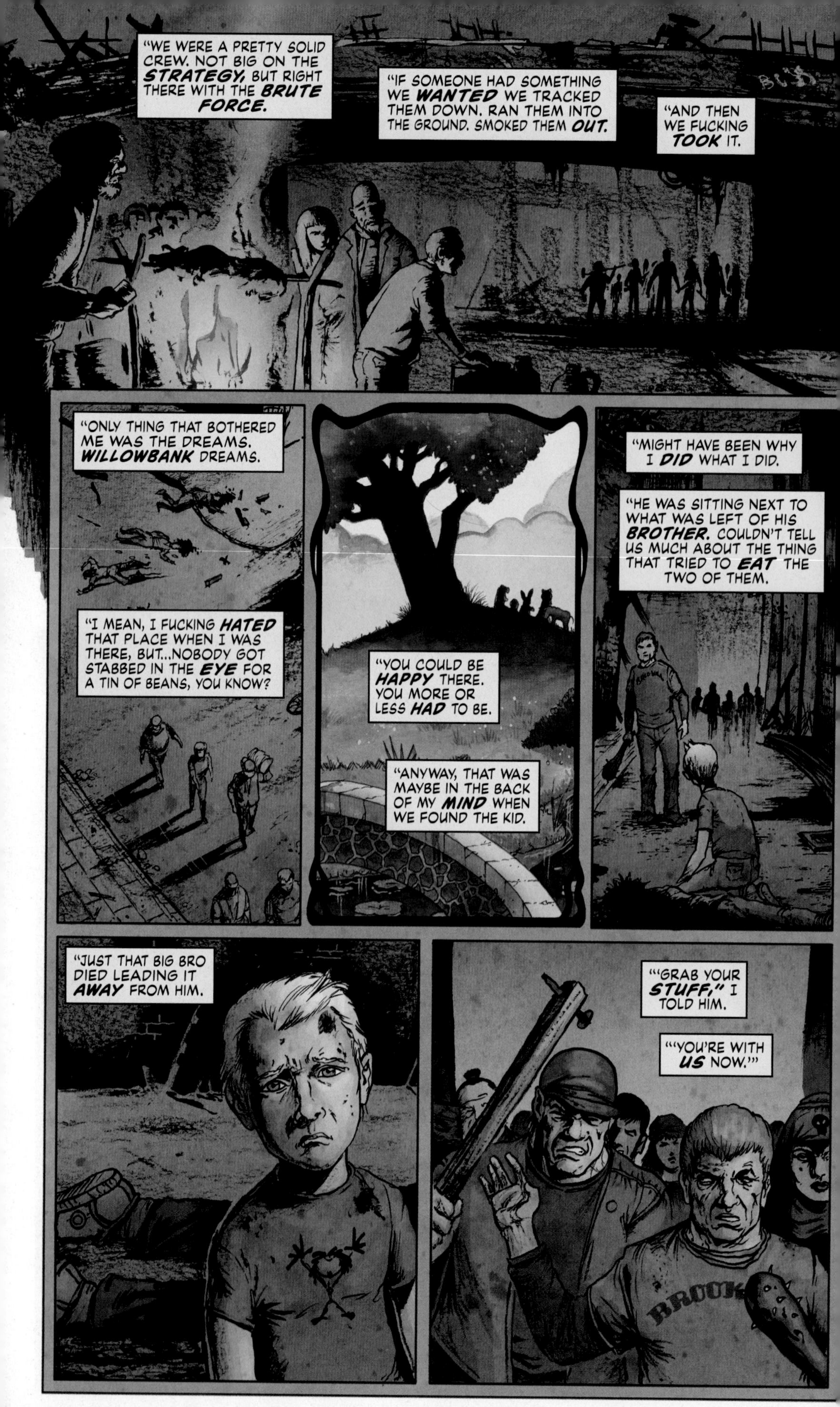
"WE WERE A PRETTY SOLID CREW. NOT BIG ON THE STRATEGY, BUT RIGHT THERE WITH THE BRUTE FORCE.
"IF SOMEONE HAD SOMETHING WE WANTED WE TRACKED THEM DOWN. RAN THEM INTO THE GROUND. SMOKED THEM OUT.
"AND THEN WE FUCKING TOOK IT.
"ONLY THING THAT BOTHERED ME WAS THE DREAMS. WILLOWBANK DREAMS.
"I MEAN, I FUCKING HATED THAT PLACE WHEN I WAS THERE, BUT...NOBODY GOT STABBED IN THE EYE FOR A TIN OF BEANS, YOU KNOW?
"YOU COULD BE HAPPY THERE. YOU MORE OR LESS HAD TO BE.
"ANYWAY, THAT WAS MAYBE IN THE BACK OF MY MIND WHEN WE FOUND THE KID.
"MIGHT HAVE BEEN WHY I DID WHAT I DID.
"HE WAS SITTING NEXT TO WHAT WAS LEFT OF HIS BROTHER. COULDN'T TELL US MUCH ABOUT THE THING THAT TRIED TO EAT THE TWO OF THEM.
"JUST THAT BIG BRO DIED LEADING IT AWAY FROM HIM.
"'GRAB YOUR STUFF,' I TOLD HIM.
"'YOU'RE WITH US NOW.'"

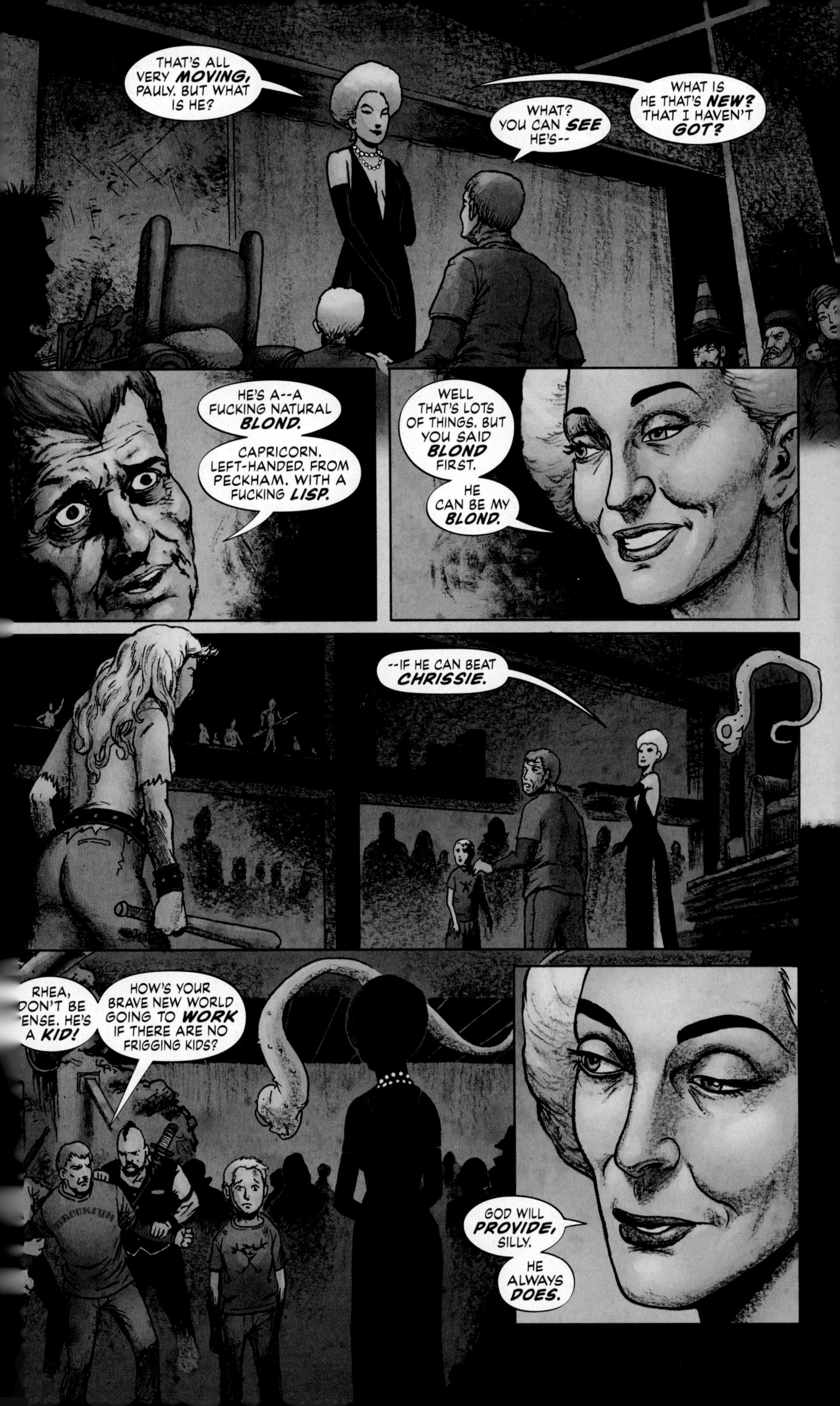
THAT'S ALL VERY MOVING, PAULY. BUT WHAT IS HE?
WHAT? YOU CAN SEE HE'S--
WHAT IS HE THAT'S NEW? THAT I HAVEN'T GOT?
HE'S A--A FUCKING NATURAL BLOND.
CAPRICORN. LEFT-HANDED. FROM PECKHAM. WITH A FUCKING LISP.
WELL THAT'S LOTS OF THINGS. BUT YOU SAID BLOND FIRST.
HE CAN BE MY BLOND.
--IF HE CAN BEAT CHRISSIE.
RHEA, DON'T BE DENSE. HE'S A KID!
HOW'S YOUR BRAVE NEW WORLD GOING TO WORK IF THERE ARE NO FRIGGING KIDS?
GOD WILL PROVIDE, SILLY.
HE ALWAYS DOES.

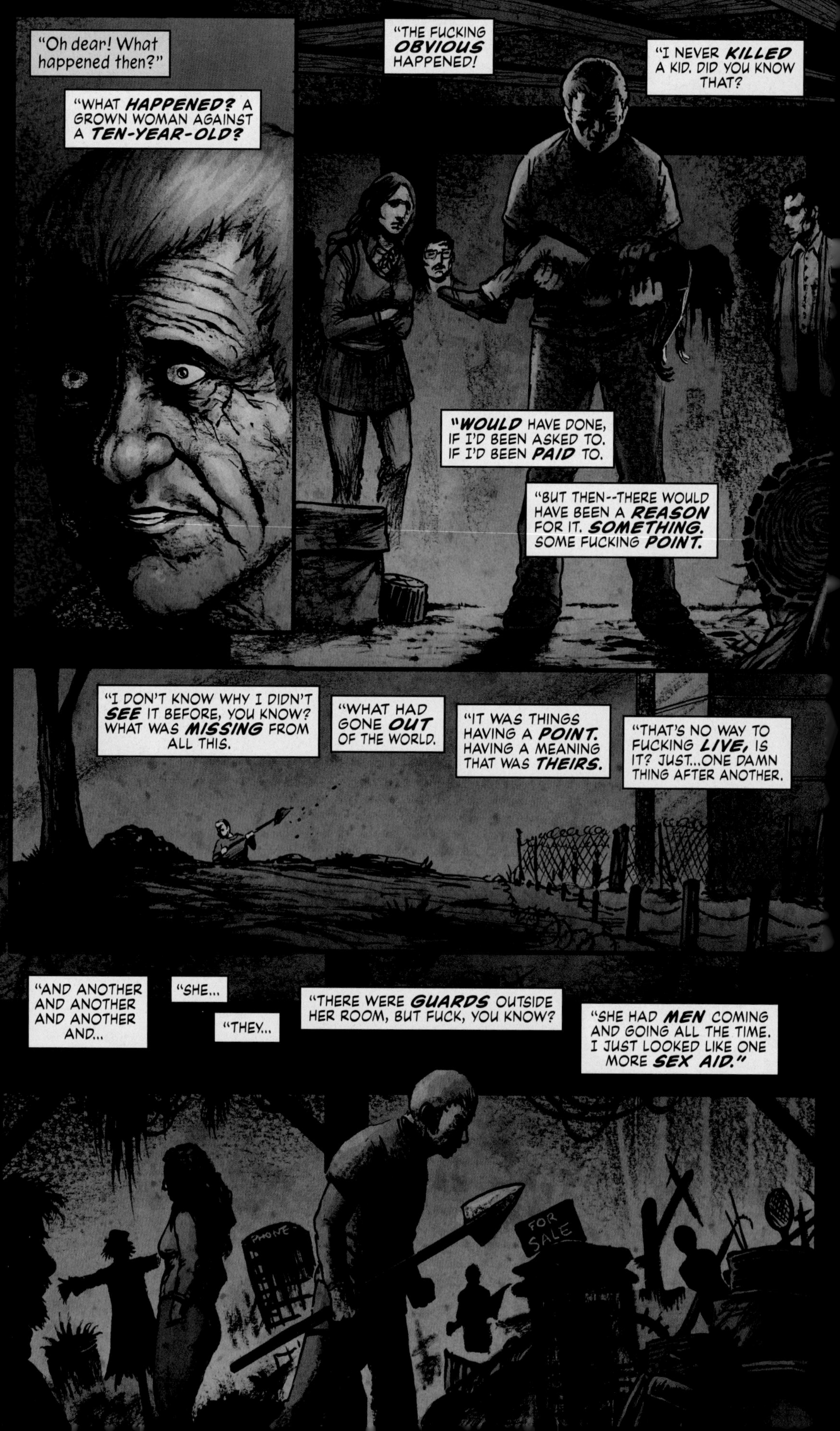

"Oh dear! What happened then?"
"WHAT HAPPENED? A GROWN WOMAN AGAINST A TEN-YEAR-OLD?
"THE FUCKING OBVIOUS HAPPENED!
"I NEVER KILLED A KID. DID YOU KNOW THAT?
"WOULD HAVE DONE, IF I'D BEEN ASKED TO. IF I'D BEEN PAID TO.
"BUT THEN--THERE WOULD HAVE BEEN A REASON FOR IT. SOMETHING. SOME FUCKING POINT.
"I DON'T KNOW WHY I DIDN'T SEE IT BEFORE, YOU KNOW? WHAT WAS MISSING FROM ALL THIS.
"WHAT HAD GONE OUT OF THE WORLD.
"IT WAS THINGS HAVING A POINT. HAVING A MEANING THAT WAS THEIRS.
"THAT'S NO WAY TO FUCKING LIVE, IS IT? JUST...ONE DAMN THING AFTER ANOTHER.
"AND ANOTHER AND ANOTHER AND ANOTHER AND...
"SHE...
"THEY...
"THERE WERE GUARDS OUTSIDE HER ROOM, BUT FUCK, YOU KNOW?
"SHE HAD MEN COMING AND GOING ALL THE TIME. I JUST LOOKED LIKE ONE MORE SEX AID."
PHONE
FOR SALE

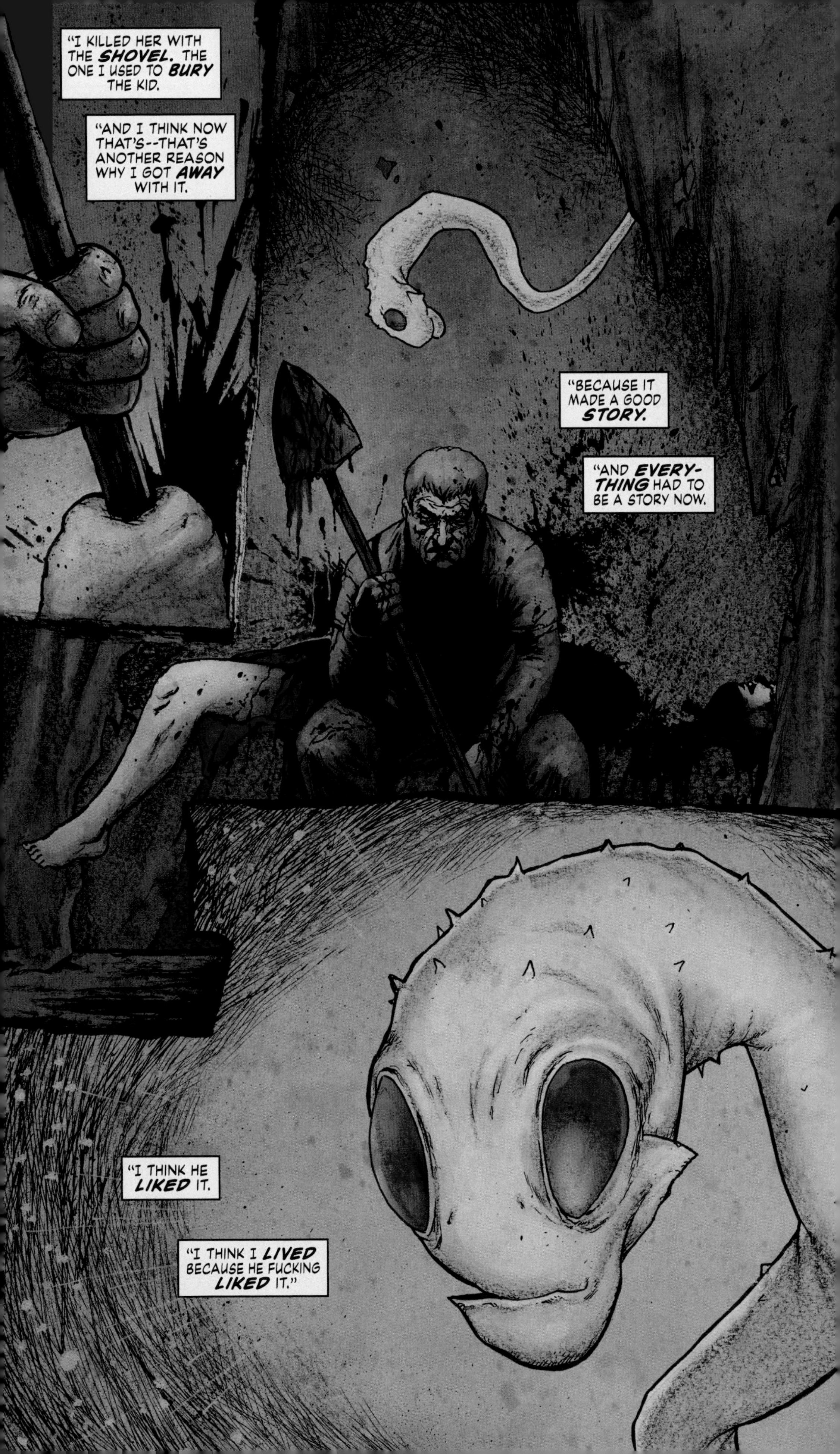
"I KILLED HER WITH THE SHOVEL. THE ONE I USED TO BURY THE KID.
"AND I THINK NOW THAT'S--THAT'S ANOTHER REASON WHY I GOT AWAY WITH IT.
"BECAUSE IT MADE A GOOD STORY.
"AND EVERYTHING HAD TO BE A STORY NOW.
"I THINK HE LIKED IT.
"I THINK I LIVED BECAUSE HE FUCKING LIKED IT."

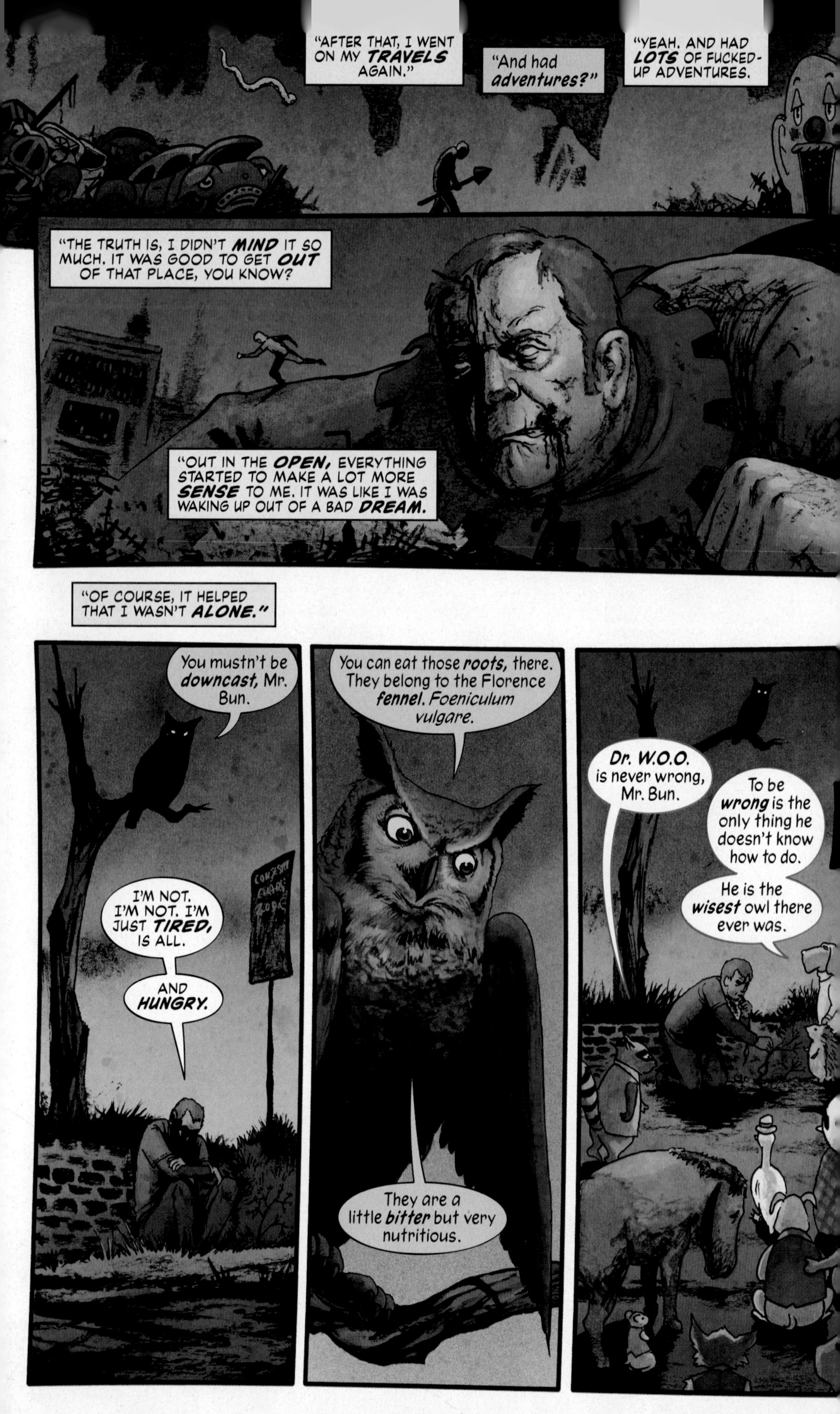
"AFTER THAT, I WENT ON MY TRAVELS AGAIN."
"And had adventures?"
"YEAH. AND HAD LOTS OF FUCKED-UP ADVENTURES.
"THE TRUTH IS, I DIDN'T MIND IT SO MUCH. IT WAS GOOD TO GET OUT OF THAT PLACE, YOU KNOW?
"OUT IN THE OPEN, EVERYTHING STARTED TO MAKE A LOT MORE SENSE TO ME. IT WAS LIKE I WAS WAKING UP OUT OF A BAD DREAM.
"OF COURSE, IT HELPED THAT I WASN'T ALONE."
You mustn't be downcast, Mr. Bun.
I'M NOT. I'M NOT. I'M JUST TIRED, IS ALL.
AND HUNGRY.
You can eat those roots, there. They belong to the Florence fennel. Foeniculum vulgare.
They are a little bitter but very nutritious.
Dr. W.O.O. is never wrong, Mr. Bun.
To be wrong is the only thing he doesn't know how to do.
He is the wisest owl there ever was.

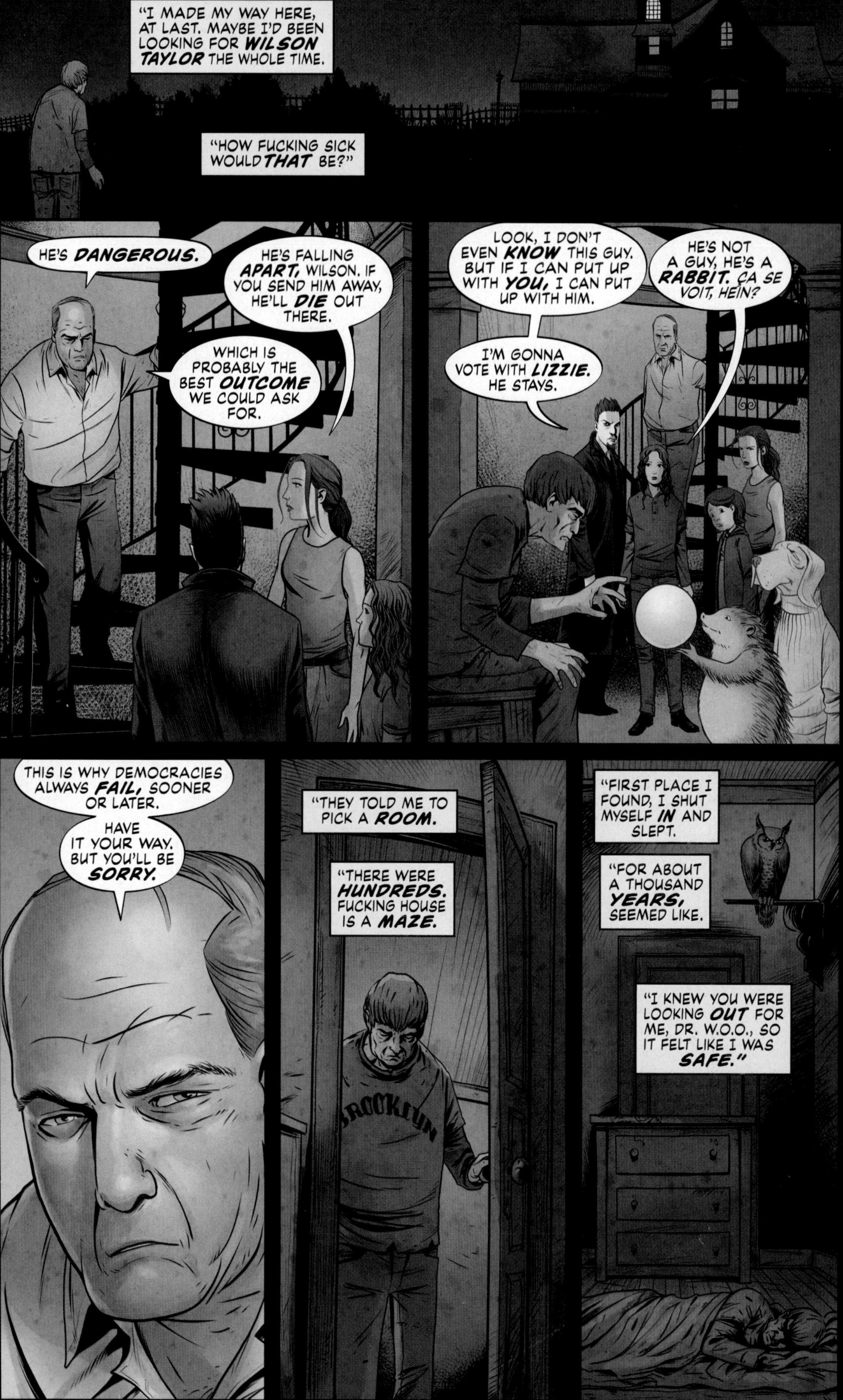
"I MADE MY WAY HERE, AT LAST. MAYBE I'D BEEN LOOKING FOR WILSON TAYLOR THE WHOLE TIME.
"HOW FUCKING SICK WOULD THAT BE?"
HE'S DANGEROUS.
HE'S FALLING APART, WILSON. IF YOU SEND HIM AWAY, HE'LL DIE OUT THERE.
WHICH IS PROBABLY THE BEST OUTCOME WE COULD ASK FOR.
LOOK, I DON'T EVEN KNOW THIS GUY. BUT IF I CAN PUT UP WITH YOU, I CAN PUT UP WITH HIM.
HE'S NOT A GUY, HE'S A RABBIT. ÇA SE VOIT, HEIN?
I'M GONNA VOTE WITH LIZZIE. HE STAYS.
THIS IS WHY DEMOCRACIES ALWAYS FAIL, SOONER OR LATER.
HAVE IT YOUR WAY. BUT YOU'LL BE SORRY.
"THEY TOLD ME TO PICK A ROOM.
"THERE WERE HUNDREDS. FUCKING HOUSE IS A MAZE.
BROOKLYN
"FIRST PLACE I FOUND, I SHUT MYSELF IN AND SLEPT.
"FOR ABOUT A THOUSAND YEARS, SEEMED LIKE.
"I KNEW YOU WERE LOOKING OUT FOR ME, DR. W.O.O., SO IT FELT LIKE I WAS SAFE."

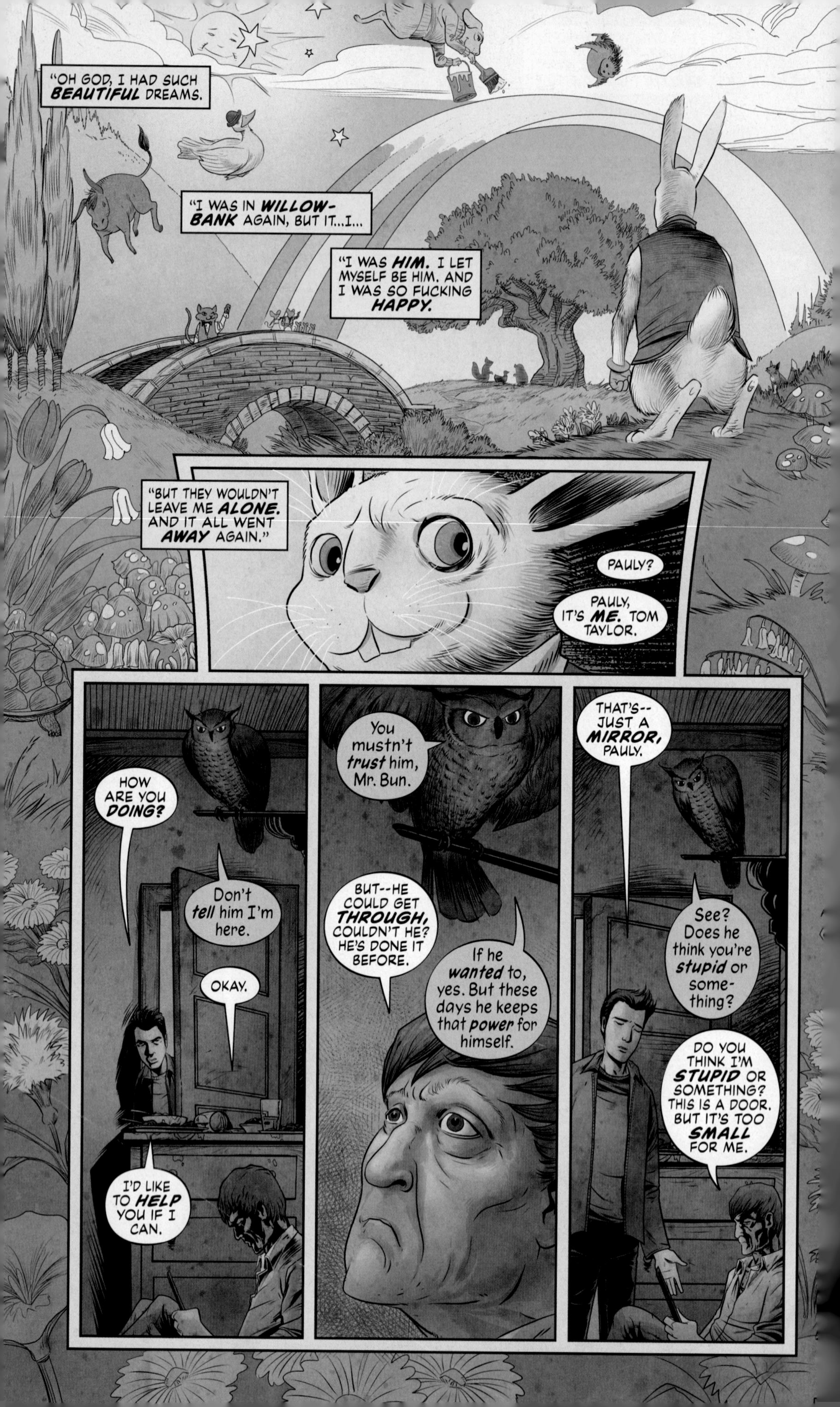

"OH GOD, I HAD SUCH BEAUTIFUL DREAMS.
"I WAS IN WILLOW-BANK AGAIN, BUT IT...I...
"I WAS HIM. I LET MYSELF BE HIM. AND I WAS SO FUCKING HAPPY.
"BUT THEY WOULDN'T LEAVE ME ALONE. AND IT ALL WENT AWAY AGAIN."
PAULY?
PAULY, IT'S ME. TOM TAYLOR.
HOW ARE YOU DOING?
Don't tell him I'm here.
OKAY.
I'D LIKE TO HELP YOU IF I CAN.
You mustn't trust him, Mr. Bun.
BUT--HE COULD GET THROUGH, COULDN'T HE? HE'S DONE IT BEFORE.
If he wanted to, yes. But these days he keeps that power for himself.
THAT'S--JUST A MIRROR, PAULY.
See? Does he think you're stupid or some-thing?
DO YOU THINK I'M STUPID OR SOMETHING? THIS IS A DOOR. BUT IT'S TOO SMALL FOR ME.

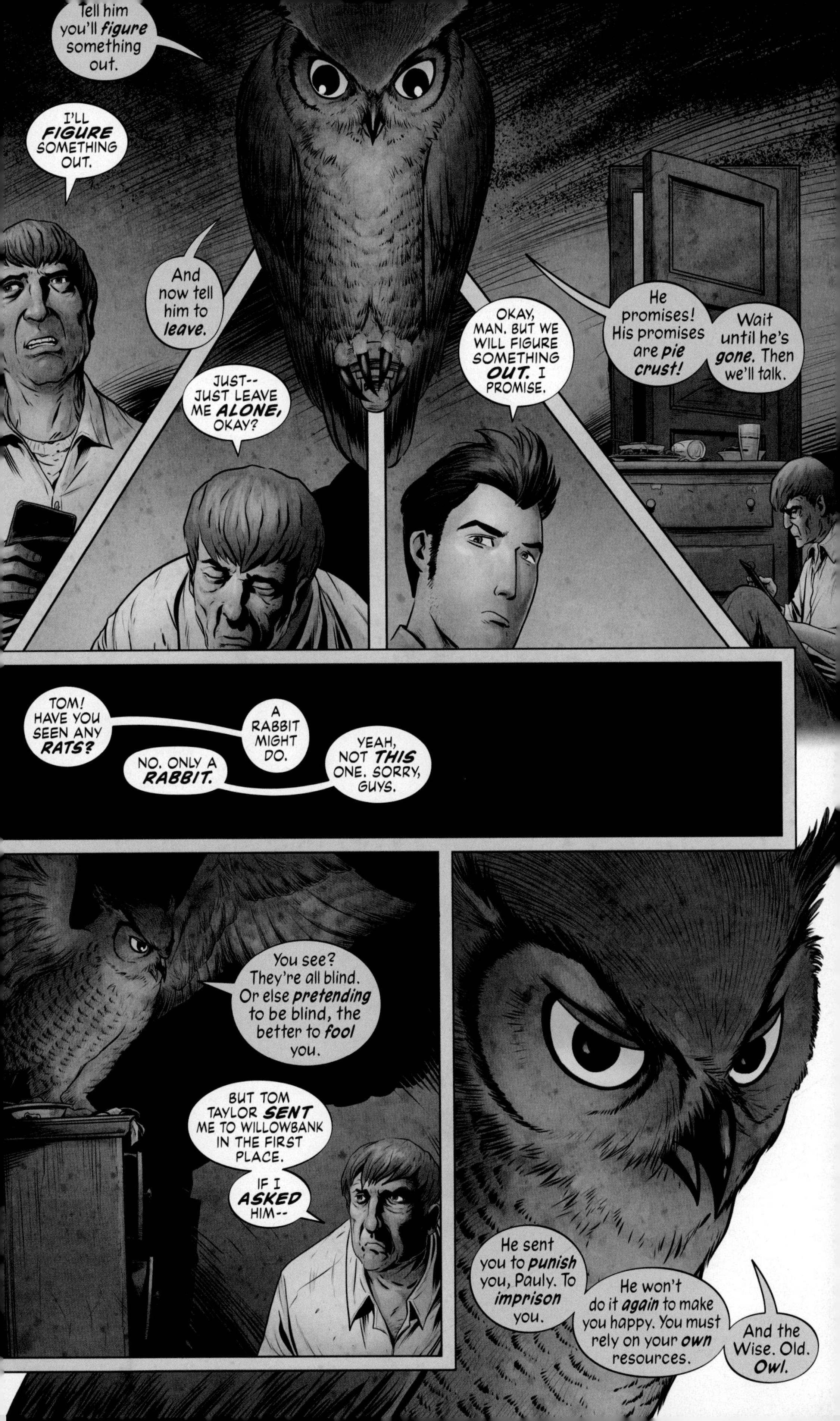
Tell him you'll *figure* something out.
I'LL *FIGURE* SOMETHING OUT.
And now tell him to *leave*.
JUST-- JUST LEAVE ME *ALONE*, OKAY?
OKAY, MAN. BUT WE WILL FIGURE SOMETHING *OUT*. I PROMISE.
He promises! His promises are *pie crust!*
Wait until he's *gone*. Then we'll talk.
TOM! HAVE YOU SEEN ANY *RATS?*
NO. ONLY A *RABBIT.*
A RABBIT MIGHT DO.
YEAH, NOT *THIS* ONE. SORRY, GUYS.
You see? They're all blind. Or else *pretending* to be blind, the better to *fool* you.
BUT TOM TAYLOR *SENT* ME TO WILLOWBANK IN THE FIRST PLACE.
IF I *ASKED* HIM--
He sent you to *punish* you, Pauly. To *imprison* you.
He won't do it *again* to make you happy. You must rely on your *own* resources.
And the Wise. Old. *Owl*.

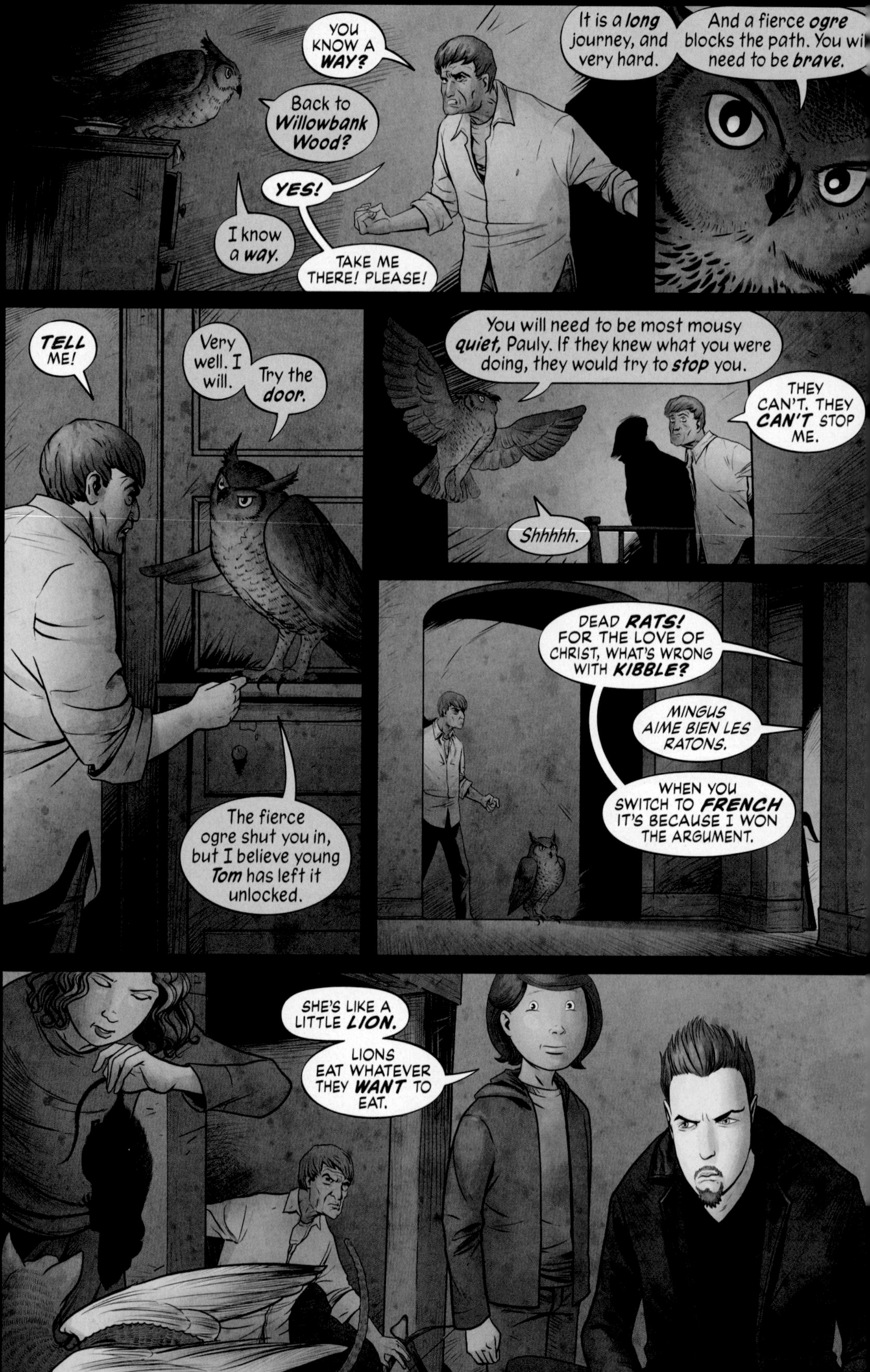

YOU KNOW A WAY?
Back to Willowbank Wood?
YES!
I know a way.
TAKE ME THERE! PLEASE!
It is a long journey, and very hard.
And a fierce ogre blocks the path. You wi
need to be brave.
TELL ME!
Very well. I will.
Try the door.
The fierce ogre shut you in, but I believe young Tom has left it unlocked.
You will need to be most mousy quiet, Pauly. If they knew what you were doing, they would try to stop you.
THEY CAN'T. THEY CAN'T STOP ME.
Shhhhh.
DEAD RATS! FOR THE LOVE OF CHRIST, WHAT'S WRONG WITH KIBBLE?
MINGUS AIME BIEN LES RATONS.
WHEN YOU SWITCH TO FRENCH IT'S BECAUSE I WON THE ARGUMENT.
SHE'S LIKE A LITTLE LION.
LIONS EAT WHATEVER THEY WANT TO EAT.

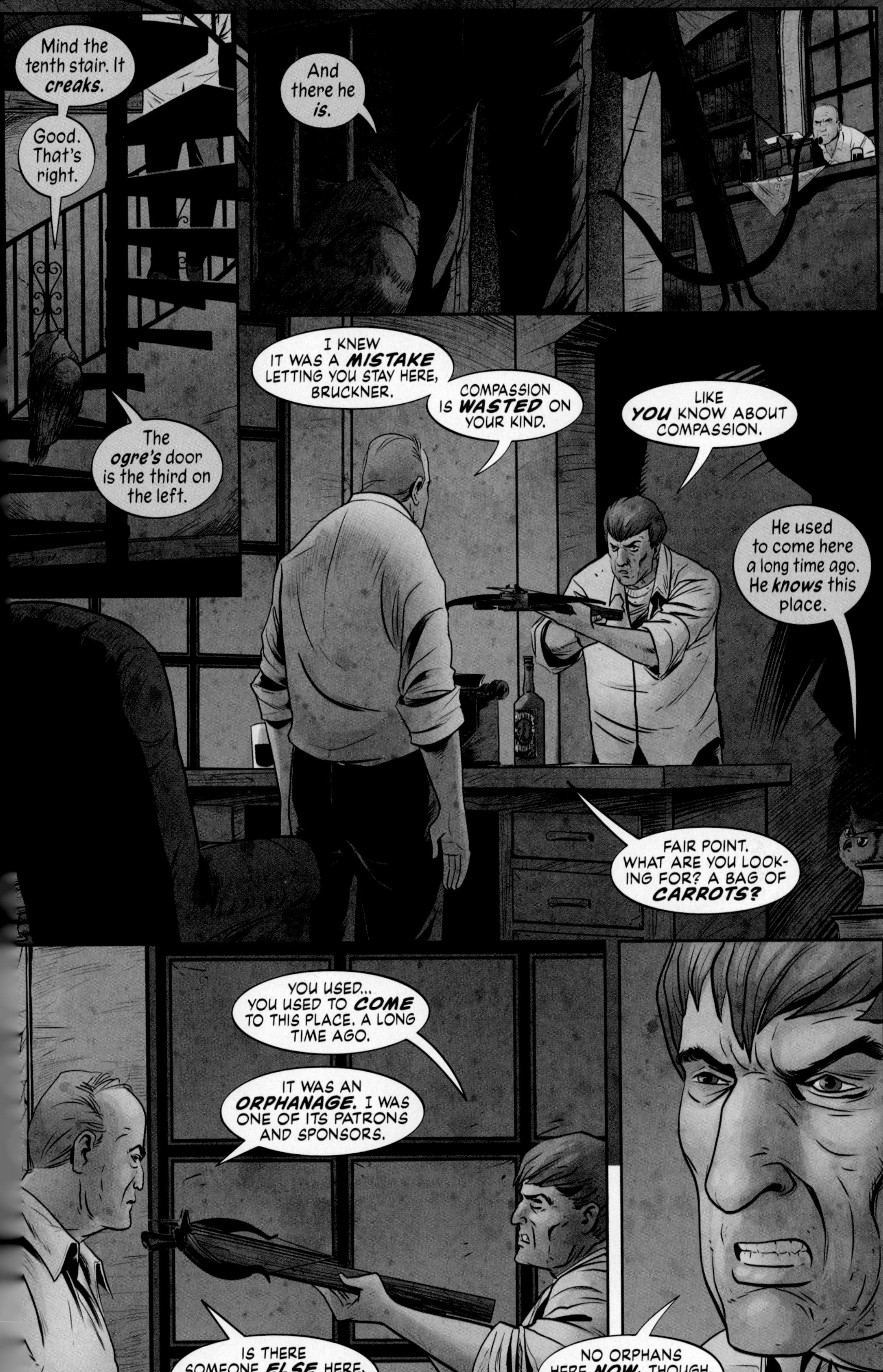
Mind the tenth stair. It *creaks*.
Good. That's right.
And there he *is*.
The *ogre's* door is the third on the left.
I KNEW IT WAS A ***MISTAKE*** LETTING YOU STAY HERE, BRUCKNER.
COMPASSION IS ***WASTED*** ON YOUR KIND.
LIKE ***YOU*** KNOW ABOUT COMPASSION.
He used to come here a long time ago. He *knows* this place.
FAIR POINT. WHAT ARE YOU LOOKING FOR? A BAG OF ***CARROTS?***
YOU USED... YOU USED TO ***COME*** TO THIS PLACE. A LONG TIME AGO.
IT WAS AN ***ORPHANAGE.*** I WAS ONE OF ITS PATRONS AND SPONSORS.
IS THERE SOMEONE ***ELSE*** HERE, BESIDES US? YOU SEEM ***DISTRACTED.***
NO ORPHANS HERE ***NOW,*** THOUGH, ARE THERE? SO WHY COME BACK?
OUT OF ***NOSTALGIA?*** I DON'T THINK SO.

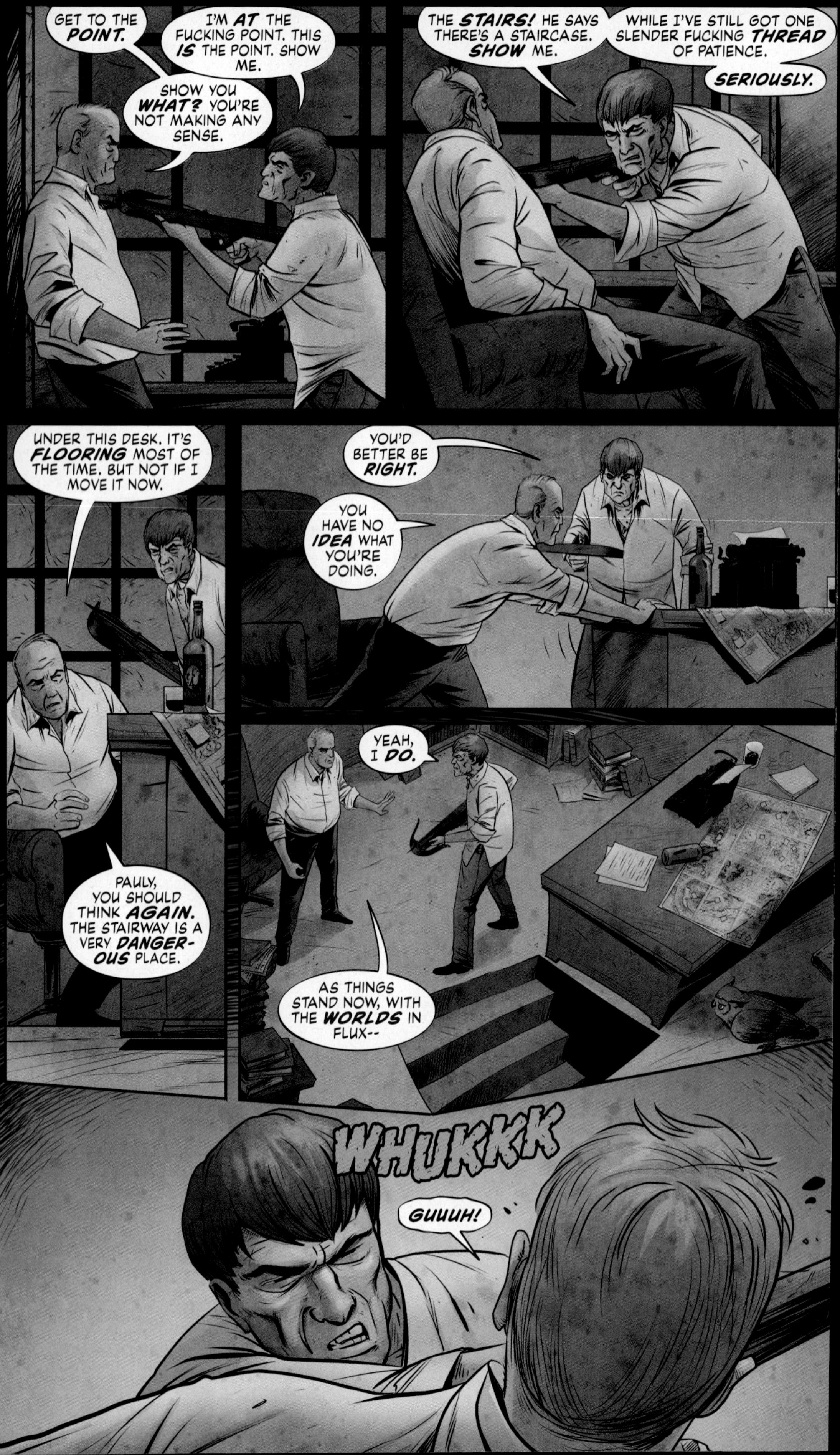

GET TO THE POINT.
I'M AT THE FUCKING POINT. THIS IS THE POINT. SHOW ME.
SHOW YOU WHAT? YOU'RE NOT MAKING ANY SENSE.
THE STAIRS! HE SAYS THERE'S A STAIRCASE. SHOW ME.
WHILE I'VE STILL GOT ONE SLENDER FUCKING THREAD OF PATIENCE.
SERIOUSLY.
UNDER THIS DESK. IT'S FLOORING MOST OF THE TIME. BUT NOT IF I MOVE IT NOW.
PAULY, YOU SHOULD THINK AGAIN. THE STAIRWAY IS A VERY DANGER-OUS PLACE.
YOU'D BETTER BE RIGHT.
YOU HAVE NO IDEA WHAT YOU'RE DOING.
YEAH, I DO.
AS THINGS STAND NOW, WITH THE WORLDS IN FLUX--
WHUKKK
GUUUH!

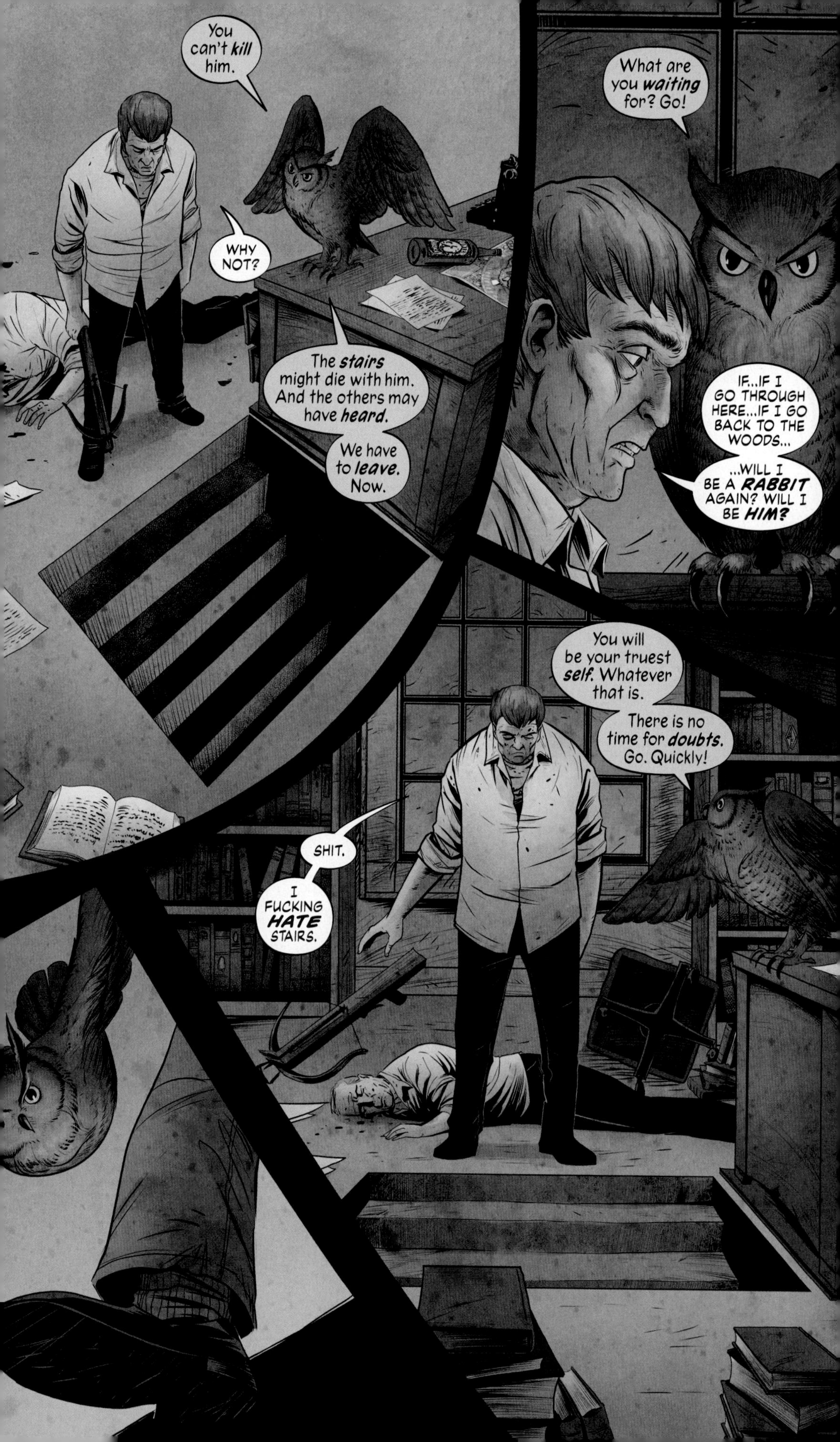
You can't *kill* him.
WHY NOT?
The *stairs* might die with him. And the others may have *heard.*
We have to *leave.* Now.
What are you *waiting* for? Go!
IF...IF I GO THROUGH HERE...IF I GO BACK TO THE WOODS...
...WILL I BE A *RABBIT* AGAIN? WILL I BE *HIM?*
You will be your truest *self.* Whatever that is.
There is no time for *doubts.* Go. Quickly!
SHIT.
I FUCKING *HATE* STAIRS.

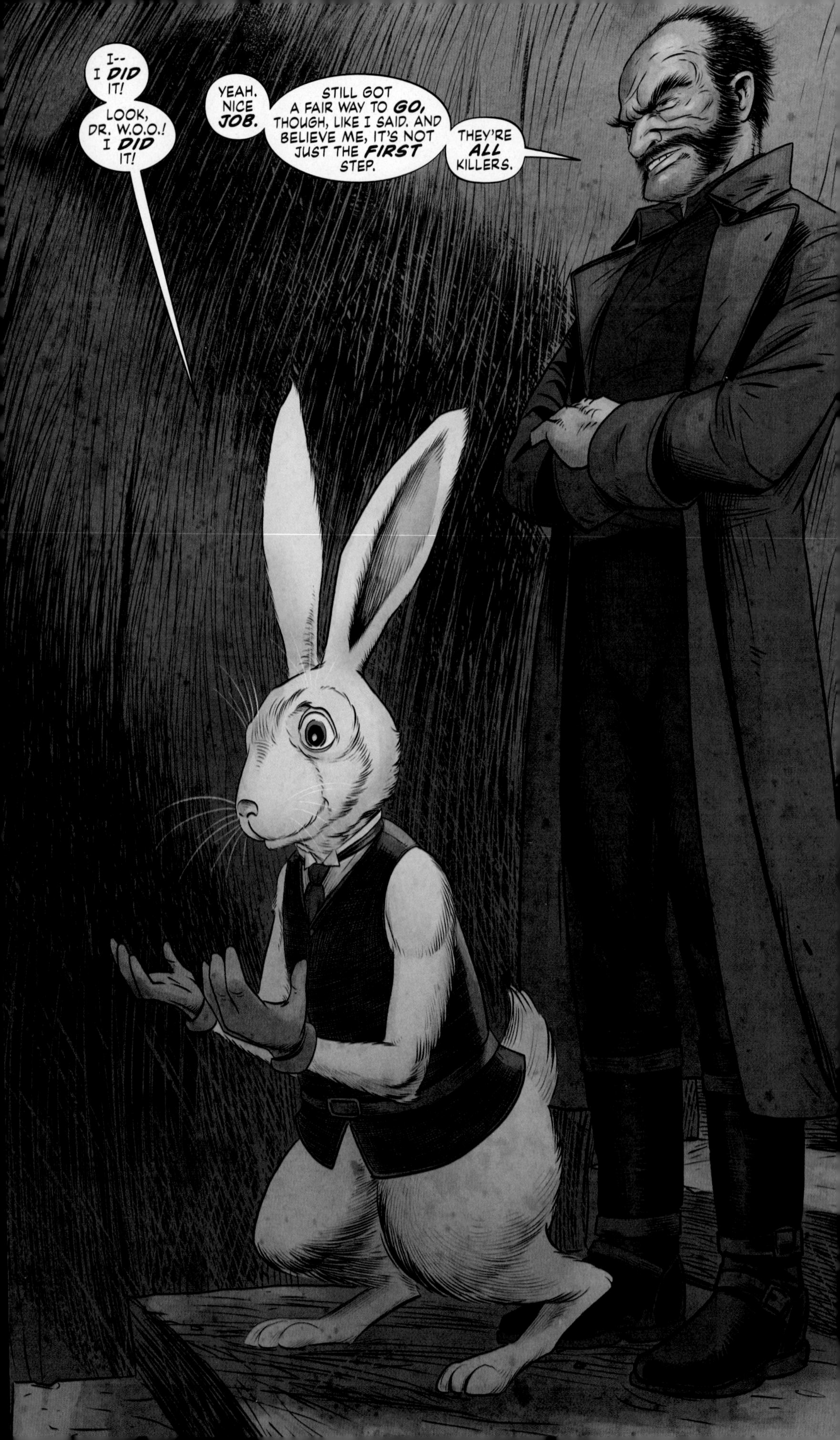
I-- I DID IT!
LOOK, DR. W.O.O.! I DID IT!
YEAH. NICE JOB.
STILL GOT A FAIR WAY TO GO, THOUGH, LIKE I SAID. AND BELIEVE ME, IT'S NOT JUST THE FIRST STEP.
THEY'RE ALL KILLERS.

Cover sketches by Yuko Shimizu

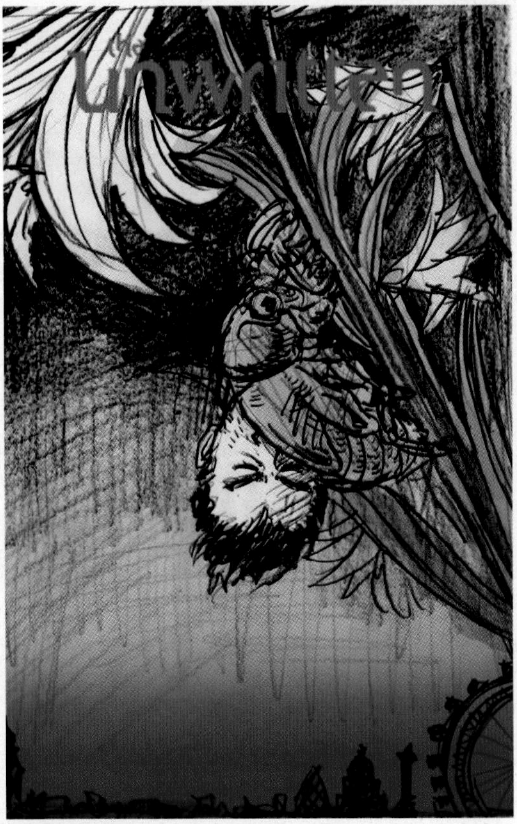
the
Unwritten

Issue #1

Variant #1 sketch by Peter Gross

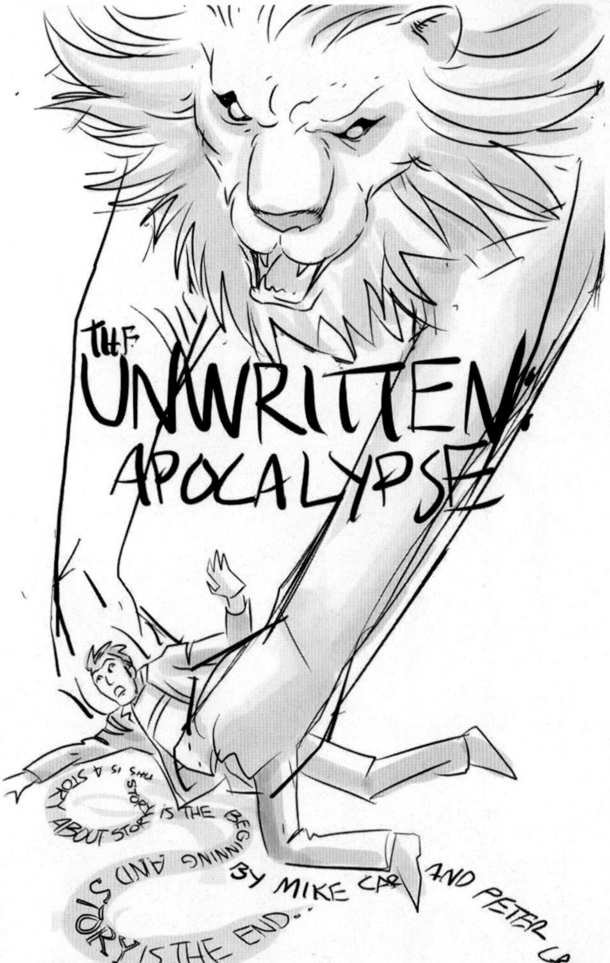
THE
UNWRITTEN
APOCALYPSE
THIS IS A STORY ABOUT STORY
STORY IS THE BEGINNING AND STORY IS THE END..
BY MIKE CAR AND PETER GR..

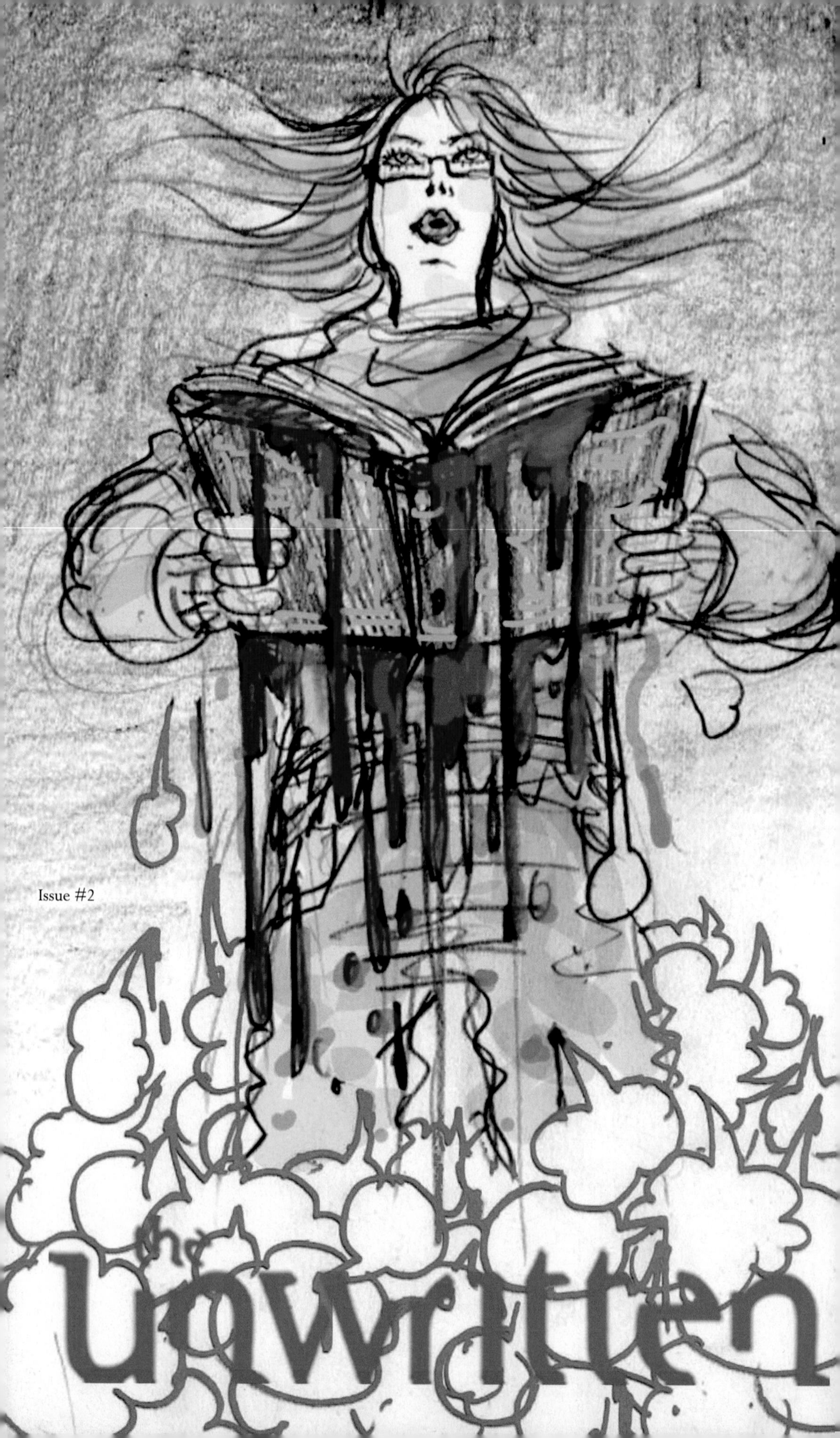
Issue #2
the
unwritten

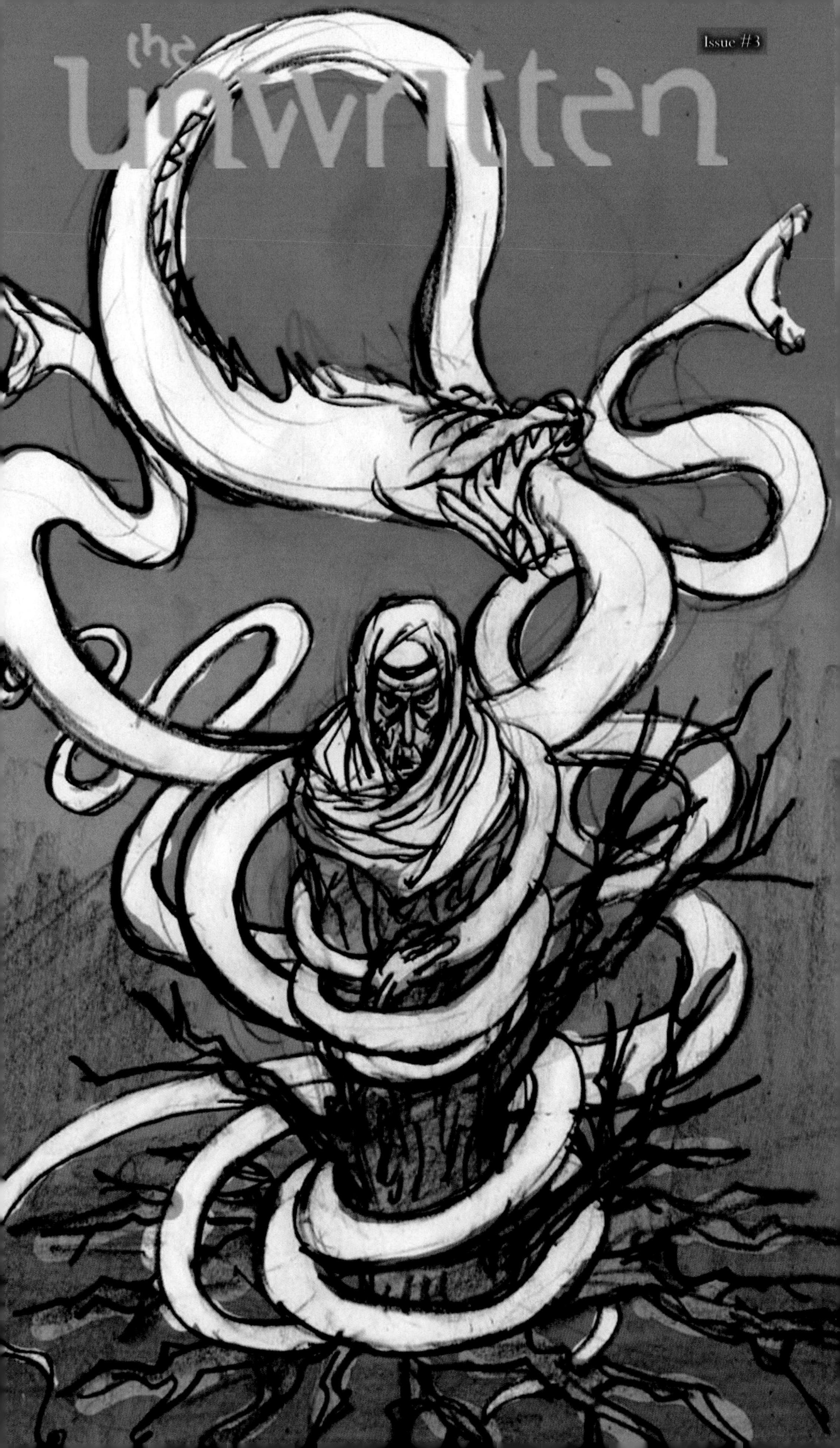
the unwritten
Issue #3

Issue #4

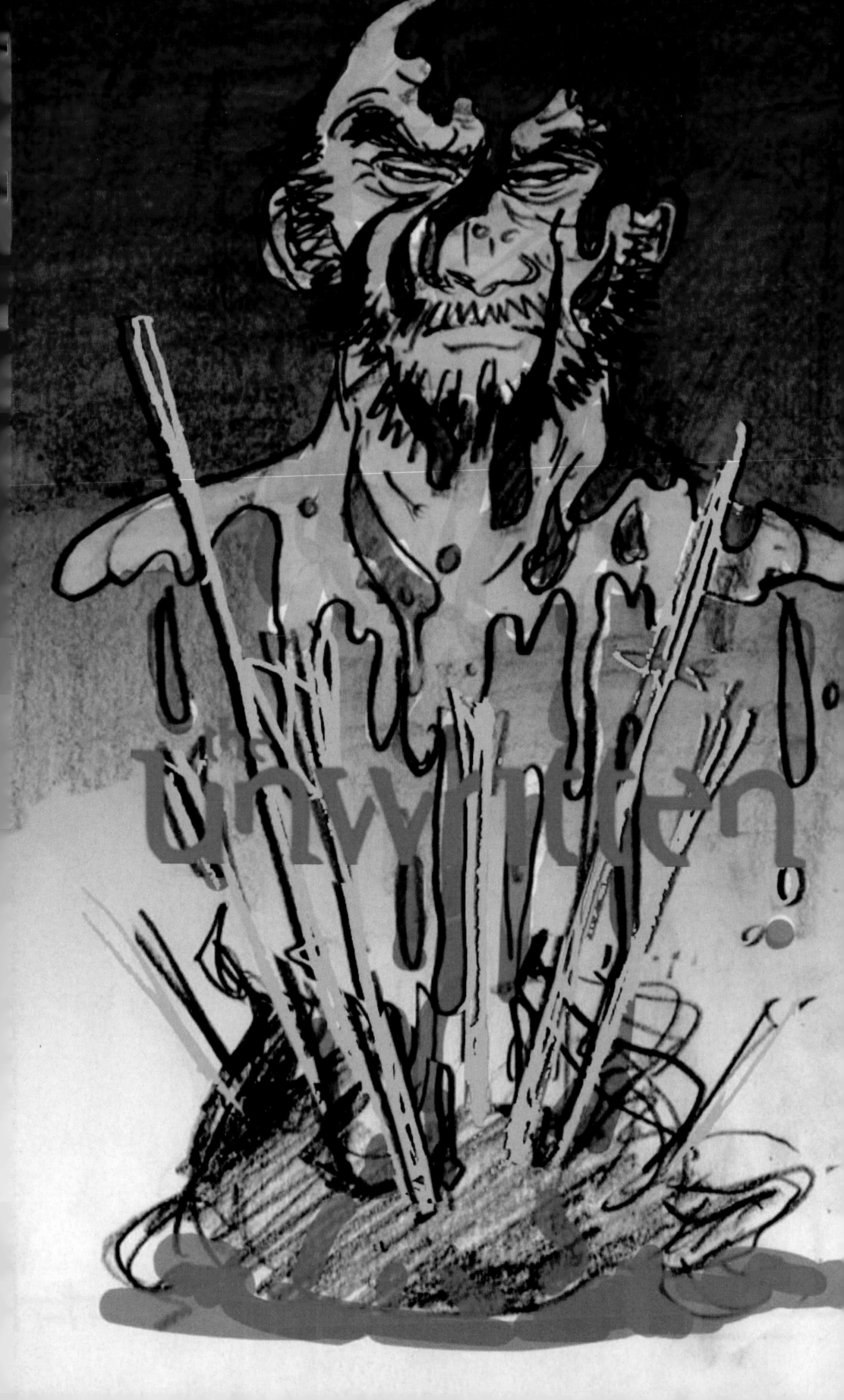
the unwritten